P9-CLN-944

Jules Verne

By the same author

IN SEARCH OF LAKE MONSTERS
THE HEART GROWN BRUTAL

Jules Verne

Inventor of Science Fiction

Peter Costello

Charles Scribner's Sons
New York

Library of Congress Cataloging in Publication Data

Costello, Peter.
    Jules Verne, inventor of science fiction.
    Bibliography: p.
    Includes index.
    1. Verne, Jules, 1828-1905—Biography.
    2. Novelists, French—19th century—Biography.
    I. Title.
PQ2469.Z5C66 1978   843'.8 [B]   78-57528
ISBN 0-684-15824-8

1 3 5 7 9 11 13 15 17 19 H/C 20 18 16 14 12 10 8 6 4 2

Printed in the United States of America

*In memory of two admirers
of Jules Verne,
WILLY LEY and R. T. GOULD
whose own books
opened portals of discovery*

16 July – After reading Edgar Allan Poe. Something the critics have not noticed: a new literary world, pointing to the literature of the twentieth century. Scientific miracles, fables on the pattern A+B; a clear-sighted, sickly literature. No more poetry, but analytic fantasy. Something monomaniacal. Things playing a more important part than people; love giving way to deductions and other sources of ideas, style, subject, and interest; the basis of the novel transferred from the heart to the head, from passion to idea, from the drama to the dénouement.

The Goncourt Journal, 16 July 1856

Imagining in excited reverie
That the future years had come . . .
W. B. YEATS

Contents

Illustrations

ACKNOWLEDGMENTS
1 Maison de la Culture, Amiens
2 The National Library of Ireland
3 Library of Congress, Washington, D.C.

Introduction

THE ITALIAN EXPLORER NOBILE IN THE AIRSHIP 'NORGE' GLIDES
over the Arctic wastes where the Swede Salomon Andrée was lost
in his balloon the *Eagle* a generation before. Captain Scott and his
party perish in a vain attempt to conquer the South Pole first. The
Frenchman Norbert Casteret penetrates into the caves and caverns
of the Pyrenees, finding lost lakes and forgotten sanctuaries of
early man. Haroun Tazieff climbs down into a rumbling volcano
in the northern province of Zaire, plumbing the secrets of the
earth's core. The American nuclear submarine *Nautilus* surfaces
at the North Pole and radios its position at ninety degrees north
to the President in Washington. A Soviet satellite circles the
earth and twelve years later an American steps down onto the
surface of the moon . . .

These incidents, and many others from the twentieth century's
scientific conquest of the universe, were all prefigured by scenes in
the novels of Jules Verne. One hundred and fifty years after his
birth, we are still living in his world.

Even in his own lifetime (he died in 1905), the word 'Vernian'
had come to stand for the romantic possibilities of the future, of
science, and of exploration. A century before man travelled there,
in fact, Verne's fiction had launched three men into orbit around
the moon. In another novel, published in 1877, he described a
journey around the solar system, which even today seems only a
distant possibility. NASA's current project to build a solar
'sailing ship' to be carried across the universe by the solar winds
to study the return of Halley's Comet in 1985 is the sort of
scheme which would have enchanted Verne, even if there will be
no place aboard the unmanned spacecraft for a Hector Servadac.

In Verne's nineteenth-century novels the twentieth century came into being. For this reason, he has often been called 'the father of science fiction'. On the wall of the house in Nantes, the capital of Brittany where he was born in 1828, a memorial plaque describes him as 'novelist and precursor'. Certainly Verne invented, among other things, a bleak idea of the future, as his vision of human history in his story 'The Eternal Adam' reveals. Not that his future is the world we live in. But he had seen enough of the science and technology, and the politics, of his own time to be able to predict some of the things we have to live with today: industrial squalor, total war, social dissolution.

Science fiction is often said to be of value for its predictions. But actually it is because it is largely a rearrangement of the present that much of it is of interest. In Verne's books the predictions and revisions go together, giving us a double vision of the last 150 years.

In this biography I have tried to place Verne as a man and a writer in the context of his own times. In discussing his books I have preferred to concentrate on their unusual features, or on their origins and sources, rather than merely provide résumés of the plots. Often Verne's plots are of little interest, while his ideas always are. In any case, reading a biography of a writer is not a substitute for reading his books.

Verne was a man who delighted in mysteries, and there are still some mysteries about his life and character. 'Le très curieux Jules Verne,' Mallarmé called him in 1874, and this strangeness is as striking today as it was then. A little more light than before, however, is cast by this book on some of the more shadowed areas of his life, especially his private life.

I have treated Verne as an adult, with adult feelings. Yet in English-speaking countries he is often thought of as a 'children's writer', a sort of Boy's Own Prophet, who appeals only to adolescents, or those with retarded sensibilities. Indeed it has been said that some of the emotional shallowness that afflicts 'space opera' science fiction today is due to him. This is largely untrue, as I hope to show. Verne is a far more varied and interesting writer than many people who have read only a few of his more famous books realise.

Certainly his stories are now part of our modern folklore. Who has not heard of Captain Nemo and Phileas Fogg? Tributes to his genius range from Rick Wakeman's rock-opera *Journey to the Centre of the Earth* to the underwater trip at Disneyland aboard Nemo's submarine. Yet for us Verne is merely good fun.

The view of Verne is very different in France and some of the socialist countries, where the level of critical and scientific interest taken in him and his writings would surprise many English-speaking readers. However, the modern manner of French literary criticism, with its emphasis on deep-structures and mythical frames of thought, precludes biography. So does the emphatic political bias of socialist literary studies. So this present book may in fact prove to be more comprehensive than much recent work not only in French, but also in Russian and Hungarian. If some of what I say seems at variance with received opinions, so much the better. The facts will speak for themselves.

The first sketch of Verne's life was written by his friend Charles Lemire in 1908, and though it contains one or two good anecdotes, it is little more than an extended obituary. It was not until 1928 that the first biography was written, by the wife of one of Verne's nephews, Marguerite Allotte de la Fuÿe. Though she had access to materials which have since vanished, she wrote her book in the form of a romantic novel, and is careless about dates and other facts. Yet for over forty years her book was the main source from which all other writers drew. In 1974 a more definitive book, *Jules Verne*, by his grandson, Jean Jules-Verne, was published. Written with the summary skills of the retired judge that he is, the book was a great improvement on the earlier work, and provides much new information about Verne. (The book should not be judged on the basis of the abridged translation published in America and Britain.) These are the 'family biographers' so frequently mentioned in the course of my narrative.

I have also profited by the slight little book of Maurice Metral, which contains some stories not to be found anywhere else; and from the diligent studies of Charles-Noël Martin, who wrote the useful introductions for the now unobtainable Rencontre edition of Verne's complete works published in Switzerland.

While I have tried to fill out Verne's personal life in some further detail, my approach has been to present Verne in relation to the science, technology and geographical discoveries of his time. I have tried to trace his sources and to show how he used them. But my main theme has been Verne's gradual loss of faith, both in the old Catholic religion of his father, and in the new science of the nineteenth century in which so many like him placed their hopes. His growing disillusionment makes Verne a very modern figure, and a man of great interest, far removed from the shallow-minded romancer of popular fame.

Any modern interpretation of Jules Verne has to combine biography, literary criticism, and the involved history of scientific development. As my old friend the Belgian zoologist Bernard Heuvelmans (himself something of an authority on Verne's use of his sources) remarked to me when I was beginning this book, a study of Verne is a study of the history and progress of nearly every science in the nineteenth century. A formidable task for one writer, but I have tried within the limits of a biography to give not only an account of Verne's life, but also of the myriad aspects of the world that took his fancy.

Verne pioneered mass production long before Henry Ford, turning out two books a year for most of his career. And as with the early Fords, quality varies from model to model. But in general the product is sturdy and well built, runs well and is reliable on less travelled roads; and, unlike the early Fords, comes with many colourful and romantic fittings. All his books can be read with interest.

It is perhaps inexact to describe Verne as 'the father of science fiction'. Such a biological metaphor suits neither his personal temperament, which was chaste and withdrawn, nor his books. I prefer to call him 'the inventor of science fiction', as the mechanical analogy fits him better. Already I can hear critics grumbling that I have not taken enough account of Edgar Allan Poe or Mary Shelley or some other figure from the early days of the genre. But as I hope to show, Verne's particular contribution was a love of exact scientific detail, such as is often lacking in Poe or Mary Shelley. And for that reason what he writes is truly the beginnings of *science* fiction.

The 103 volumes that contain the *Voyages extraordinaires*, as his series of strange journeys into worlds known and unknown was called in France, is in any terms a formidable achievement in itself. But the wonders of his books were almost equalled by Verne's own strange journey through life.

Jules Verne

Chapter One

The Artificial Island

IN THE NOVELS OF JULES VERNE, WRITTEN OVER SO MANY YEARS, one image persists: the image of the man-made island. The iceberg in *The Fur Country*, the giant raft floating down the Amazon in *La Jangada*, the great ship in *The Floating City*, and of course, the bizarre craft in *Propeller Island*: these prodigies of fiction had their origin in reality, for the idea of an artificial island went back to the setting of Verne's childhood and his earliest days on the Ile Feydeau in the Breton seaport of Nantes, where he was born in 1828.

Today Nantes is one of France's most flourishing cities, for trade and industry have been part of its heritage. Straddling the Loire, forty miles inland from the Atlantic, and the largest city in Brittany, Nantes was the centre of the old spice trade with the West Indies: nutmeg is still a dominating flavour in the local cuisine. The city's traders, locally known as 'the San Domingo planters', made their fortunes in the three-way trade of European goods, African slaves, and tropical spices, fruits and woods. The first families of Nantes are descendants of *les négriers* whose prosperity was created by *la traite des noirs*, or more simply, *la traite*.

Slavery, which Verne detested, was only abolished in France and her colonies in 1848. That year of revolution was also a year of personal liberation for Verne himself, for it was the year in which he escaped from Nantes to live in Paris. But the influences of his childhood were something he could not so easily escape from, and a city built upon African slavery appears in the very last of his books in 1919.

Back in 1713, twenty-four of Nantes's wealthiest merchants combined to buy out the rights of a miller in a small, sandy island, lying in the river at the heart of the city, almost beside the Bourse. They laid down piles and on the artificial island thus created, which they named after the royal administrator of Brittany, Feydeau de Brou, they erected twenty-four great mansions. Today the channel between the island and the shore has been filled in. The Ile Feydeau is no longer an island. Urban expressways cut through it, bringing into the once quiet quarter of the city the noise and bustle of the twentieth century.

But in the early nineteenth century the Ile Feydeau was still a real island, shaped like a great ship at anchor. From the Petite Hollande at the west end there was a splendid view over the busy port. Many of the great merchants had been ruined when their estates were confiscated after the Negro revolt in the Indies in 1791, and the mansions were now let out in apartments, and the once fashionable streets were lined with fishmongers and other traders. However, at 4 rue Olivier de Clisson, on the corner of rue Kervégan, the descendants of one merchant prince, the Allottes, still resided in the same house. It was there on 8 February 1828, that a son and heir was born to Pierre Verne and his wife Sophie Allotte de la Fuÿe. Today a plaque in the usual French style for commemorating notables of all kinds marks the house as the birth-place of Jules Verne, 'Romancier, Précurseur des découvertes modernes'.

Pierre Verne was originally from Provins, in the Brie district south of Paris, where his father was the local magistrate. Pierre became a lawyer also, and on his graduation acquired a legal practice in Nantes. There, in 1826, shortly after his arrival, he made the acquaintance of Sophie Allotte de la Fuÿe. They fell in love and were married on 27 February 1827.

Sophie Allotte de la Fuÿe was more than a descendant of one of the merchants who had built the Ile Feydeau. Her family traced its lineage back to a Scottish archer who had taken service with the French king in 1462. By a Royal Patent granted before the Revolution they had acquired the right to own a dovecote. This was called *droit de fuie*, hence the pseudo-noble name of de la Fuÿe. Such petty, but valued privileges were an essential part of the aristocratic system before the Revolution of 1789.

Pierre Verne's ancestry has been traced back to a Fleurie Verne who lived in Paris in the reign of Louis XV. On both sides of his family, then, Jules Verne came of gentry, merchants and lawyers, the sort of people who had come to power in France after the Revolution had broken the power of the aristocracy. Even in 1828 under the restored monarchy of Charles X, they were a force to be reckoned with in France. Men like Pierre Verne saw themselves as the conservative backbone of the country.

During Jules Verne's lifetime there were claims that he was in fact a Polish Jew named Olscievitcz. His family biographers have done their best to scotch such legends: so eminent a French author born of good Catholic stock clearly was not Jewish.

Pierre and Sophie were not happy together at first, as she did not care much for cooking and other domestic duties. They lived with her mother, as her father was almost perpetually absent on long journeys. The missing father so common in Verne's novels may well have had its origin here. Sophie, according to Maurice Metral, in his brief but well-informed biography, was 'sweet, cordial, but a little coquettish'.

Jules's was not an easy birth. In January there had been a false alarm, and the doctor had been called. When the baby did arrive, it was sickly, and during its first few days could not stomach its mother's milk. Sophie spent most of the time watching by the infant's bed.

Pierre Verne, who was of a nervous disposition with bad digestion and rheumatism, was troubled by the baby's continual cries. Sophie, intent on her child, continued to neglect the housework, and paid little attention to her husband. Days passed without a word between them. Their maid, tired of the tense atmosphere, left. Pierre blamed Sophie for this. He wanted to send the baby out to a wet-nurse as it seemed to be too much for Sophie to cope with. Sophie took this suggestion badly and threatened to leave him. That evening, however, all was in order when he came home and Pierre swore he would behave better to Sophie in future. But by the morning he had forgotten his promise. They started fighting again, and the baby joined in the noise.

Eventually a doctor was brought in to see what he could do for the child. He found a splinter of wood in the baby's foot. After this was taken out, Jules became a model baby, who cried only when he was hungry. Relations between Pierre and Sophie improved as well.

The baby was not baptised until the spring, so that the

scattered Verne family could travel to Nantes to attend, as they had come for the wedding the year before. Other relations also came. In the parish register can be seen the names of Gabriel Verne and Adelaide Allotte-Laperrière, the godfather and godmother, and as witnesses two maiden aunts known in the family as 'the Roses of Provins'. M. de la Celle de Chateaubourg and M. Tronson, the husbands of Sophie's elder sisters, also signed as witnesses.

Another relative, a dandy known in the family as 'le bel Allotte', arrived for the ceremony in all his finery, but Madame Allotte-Laperrière refused to have him at the reception afterwards. The very sight of him, 'that fop, that popinjay', upset her. Another uncle, Prudent Allotte, who had walked all the way from La Guerche-en-Bains, nearly twenty miles away, was there and took the place of her husband, absent as usual on business abroad.

Family portraits, of François Guillochet de Laperrière, descended from a long line of Norman seamen, and of Alexander Allotte de la Fuÿe, looked down on the assembled guests. François Tronson, an examining magistrate, recorded that the conversation turned that evening on genealogies, and that Pierre Verne expressed the wish that his infant son would also be a lawyer and inherit his prospering practice. This was a wish they all drank to.

The wine was a special vintage, and heady in its effects according to Maurice Metral. As the evening wore on the discussion became a little heated. The grandmother (maternal) said the boy would be a sailor. The grandfather that from the shape of his neck and forehead he would be a poet of genius. Pierre listened to all of this discontentedly: the boy would be a lawyer, if he could make him one, and no sailor or poet.

Excited by these great plans for the child, the relatives argued in loud voices. Some even went as far as menaces. The morning found some of them asleep on the floor, with the baby in his cradle happily tearing up the contents of his father's brief-case. Jules had opened a client's will which was to involve Pierre in making compensation to this client. A few days later he talked to Sophie about the boy's future: this son would be the lawyer, the next one could be a sailor. (Though only recorded by Metral, these stories, highly coloured though they may be, fit in well enough with what we know from other sources.) And true to this promise, the second son Paul (born in 1829) did indeed become a sailor. There were also three daughters by the marriage: Anna (born 1837), Mathilde (born 1839) and Marie (born 1842). But in those days one did not have to worry about careers for them.

A short time after Jules was born, the family had moved to an apartment in the same building as Pierre's office, 2 Quai Jean-Bart. Here, only across the channel from where he was born, Verne lived until 1841, when he was thirteen.

This sober-minded professional background was, however, also shot through with romantic colours. These were not merely the tropical trade of Nantes, and the relics of the old traders with which his childhood was surrounded. On visits to his uncle, Francisque de Chateaubourg, who was a painter and the son of a painter, he heard of yet more exciting adventures. The painter had been married to the sister of Chateaubriand, and he had seen much of the famous writer in his later years.

By the time of Verne's childhood René de Chateaubriand was living quietly on his estate in Brittany after a turbulent life, slowly composing his *Mémoirès d'Outre Tombe*. But what caught the imagination of the young Verne was the moody youth who had escaped from revolutionary France to America in quest of the North-West Passage, that almost legendary route to the Far East. Chateaubriand had travelled with fur trappers through the forests of New York to the shores of Lake Erie and the Niagara Falls. The virgin forest ravished his soul. The author of *Atala*, who had brought into French literature the novelty of exotic natural descriptions, had perhaps some slight influence on the original imagination of Jules Verne. The romance of adventure in the wilderness was a literary genre which Verne would make peculiarly his own.

But there was nothing exotic or romantic about the domestic life of Pierre and Sophie Verne. The temperament of the father, a strict man who insisted on regularity in life and religion, was puritanical. He was given to self-flagellation. Sophie, though also religious, had little of such austerity, for the Allotte imagination was light and fantastic.

One of the earliest surviving letters from Verne was written on 30 March 1836, when he was seven, to his aunt 'Madame de Chateaubourg, third floor in the Orient' – she lived in Lorient – which was kept because of his amusing version of her address.

Please come and visit us again, because I love you very much. And then, could you please bring those little 'telegraphs' you promised us? Paul must have one too because Paul doesn't know how to write, he is only beginning, but I have already spent a year at boarding school.

Hardly the letter of an infant prodigy, and his family do not seem to have thought young 'Julian', as he was called then, in any way exceptional. But one is struck by his devotion to his brother Paul, a year younger than himself. And, of course, by his early interest in the telegraph – not the real electric telegraph, but a mechanical forerunner of the instrument which was soon to transform the world by making communication over long distances almost as fast as thought.

The infant school which he attended was run by a Madame Sambin. She was the wife of a sea captain, and was surrounded by an aura of mystery according to Francis Lefeuvre, a school friend of Verne.

Sambin must have left his wife while they were still on their honeymoon. Thirty years later, she was still without word of him. Had he spent all those intervening years roaming the seas like Sinbad the Sailor? Or had he been shipwrecked on some desert island, from which he would return like Robinson Crusoe, with a Man Friday and a parrot?

Often this Nantais Penelope would relate her strange story to her small pupils and so it is not extravagant to suggest (as Marguerite Allotte de la Fuÿe does) that she was the original of Mrs. Branican, the woman in Verne's novel of that name who was to spend fourteen years searching the coral seas of the Pacific for her lost husband, whom finally she was lucky enough to find alive. But her story was not published until 1891: Verne had stored away in his memory the strange tale of Madame Sambin for over fifty years. His tenacious memory was to serve him well in his writing career.

After this school Jules and Paul were sent at nine and eight to St. Stanislaus College in Nantes. Jules's school record shows that he took prizes in geography in 1837 and 1838, as well as in Latin, Greek and singing. His teachers later recalled him as 'a slender boy with hair all awry, running on stilts, throwing himself passionately into all forms of sport, a real king of the playground'. Though nothing exceptional as a student Jules worked diligently enough.

After the fifth class, Jules went on to St. Donatian's Seminary to begin the fourth class in 1840. From 1844 to 1845 he was at the Royal Lycée. Here again he failed to shine.

When grown up Verne himself was no lover of studious children, as he said in a later letter to his father (14 March 1853):

Oh! Yes! Children, they never study during childhood. But it is always like that; happily the studious children are always the stupid youths and the imbecilic adults.

Years later, when he was famous, Verne's schoolmates inevitably recalled how he filled his notebooks with drawings of ships and flying machines. One of them even claimed to have heard Jules describe a steam-driven vehicle and that he drew it out on the blackboard complete with a steam elephant. But here recollections seem to have been created out of reading the author's later books: that steam elephant appears in *The Steam House* of 1880. But in a letter written in December 1842, Jules asked his mother for the words of an old song 'Adieu mon beau navire' and for his set-square. So perhaps his romantic imagination was already playing with mechanical inventions of some kind, though no written record to substantiate this seems to exist.

Whatever he felt about school, it seems clear that for Verne himself, his real education was in the holidays, when he and his brother could escape from the city into the countryside. Around 1838 his father had bought a small estate on the banks of the Loire at Chantenay, where the family spent their summers. There the boy's imagination had full rein as he later described in an article which he wrote for the Boston paper *Youth's Companion* in 1889.

From the window of his small bedroom he could see the river and the wide meadows which were flooded in the winter. In summer there were great bands of sand along the banks and small islands in the river. He loved the Loire, even 'if one can't compare it with the Hudson, the Mississippi, or the St. Lawrence, it is at least one of the great rivers of France'.

But it was the sea and his dreams about it which absorbed him.

From the ships at the quays in Nantes which brought in the monkeys, parrots, parakeets and canaries, which crowded the cages of the bird-catcher on the Quai Brancas, to those that sailed past their summer home, to those in the pages of Fenimore Cooper's romances: he was enchanted by them all.

Somewhere Verne picked up the faded journal of a frigate captain named Pierre Leguerte. He spent hours reading the badly written entries jotted down between battles. There was a bloodstain on the last page, and he often speculated about what had happened to the writer.

To live out their dreams, he and Paul would sometimes hire a boat – at a franc a day, this was hard on their meagre resources – and play at naval battles on the river. But the most daring of his escapades, Jules made alone.

One day in the summer of 1839 he failed to return at noon for his meal. He had been up and out of the house early, for his old nurse (who now ran a pork shop) had seen him cross the square at six in the morning. His mother was fearful. Jules might have been drowned, like his Tronson cousins who had died on a shooting expedition two years before. His brother and sisters thought of the 'outlaws' who lived in the nearby quarries, they were dangerous and might have kidnapped him. Very worried, Sophie called on Colonel de Goyon, who lived in the château, to ride into Nantes and alert Pierre Verne.

Word came that the boatman who kept the ferry at Grenouiltère had seen Jules being rowed out to a three-master called the *Coralie*. But the *Coralie* had sailed that morning for the Indies. However, as it was calling into Paimboeuf farther down the Loire, they might yet catch it before it put to sea.

Pierre Verne caught one of the fast steam launches, the 'pyroscaphes' that plied the river, and was in Paimboeuf by six o'clock. Jules had bribed the cabin boy of the *Coralie* to get him aboard the ship, but by the end of the day he must have begun to regret his rashness for he seemed glad enough when his father appeared to rescue him. He got a good hiding and was put to bed on a diet of bread and water. 'From now on,' he promised his mother, 'I'll travel only in my imagination.'

His motive in running away was not just to see the sea, but to bring back a coral necklace for his cousin Caroline with whom he had become infatuated. She was two years older than him, but he used to bring her flowers at the gate of her school. She did not take him seriously, and he hoped the necklace would change her attitude to him.

Verne himself, in his own account of his childhood, makes no mention of this adventure. He does say that it was not until he was twelve, that is in 1840, the year after he 'ran away to sea' on the *Coralie*, that he actually saw the Atlantic Ocean for the first time. He and Paul got permission to travel on the No. 2 pyro-scaphe, which went down to St. Nazaire at the very mouth of the Loire. On the way they passed Indret, where the state yard built ships for the navy; past Paimboeuf; and so to St. Nazaire. Tasting the water Paul was disappointed to find it was not salty (because of the fresh water from the Loire trapped in rockpools on the shore). But elsewhere they found the sea was as briny as they could have hoped for.

Sea stories fascinated both boys. But of all the books of his childhood, the one that Jules loved best, even more than *Robinson Crusoe*, was *The Swiss Family Robinson*. As he was to explain to his young American readers in 1889:

I am well aware that the work of Daniel Defoe has a weightier philosophy. It concerns a man in command of himself, a man alone, a man who finds one day a naked footprint in the sand. But Wyss's book, rich in facts and incidents, is more interesting for young minds. It has the family, the father, mother, the children and their different aptitudes. How many years I passed on their island! With what ardour I involved myself with their discoveries. How much I envied them their fate! So it is not surprising that I was forced to create in *The Mysterious Island*, the Robinsons of Science, and in *Two Years Holiday*, a boarding school for Robinsons.

For Verne the novel, like the Ile Feydeau of his birth, was another form of artificial island.

However it was Defoe's hero who inspired him on the little island in the Loire below Chantenay where he pretended one day to have been shipwrecked. Alone there, he made a hut out of branches and would have settled down. But soon his hunger overcame him. Now he really knew what it was like to have been Alexander Selkirk and those other famous castaways. Hunger was a thing he always dreaded. So as soon as the tide went down, he hurried off home to eat his dinner at the family table.

Summer over, the family returned to Nantes. Verne was four-teen and by now the family had moved to a new house, a large one at 6 rue Jean-Jacques Rousseau, which was almost halfway between the Bourse and the courts, where most of his father's business was done. The house was only a step up a short hill from the river bank, so that Jules was still able to haunt the docks and listen to the strange tales of the Cape Horners about the lands they had seen.

Winter also meant a return to school. The school lists for the Royal Lycée in 1844 show that Jules was still an undistinguished schoolboy: he was fourth in French composition and fifth in Latin. However he easily passed the all important final exams for his Baccalauréat, along with his friends, Charles Maisonneuve, Couteloux de Testre and Ernest Genevois.

These four friends were part of a group that used to meet together after school at Bodin's bookshop, between the Place de Pilori and the main street of Nantes. Here Jules wrote a verse tragedy, his first serious attempt at literature. He showed the manuscript to the director of the Théâtre Riquiqui, a puppet theatre, but he rejected it. Perhaps it was too 'literary'.

Disappointed, he read his play to his Tronson cousins at La Guerche, where he often went in summer, hoping to impress once again the cousin whom he had loved for years. But Caroline only laughed at him and his 'so serious' play. Only Marie Tronson was kind to him, and in gratitude he wrote her a sonnet:

> With true compassion you have shared my pain;
> Your soft caresses, ne'er bestowed in vain,
> Alone have power to dry my sorrowing tears . . .

But it was still Caroline that he loved.

From two paintings by their uncle Francisque de Chateaubourg we know what Jules and Paul, as well as Marie and Caroline, Tronson looked like about this time. The boys with their hoop, their girl cousins with bunches of flowers; all of them with the serious expressions of awkward adolescents.

Jules had been infatuated with Caroline since he was twelve, but she had never taken him seriously. Once he had been so provoked that he slapped her across the face. Years later he was to be heavily sarcastic about her in a letter to his mother written on 14 December 1854. In this he reveals that he had fallen in love with other girls, but with no better success. He refers to a girl named Heloïse David, who was marrying at the end of the year:

Mlle. Heloïse and all the other young women whom I have honoured with my kindnesses all marry within a short time. Look at Mme. Dezaunay [that is, Caroline], Mme. Papin, Mme. Terrier de la Haye [sic], Mme. Duverger, and not least Mme. Louise François.

This is a long list of girls for a man whom his family biographers call a misogynist.

Though he might joke about it, Jules's chagrin over the ingrate Caroline lasted a long time, and in some of his work there is indeed a misogynist streak. In *Broken Straws*, his first play to appear on the Paris stage in 1850, he was particularly harsh about faithless young women. And in a novel written in 1888, a very long time later indeed, he ends the story with a terrible scene in which the two lovers are swept to their death in a burning boat over the Niagara Falls. The name of this funeral wedding-boat was *La Caroline*.

Certainly, as a young man, his feelings had been badly hurt. He wrote of his despair to his old school-friend Aristide Hignard, a candidate for the Prix de Rome, who was studying music in Paris under Halévy. Hignard urged Jules to come to Paris and to forget the ungrateful Caroline.

Pierre Verne, however, wanted Jules to make a start on his legal training. So he settled down obediently after leaving school to study his law books in his father's office in Nantes. Then his parents relented a little, deciding that as Caroline was marrying her Emile Dezaunay on 27 April 1847, Jules might go up to Paris to sit his first law exam and so be out of the way.

So Jules took the pyroscaphe up the Loire to Tours and caught the train to Paris. Strange as it may seem, this was his first train journey, for the railway had only reached Tours shortly before in the great expansion of the railways across France. The railhead at Nantes was established in 1851. Before that the port had been closer in some ways to the West Indies than it was to the capital.

In Paris he stayed with his great-aunt Charruel, a peevish old woman whose house at 2 rue Thérèse was 'like a well, airless and wineless'. Here he finished off a five-act tragedy in verse, *Alexandre VI*, which he had begun the winter before. The manuscript is dated 8 May 1847. He also managed to pass his exams despite 'the ferocity' of the examiners.

He then went on to stay with his aunts at Provins. From their house he wrote home, to confirm that Caroline was married. And so back to Chantenay and his law books. There he was bored and moody. He no longer visited La Guerche: the Tronson family there had lost the charm they had had when he was in love. His letters to his friends such as Hignard and Genevois spoke of what a family biographer calls 'other coarser distractions'. He worried his mother by disappearing for several hours at a time. He was rude when he went visiting and would not dance with the girls.

Very little is known about Verne's life during the winter of 1847–48. But his moodiness might be explained by the fact that he was in love again and writing poetry about it. He was deeply infatuated with a girl called Herminie Arnault-Grosstière. Preserved among his private papers, inherited after his death by Michel and Jean Verne, are two notebooks containing a series of poems, some of which are dated 1847 and 1848. One of them is an acrostic of her name, beginning 'Hélas! je t'ai donné mon cœur faible et sans armes'.

This poem is No. IV in the first notebook. No. XI 'La Fille de l'Air' is dedicated to Herminie. No. XVIII, still from 1847, with an epigraph from Victor Hugo, also refers to Herminie. In the second notebook, poem No. XIV is full of regrets, doubtless due to Herminie's marriage on 19 July 1848 to Auguste Terrien de la Haye, a Nantes landowner.

These poems, then, were mostly written during the summer of 1847 and the early months of 1848, to girls whom Jules had met in his social circle in Nantes and Chantenay.

These emotional disasters made Verne restless. His brother Paul, having failed the medical examination for the Naval School, had gone to sea on 23 December aboard a merchant ship bound for Reunion. He at least was free to do as he pleased. But Jules must bend to his father's will, and Pierre would allow his heir no other career except the law and a future in his Nantes office.

Though a career in literature seemed impossible, Jules continued to write. A piece he had written, probably a poem, was passed around the Nantes literary society, Le Cercle de la Cagnotte. It was very 'free' and had to be read surreptitiously. Its content might have shocked his father. The members of the group assured him of his potential as a popular playwright.

Then in February 1848, revolution broke out in Paris. On 24 February Louis-Philippe abdicated. A provisional government led by the poet Lamartine emerged to take charge. These events in Paris were only a small part of the revolutionary tide that swept across Europe that year.

According to Verne himself, his earliest memory had been the sound of rifle fire in the streets of Nantes as the people fought with the Royalist troops in the Revolution of 1830 which had overthrown Charles X and put Louis-Philippe on the throne. So he had already seen a revolution at the age of two and been scared by it. The events of 1830 had inspired Delacroix's painting 'Liberty Leading the People', a revolutionary icon better suited to the headier romanticism that surrounded 1848. Like many young people of the time, Verne responded to that romanticism. During the election in April he distributed literature in support of the Provisional Government in the streets of Nantes.

In these elections the socialists were badly defeated, gaining only a quarter of the votes. An attempted rising was quickly quashed, but after the National Workshops were closed (because they were thought to be hotbeds of socialist sedition), worse trouble broke out on 23 June.

Fifty thousand workers fought in the Paris streets with soldiers and armed bourgeoisie. The government created a military dictatorship under General Cavaignac, and in three days of bloody fighting the insurrection was put down. Ten thousand workers were killed. So were two generals, the Archbishop of Paris, and more officers than had died in the Napoleonic wars. Anyone found with arms was shot on sight. The National Assembly set about restoring order, one result of which was a new French Constitution in October.

Verne's response to these events was to write a play *La Conspiration des Poudres* about Guy Fawkes' attempt to blow up the British Houses of Parliament. Fawkes, argues Jean Jules-Verne in his biography, is seen by Verne more as a religious than political hero. But in the light of all the explosions that feature in his books and the political feelings of his old age, it strikes one that the young Verne was either something of an anarchist or a latent pyromaniac. Blowing up people, even on paper, can indicate deep frustrations. There can have been little freedom in his father's strictly ordered home, dominated by the twin authorities of law and Roman Catholicism. Verne was to spend his life trying to escape from both, moving as he grew older towards anarchy and a more generalised deism.

It was after these desperate days, at the beginning of July, that Verne went up to Paris to sit for his second law exam. From the capital where he was staying with his cousin Henri Garcet (his great-aunt Charruel having fled the city when the revolution began), Jules dutifully informed his father about his expenses and made some passing remarks about the recent events. He had been out to look at the scenes around the rue Saint-Antoine, at the bullet-battered houses and wrecked buildings. He thought them a frightening sight, and the street fighting was incomprehensible to his provincial mind.

Ten days later, on 21 July, he wrote again. But this time with something more personal in mind.

> Good heavens! I was forgetting, there is something else which nags me in the midst of my absorbtion with Paris. What has happened about the marriage of a certain young lady whom you know well and which was to have taken place on Tuesday? I would like to know what has been finally fixed up.

Writing again to his mother on 30 July, he reverted more bitterly to Herminie.

> Alas, my dear mother, all is not rosy in this life, and those who built brilliant castles in Spain, find themselves alone in their own country. So it is true that the wedding has taken place!

There then follows a most astonishing description of 'a dream' which he had had recently, in which a wedding was being celebrated in the most expensive style, over which a weird figure presided.

> The bride was dressed in white – symbol of simplicity of soul; the groom was in black, a symbolic allusion to the colour of her

soul . . . The bridal chamber was opened before the trembling couple and the joys of heaven filled the hearts of the pair . . . and all night, all the long black night, a man in rags sharpened his teeth on the door handle. Ah, my dear mother, at this dreadful idea, I awoke with a start, and now your letter tells me my dream was a reality. What misfortunes I foresee. Poor young man. But I'll always say: Father, forgive him, he knows not what he does. As for me, I will console myself by killing the first black cat I meet . . . It was necessary to record on paper the memory of this funereal ceremony.

It needs little knowledge of psychoanalysis to see in this dream the frustrated longings of a jealous man. The young Verne was cultivating a bitterness about women and marriage, based perhaps on little enough experience, which was to last a long time.

Unlucky in love, Verne had deeper resources. From his childhood, music had been one of Verne's great loves, the consolation he fell back on in times of stress. We hear very little about it in his letters, but with his growing enthusiasm for opera and musical comedy, it is always there, a motif in the varied pattern of his life.

He passed his exams once again, and went down to Provins to visit his relatives. Then back to Nantes. His third year of law was the most important, and so it was decided that it would be better for him if he studied for it in Paris. After all, the exam questions were keyed to lectures which he could not hear by studying at home.

He spent the summer at Chantenay writing: a short farce *Une Promenade en Mer*, and the outlines of three other comedies, the manuscripts of which were inherited by his son, and after him by Jean Jules-Verne. They were never performed or published. And also more poems to go into his notebook.

Paul came back to Nantes from his first voyage at the beginning of September. He was preparing to depart again in November to return to Reunion on another ship. Jules packed up his manuscripts and made ready to leave also. He was to take quarters in Paris with his old friend Edouard Bonamy.

This was a definite break in his life. He, like his brother, was escaping from home at last, even though it was not to go to sea; escaping from the city of Nantes and the ever-present influence of his father. Admittedly some of the quirks of his later character may have their origin in his early years. The roots of the 'romancier' can be seen easily enough in the romance of Nantes and its ships, in Chateaubriand and his tales of the virgin forest, in *The Swiss Family Robinson* and the games of castaways with his brother. Yet there is nothing in the least scientific or progressive in his origins, so sternly conservative and Catholic, pious and orthodox. The secret core of Verne's personality lies in his relations with his parents, with his brother Paul, and with those girls who took his fancy so easily. But the writer to be, the 'précurseur des découvertes modernes', the creator of the *Strange Journeys*, was still in the making.

In a letter to his friend Hignard he washed his hands of Nantes and all it stood for.

Well, I'm leaving at last, as I wasn't wanted here, but one day they'll see what stuff he was made of, that poor young man they knew as Jules Verne.

And off he went to a Paris still recovering from the revolutionary months of 1848, and settled down as a student on the Left Bank.

Chapter Two

Paris 1848

On 10 November 1848 Jules Verne and his friend Edouard Bonamy started for Paris. For the inauguration of the new Republican regime, the National Assembly was holding a civil and religious ceremony in the Place de la Concorde during which the whole of the new liberal constitution was to be read out and a solemn *Te Deum* sung by the Archbishop of Paris, who was also new. Naturally the young men were anxious not to miss this splendid occasion. So they took the stagecoach to Tours, where they tried to slip aboard an official train which was carrying a contingent of the local National Guard to Paris.

They were thrown off the train, and in consequence missed the inauguration, as Bonamy explained in a letter to his family a few days later:

Reaching Paris only on Sunday night, all we saw of this much talked about celebration of the Constitution were the last candles guttering in their sockets. The Concorde was a basilica of velvet and gold above a forecourt of snow. After trudging many streets and climbing many flights of stairs, we finally discovered two suitable rooms at 24 rue de l'Ancienne-Comédie, at thirty francs a month.

Paris in 1848 was the epicentre of the revolutionary tremors which had shaken thrones all over Europe. The atmosphere of the capital was heady with political excitement, for a young man like Verne this was a lively time to arrive there. What in Nantes had seemed to Verne's father a profound threat to his way of life, was in Paris the fashionable fervour of the literary élite.

Verne was of an age with those liberals who had hoped to see in 1848 the flowering of their political ideals. They were to be disappointed. The monarchy had been overthrown, and a new Republic established, but the communist rising had brought havoc to the city. The election of Louis Napoleon as President was to be followed in 1851 by the coup d'état which made him master of France. There was much disillusionment with politics; some literary men, like Hugo, went into exile, others concentrated only on literature.

This mixture of idealism and defeated hopes provided a theme which was to run through much of Verne's later work. Balzac has remarked that as men we all belong to the generation in which we are between twenty and thirty. Verne was one of the generation of 1848. Later this would be an evocative phrase, redolent of freedom, of liberal and democratic hopes for a better future. But for Verne at the time the freedom of 1848 was the freedom of Paris, the freedom to do as he liked. For a young man of twenty that was as important as any political belief.

And the young men who arrived on the Left Bank that Sunday evening had more immediate concerns than politics or the state of society.

They had found their rooms soon enough, but, as with all students, money was short. Their landlady was always asking for money to cover her housekeeping. Jules ate at a restaurant where there was a set menu for thirty-two sous. In this way he could keep his daily expenses down to forty sous, the sum his careful father had suggested when he left home. But as he explained in a letter home, sometimes he could not get to the restaurant. So then

> I dine in my own quarters, but it's dearer, a simple meal costs forty sous; besides breakfast with bread and milk costs me five sous, and often a single roll at two sous isn't enough. Then there's the inevitable five centimes for the waiter. In short, my food here often costs forty-seven to forty-eight sous a day, even when that includes only one full meal. I hope you will give the matter some thought, my dear father, so that in fixing my allowance you take account of all the necessary items.

With so little money to spare, his social life might have suffered. However, shortly after Jules's uncle the painter

Chateaubourg came up to Paris to visit the Salon and to see his friends, he introduced Jules into the salons of Mme. de Jomini, Mme. de Mariani and Mme. de Barrère (who was an acquaintance of his mother Sophie). All of these were frequented by celebrities. Mme. de Jomini's was political in tone, which Jules did not really care for. As for the others:

> The conversation of Mme. de Mariani and her guests is rather like those crude bronze figures that take on a superficial polish from constant handling. And like the bronzes that sort of conversation costs little to acquire. On the other hand, at Mme. de Barrère's salon at the rue Fermes-des-Mathurins, one can breathe freely.

Even so her guests were very elegant, and between them the two boys had only one evening suit and one pair of patent leather shoes. They had to take it in turns to wear them on evenings out. This they found amusing rather than inconvenient. But one thing they could not do without was books. At the beginning of December Jules was telling his father about buying a complete Shakespeare and a set of Scott. He got nervous shudders when he stood outside a bookshop, so great was his desire for books of all kinds. He went through 'all the torture of unsatisfied passion' when he could not buy them. He had been unable to resist the temptation of the well-bound edition of Shakespeare and had to live on dried prunes for three days.

At this time the dominant concern of all Paris was the coming election for President of the Republic, for which Lamartine, Cavaignac and Louis Napoleon were standing. 'Who will be for order?' was what Verne asked himself in his letters home. Earlier he had told his mother that he had no plans to join the rioters. He had been impressed at that time by 'the calm and moderation of M. Thiers and his colleagues, who represented *order*' – which was the obsession of his parents' social class.

Secretly, perhaps, he now felt that politics were not really his affair. He was more concerned with social life. Mme. Barrère introduced him to the Comte de Coral, the editor of *La Liberté*. Coral was a friend of Victor Hugo and promised Verne that he would take him to see the poet as soon as he would receive him. Hugo was Verne's demigod. He admitted to his father that there were good citizens of Nantes who were as worthy of curiosity as any eccentric Parisian literary man, but all the same he felt an irresistible attraction to the literary life he saw in Paris.

And in that attraction, it was Hugo and the Romantics who were to be the greatest influence on Verne. And Victor Hugo, in his opposition to Louis Napoleon, was not quite a representative of the order that young Verne had told his parents he admired.

For of course he did not tell them everything, nor about everyone whom he met at Mme. Barrère's social gatherings. She had in her service a young lady, probably of Spanish-Jewish origin, named Maya Abanes, whom Dumas courted in his spare moments. The girl was not slow in noticing Verne, the large shy boy who always arrived alone. One evening she approached him and said she had two tickets for the Etoile the next day – Dumas had given them to her. She thought he might go with her.

The young man could not have hoped for more. They passed a pleasant evening, and then went to dine in a little restaurant on the banks of the Seine. There Verne declared his love.

But now Maya had learned to turn a deaf ear to such little speeches from men of any age. But for once, perhaps, she did not listen to the wise voice of her conscience. The next morning she awoke in the student's glacial room – a little ashamed of herself. Verne himself was not to be seen. He had not dared to stay, but when she got up she found he had left a note for her on the bedside table:

> Please Mlle. excuse the poor man who yesterday, late in the night, wished to abuse you, led you to this miserable lodging.

The young lady must have laughed at this, for she wrote an answer on the same sheet of paper:

> I will wait for you at the same place. And believe me your bed is the best in which I have ever been.

Their affair continued. Years later, when he bought one of the boats which were then his greatest passion, Verne confessed that he was as excited about it as if he 'were twenty and she were my first mistress'. That cold winter he was twenty, and the beautiful

Maya was the first girl who had responded to his attentions.

But this relationship, important as it must have been for Verne, was not as influential as another begun through Mme. Barrère. At her salon Verne met the Chevalier d'Aspentigney, an expert on palmistry, a fashionable pseudo-science in which Alexander Dumas was very interested. D'Aspentigney introduced the young man into the author's circle, and soon Verne was a frequent visitor to Dumas's apartment, where a hospitable host would feed his young and hungry friends with dishes of his own special creation. There Verne became acquainted with Dumas's suddenly famous son, author of *The Lady of the Camelias*. Verne enjoyed these evenings very much indeed.

Indeed, I find it an entirely new and marvellous pleasure to be in immediate contact with literature, to sense it as something alive and on the move, as the talk switches from Racine to Shakespeare, from Scribe to Clairville.

But his enthusiasm and his studies – about which his father had to be reassured, for there was an exam at the end of February – were disturbed by the more public enthusiasms of the moment.

Unfortunately, infernal politics cast their drab mantle over the beauty of poetry. Let Ministers, President and Chamber all go to the devil, as long as there remains in France one poet who can touch our hearts. Politics, as history proves, are purely contingent and ephemeral. I think and repeat with Goethe: 'Nothing that makes us happy is an illusion.'

His austere father thought that a dangerous notion for a young man and remonstrated with his son. But Verne was adding poems to his notebooks, inspired by his affair with Maya, and must have felt that happiness was indeed no illusion.

Yet history as drama was being played out around him in the Presidential elections. And that autumn, on the stage of the Théâtre Historique dramatic history was also re-enacted, this time under the direction of Dumas. The theatre reopened on 21 February 1849 with a production of *The Youth of the Musketeers*. Verne attended the first night as a guest of Dumas in his own box.

It was extremely amusing. The play is taken from the first volume of *The Three Musketeers*, and although it has no particular literary pretensions, it shows an almost miraculous sense of theatre. Dumas was wonderful to behold while the play was in progress. He couldn't help telling us everything that was going to happen next. I saw a lot of well-known people come into the box: Girardin, Théophile Gautier, Jules Janin, etc. These little privileges are not to be scorned.

Verne was hopeful that his connection with Dumas would advance his literary ambitions, even when he became a lawyer. He had hopes of having one of his plays, such as *The Gunpowder Plot*, performed at the Théâtre Historique. He showed these plays to Dumas together with a one-act play in verse *Les Pailles Rompues* (*Broken Straws*). Bonamy thought the last was charming, as Dumas must have, for it was *Broken Straws* that he selected for production.

The first night was 12 June 1850. *Broken Straws* was only a trifle but it was also a beginning. The plot revolved around an old man, his young wife, and her handsome former suitor. She wants a necklace which her husband refuses to buy her. The broken straws refer to a wager: if either of them gives the other anything, the necklace will be forfeit. The suitor appears on the scene. He hides in a cupboard and the husband demands the key from his wife while looking for him. Henriette the wife gives it to him, but the wager is won, and the necklace is hers.

This play was typical of the boulevard entertainment of the period. But the lines had a certain bite, and there was an underlying cynicism directed against women throughout the piece. The painful memory of how he had been treated in Nantes had made the young Verne bitter at heart.

The play was a success with the critics, perhaps because it was generally thought that Dumas had had a hand in rewriting it. The young Verne found himself applauded by polite society and that was something he wanted very much indeed. A party for him was held at the apartment of Adrien Talexy, the composer, which all the younger poets and composers attended. Later ten of these young men and Verne formed a dining club which met once a week at the Tête Noir restaurant. They called themselves the *Onze-sans-Femmes* (Eleven without Women). Also at the party were Hignard and Charles Maisonneuve, who paid for *Broken Straws* to be printed. The play ran for twelve nights and the printed copies were soon sold out.

In Nantes, Pierre Verne was a little disturbed at the play in spite of its success. As a good Catholic he found the plot distasteful. Was his son becoming 'a dangerous writer'? Jules had to mollify him as best he could.

These plays are not meant to be taken seriously. I have plenty of other ideas in my head, thousands of projects that I'm not able to put into shape; if these things turn out well, you will see them one day, but what I need now is time, and patience and tenacity.

On his return to Nantes that summer Jules found himself famous there. Friends and acquaintances (in the usual way known to all writers) asked to borrow copies of the play. They could as easily have bought one before they were all sold out, Jules observed to Maisonneuve. The Théâtre Graslin in Nantes put on the play and all of fashionable Nantes turned out for the first night on 7 November. The local critics were kind, though one of them felt the plot was so *risqué* 'that only the author's grace and wit made the play acceptable'. Another thought 'this courtly trifle held a sad moral for all old men, indeed a desperate one for any husband over fifty'.

His family were put out by the 'risqué' part. But Jules recognised that the play was of little importance. Returning to Paris he reproached himself with 'lingering on well-trodden paths, when science is performing miracles and thrusting forward into the unknown'. He had found a new interest, which was to absorb him more and more.

He now settled on the Right Bank of the city, away from the student quarter. He was supposed to be working on his thesis for submission to the university, but in reality he was brooding on those miracles of science and what he might make of them for literature.

Yet he did not abandon the theatre. He wrote a three-act play *Les Savants*, followed by a music-hall sketch *Qui me rit*, and in collaboration with his friend Michel Carré, the libretto for a mime-play for which Hignard wrote the music, called *Colin-Maillard*.

Jules by now had graduated. His father expected him to return to Nantes and to take over the family law firm. But Jules was determined to stay on in Paris and be a writer.

It is fate that keeps me in Paris. I may become a good writer but I would never be anything but a poor lawyer, since I habitually see only the comic or the artistic aspect of things, while their precise reality escapes me.

So he refused his father's practice, which caused the old man some pain. Since Jules had been born he had planned that his son would follow after him. But Jules was adamant:

The only career for which I am really suited is the one I am already pursuing: literature. I am deeply moved by your suggestions, but surely I must trust my own judgment in this matter. If I took it on, your practice would only wither away. Please forgive your respectful and loving son.

So Verne gave up the law, determined to be a writer, no matter what the future held.

While he was arguing with his father, Maya Abanes came to see him. She told him she was getting engaged to an industrialist from Lyons. She preferred an easy life to the hardships of love. Verne told her she was quite right, and he would have thought the less of her if she had done otherwise. The fact that she was choosing to marry an industrialist rather than an aristocrat is striking however: since Verne's childhood, the Industrial Revolution had spread to France. Prosperity and change were imminent. And the science and technology that made these possible were becoming of increasing interest to Jules Verne.

Chapter Three

Boulevard and Bourse

LONG YEARS WERE TO PASS BEFORE VERNE COULD CLAIM TO
be a literary success, longer still before he became wealthy.
Naturally his family, especially his mother, worried about Jules.
Would he really be able to make his living by writing? These
worries were only increased by his raffish way of life. During the
winter of 1852 poverty kept him in lodgings with a rowdy set,
who gave him little peace with their comings and goings. But
slowly things began to improve for him.

He had placed two stories with the editor of the *Musée des
Familles*, Pitre-Chevalier, who was a Breton and perhaps sym-
pathetic to a fellow-countryman. The first story, *Les Premiers
Navires de la Marine Mexicaine* (*The First Ships of the Mexican Navy*),
had appeared the year before. With Pitre-Chevalier he wrote a
play about the Californian gold-rush, *Les Chateaux en Californie*
(*Castles in California*), with the punning subtitle *Pierre qui roule
n'amasse pas mousse* (*A Rolling Stone Gathers No Moss*). But money was
scarce all the same. There was very little from home. Maurice
Metral suggests that his father even cut off his allowance, and that
with his last few coins he bought a gold-fish. He tried coaching
students for their law exams. Then he entered a law office as a
clerk, but he found he would have to work there for eighteen
months before he was paid. Even after that, he would only have
got 600 francs – workmen on the roads got hardly any less.

He continued to work at his plays and librettos, for he still saw
himself as a man of the theatre. Between 1851 and 1863 he
wrote some fifteen dramatic works of various kinds. But these were
inconsequential pieces for the most part, and would have no
interest now if it were not for his later work. However his plays

taught Verne a great deal about writing. His novels are often constructed like plays in set scenes, with vivid dialogue to move the action along. Though they were a hard grind at the time, these years of apprenticeship were not really wasted.

Even though his plays came to nothing – nine of them were never even produced – he still worked away in the Bibliothèque Nationale. Here his studies were taking a different direction. He was already building up the idea for his future work and spoke about it to Dumas: he hoped to do for science and geography what the author of *The Count of Monte Cristo* had done for history. Dumas encouraged him. Hence he was obdurate to further pleas from his father to have second thoughts about the law.

> You ask me to give the matter further thought. But what's the use? You know Dumas's opinion. In my own mind, my decision is irrevocably fixed. Further reflexion belongs to the polar zones of uncertainty. But the region I inhabit now is less to the north, and much nearer the passionate tropical zone.

Geography, as that strange polar metaphor indicates, was Verne's great passion. In his father's office he had met one Jacques Arago, who was helping some mutinous sailors in their defence. In Paris he got to know Arago quite well.

Though now blind, Arago still travelled widely. He had only recently taken a party out to the Colorado gold fields – the 'Argonauts' they called them in Paris. The brother of the well-known astronomer Françoise Arago, Jacques Arago was famous himself as the author of *Tour du Monde*, perhaps the most successful travel book of its day. Jules listened with rapt attention to Arago describe a giant liana, 'several leagues long', which he had followed on the hills above Rio de Janeiro: years later such a vine would appear in *La Jangada*, guiding Verne's heroes through the Amazonian forest.

By now he had rooms with Hignard at the top of a house in Boulevard Bonne-Nouvelle, between the Opéra and Montmartre. He had 'a light, airy room in which I can put my ideas in order'. Not that he was adverse to the more Bohemian entertainment which the *Onze-sans-Femmes* still provided.

In December 1851 Paris was thrown into turmoil by the sudden coup d'état of Louis Napoleon, who was shortly after to restore the imperial dignity of France by making himself Napoleon the Third. Radicals and Republicans were sent into exile in their thousands to Brussels and London.

But early in 1852 Verne was saved from his own turmoil when he was appointed secretary to the director of the Théâtre Lyrique, Jules Seveste. Jules was excited enough by this job, even though it did not bring him any money. It meant he was in direct contact with theatrical affairs and that was worth a great deal to him. However his parents thought the position 'bizarre' and were careful not to mention what they considered a shameful secret to any of their friends in Nantes. Though he continued to write to them, now on paper headed Théâtre Lyrique, Jules filled his pages with trifles. He told them little about his work, even less about his private affairs.

Jules enjoyed the free and easy atmosphere of the theatre, and was fascinated by backstage life. His friend Haucilly recalls him as something of a gad-about, and recalls an amusing story of a feud between Verne and a stage-singer called Marie Cabel. Feeling the cold in his draughty office one day, Jules borrowed a false-ermine property cloak from the wardrobe-master. While walking round the theatre he wore the cloak much to the amusement of the minor actors and actresses, who were overjoyed at his prancing impersonation of the great singer's manner. Haucilly also recalled the icy disgust of Marie Cabel when she discovered what the mere secretary of the theatre was doing.

His first biographer, Marguerite Allotte de la Fuÿe, with due regard to family feelings, says that at this time Verne was a typical provincial product of his time, 'free in his language, yet chaste in his conduct'. One naturally enough takes this with a grain of scepticism. After all Verne moved in *louche* literary circles, and any lapses from the stern code of conduct his father held would not be reported home. Or so he hoped.

Yet he was not completely happy. Marriage he came to feel was the only answer. 'You must marry me off, dear mama,' he wrote in a letter home. 'I'll take any wife you care to choose. I'll take her with my eyes shut and my purse open.' When a Nantes girl, Heloïse David, and her father turned up at the theatre looking for free tickets, he wondered what her real reason was. Could she be looking for a husband? She was one of the girls he mentioned to his mother as having lost his heart to. Whatever he did about making his feeling known came to little, for she married a M. le Marchand in 1854 at Nantes.

If love still eluded him, there was always his work. His father, having asked which of the current literary schools he would attach himself to, was put out by his son's disrespectful remarks about both the Classical and the Romantic groups. Jules felt that the only school he could belong to would be his own.

At this time he was writing *Mona Lisa*, a play about Leonardo and the Giaconda, a comedy like those Musset used to write. However nothing came of this, for the finished play was another of those that remained unproduced.

Of far greater interest and significance was a short novel which appeared in the *Musée des Familles* in 1852. This was *Martin Paz*, an historical story which he wrote around a set of paintings by the Peruvian artist Merino, whom he had met at Arago's house where he was staying for some months. A dramatic story of love and revolution in Lima, this book is marked as an emphasis on Catholicism which is lacking in later books. The beautiful heroine was a Spanish-Jewish girl – an oblique commemoration of Maya Abanes perhaps. The reception of *Martin Paz* by the critics stimulated Pierre Verne to ask Jules to put the book forward for an Academy Prize. But Jules did not think the distinction, if it was one, was worth the trouble of soliciting Academy members.

Despite these small advances in his career, life was still hard enough for Verne. His socks and shirts were the subject of continual maternal concern. There was an obvious solution to the problem. In a letter written about this time to his friend Ernest Genevois in Nantes he urged him not to marry with such solicitude that we can have no doubts about the ache in his own heart to be doing just that. Their friend Stephane Halgran had also recently married. Verne affected to think that marriage was the worst blunder that a young man could make. He gave Genevois some jocular advice. Sooner or later, Verne suggested lightly, he would have to become the consoler of his wife. Genevois knew his tastes. If he must marry, he should choose a girl to suit Verne.

Hardly the letter to someone chaste in his behaviour, if Jules had by now been able to develop a definite taste in woman. Unfortunately this letter was shown around the Fine Arts Club in Nantes where it was read by Pierre Verne. (Another letter to

Genevois exists in Nantes Public Library which Pierre does not seem to have read and which I deal with below.) Pierre wrote to his son that he was in danger of becoming the object of scandal; but Jules was unperturbed.

So now I'm supposed to be an object of scandal? The truth is quite the opposite. I'm becoming as old as the hills, as wise as the Seven Sages, as keenly observant as Arago, as deep as the well of Grenelle, as moral as any professor of ethics.

Ah! so dear old Genevois finds me frivolous? But it is wisdom to find life as black as Avernus, as black as the American cap of Independence, as black as a coal-heaver's family. I have never been so merry as I am today, in spite of the anarchy which reigns in the Ministry of my Interior. Whence comes all this anarchy? For, after all I lead a model life, and even Simon Stylites, who spent years on top of a pillar to make himself agreeable to Heaven, cannot hold a candle to me in virtuous conduct. I am not exactly reduced yet to eating the droppings of birds, but the meat which I put up with must have dragged a good many omnibuses through Paris.

This view of his life may well have been improved for home consumption. It is true, however, that Verne's health, like his father's, was uncertain, that he suffered from neuralgia and from terrible stomach pains, which he tried to assuage with large helpings of food when he could afford it. When he could not he suffered terribly from cramps.

His mother, worried at the thought of her son eating horse-meat, sent him money in secret. He wrote to thank her, assuring her that his mime-play *Colin-Maillard* would make him rich when it was soon produced.

At this time he was writing a strange Hoffmanesque story called *Master Zacharius*, about a Swiss watchmaker who sells his soul to the Devil. The story features a sinister clock which was actually a time demon. The fleeting nature of life was brought home to Verne by the death of one of his friends in the *Onze-sans-Femmes*, David Pitfold, in March 1853. Then another friend, Lorin, died, and Michel Carré was far from well. The time demon seemed to be carrying away his generation.

In a letter to his father Jules explained that Lorin had lived with a young woman he was not married to. They were very respectable people otherwise, and her father and mother were part of the household, and Lorin's parents often dined with them.

What will shock you in all this, my dear father, was certainly no offence to the delicacy of most of these people.

Lorin was, besides, an excellent fellow, warm-hearted and generous and loyal. He had in short, a fine, frank, courageous, open character. He certainly believed in God, but rather less, I feel, in the Catholic teaching of the doctrine of the immortality of the soul, and not at all in organised Christianity. He was one of those people who detest priests without knowing anything about them, and I have had many a discussion with him on the subject.

However, his Henrietta loved him deeply and well and shed many tears at his going, and how he had died, naturally without the least religious consolation. Through his love, charity and devotion, he filled his life with every possible good action, and he died feeling that he had done nothing to deserve a reproach. All the same, that is how he died. Where is he now?

A strictly orthodox view, such as that held by Pierre Verne, would have placed him in Hell. But what he actually replied to his son we do not know. Latent in Jules's question he must have seen, as we can see now, the seeds of doubt by which traditional dogmatic religion is constantly undermined. After this exchange father and son seem to have grown closer together. At this period Jules was still an orthodox Catholic himself, but a deeply troubled one, beset by personal and emotional problems for which the stern verities of his father's generation did not provide an answer. He was slowly becoming a modern man.

The story of Master Zacharius seems to have originated in such doubts, for in the original version there is a scene in which the old clockmaker refuses to honour the elevated host in his parish church. A later version made this explicit Catholic scene more pointed, the old man's defiance echoing that of Nemo and other Verneian heroes.

His operetta *Colin-Maillard* had its première at the Théâtre Lyrique on 20 April 1853. Though it was acclaimed by the press, it did little to make the fortunes of either Verne or Michel Carré who had written the libretto, or Aristide Hignard who did the music. Again Verne shrugged this off. The play was a trifle, 'no more than ballast to help me keep my head above the surface of this dazzling, dizzying whirlpool that is Paris'.

Later that year he wrote yet another play with Michel Carré, again with music by Hignard. Called *Les Compagnons de la Marjolaine*, this too was accepted by the Théâtre Lyrique and was produced in 1855.

For his employer Seveste he obtained a translation his father had made of the *Ave Maria Stella*, which Seveste's daughter needed for an entertainment at her convent. He was so pleased with Verne that he gave him a much-needed holiday from his unpaid labours, which Verne wangled by getting his father to write to say he was required in Nantes on family business. This was true enough, as Pierre Verne was selling his practice and Jules felt he should be there to give him some moral support at this critical time.

And then there was the question of a wife. His friend Haucilly felt that Verne was out of place in Paris and that he should give up the Bohemian life he was leading. Verne felt the solution to his restlessness was to get married. Haucilly and he discussed the various young ladies of Nantes, and the name of Laurence Janmar seemed likely. Verne planned his return to Nantes like a military campaign.

He wrote an entertainment in which he and some of his friends would appear at a fancy-dress ball given in the new year of 1854. As a costume he wore the 'incroyable' dandy suit of his uncle le Bel Allotte that had made such a stir at his baptism. Naturally with his Parisian airs the girls found him immensely attractive. Their fathers were less enthusiastic and eyed him suspiciously.

Laurence Janmar was there in a gypsy costume. Later that evening, after the entertainment, she was talking to Ninette Cheguillaume (a girl for whom Paul Verne had conceived a hopeless passion only to see her marry someone else). She remarked that her whalebone corset was pinching her ribs. Jules, overhearing her, murmured after bowing to her, 'Ah, that I might go fishing for whalebone on that coast.'

Her father when he heard this was furious. A M. Charles Duverger, Verne's rival, bore Laurence away in triumph. Such a joke might be all very well in Paris (where a play called *La Pêche aux Corsets* had opened shortly before), but certainly not in provincial Nantes.

Jules was determined, however, not to leave it at that. Pierre Verne was sent around to the Janmars to see what could be arranged for his son. But it seemed that Laurence really preferred Duverger and had only been flirting with Jules. As his father explained to him:

> My poor boy, Janmar thinks that your position at the Théâtre Lyrique is far too uncertain. And then felt that your joke about his daughter's corsets was out of place . . .

Once again provincial mores had triumphed. Verne retreated to Paris.

Verne seems to have made more efforts to gain a wife however. There was a Louise Françoise, a year younger than he , who attracted his interest, but she too went elsewhere in the end, marrying a Stanislaus Prevost in December 1854. Laurence married Duverger in August of the same year.

In April 1854 Jules had been at Mortagne, where he was visiting a family with a view to marrying the daughter of the house. But though Jules was prepared to go ahead, nothing came of this effort either, much to his mother's regret.

On 29 June 1854 Verne's director at the Théâtre Lyrique, Jules Seveste, died of cholera (which was spreading in an epidemic across Europe from the Crimean War which had begun in March). His contract dissolved with Seveste's death. This meant that he could now leave the Théâtre Lyrique, which delighted him. But in fact he had to stay on until November 1855, to help in the transition of management. He turned down subsequent offers to extend his contract, even to take a share in the profits. He wanted to be free to write.

His mind was moving in new directions. An indication of this is given by a footnote in a letter to his father. 'Please send me Henri Garcet's new book, *Elements de Mécanique*, which I left behind me at Nantes.'

He was able to see his friendly cousin Henri Garcet at the Lycée Henri IV only on occasions. Most of his time was taken up at the Théâtre Lyrique making arrangements for new productions and in keeping the peace between the artistes. He was unable to get to Nantes for his sister Marie's communion, and she had to be content with a poem.

Verne's new play *Les Compagnons de la Marjolaine* was produced in 1855 at the Théâtre Lyrique. Though Verne thought the theatre's mime plays were in the true tradition of Molière, the critics merely thought them childish. He was fraught with worries which a present of apricots from Chantenay did little to assuage. He could no longer sleep at night, and it was often six o'clock before he dropped off. He was glad the theatre was closing for the summer.

His nervous tension gave rise to symptoms of psychosomatic distress, insomnia, bilious attacks, ear-aches, then facial paralysis affecting his left eye and mouth. The symptoms were to reappear later in his life whenever he was under strain.

My nerves are strung up to breaking point. My tongue is coated and I have a persistent temperature. I can no longer close my mouth properly. It's absolute torture! I dribble like a boa constrictor digesting a meal, or a dramatic critic at work. Even so, in spite of my exhaustion, I used my last five francs to make a journey of eighty leagues. On Saturday evening, I took an excursion train to visit the Allottes at Dunkirk, a pretty little seaport, completely Dutch in atmosphere. So at last I have seen the North Sea.

This visit inspired a short novella about the fishermen of the northern seas called *A Winter Among the Ice Floes*, published in the *Musée des Familles*.

In October 1855 another secretary, Verne's friend Philippe Gillé, was found for the Théâtre Lyrique and Verne handed over his duties at the beginning of November.

At last he was free. He had managed to save some money. All he wanted to do now was retreat to his room on the Boulevard Nouvelle and put his ideas in order. He was working on his style (rather as the young Stevenson did) by improving his vocabulary, using nothing but technical words to avoid cumbersome periphrases. (Later Apollinaire was to remark on this: 'What a style Jules Verne has, nothing but nouns.') This was how he spent his time; it might seem the merest literary drudgery, but he enjoyed it.

His new stories had appeared in the *Musée des Familles*; now he started a comedy of manners *Les Heureux du jour*, which provided him with an excuse for conducting research in some of the seedier quarters of Paris.

In December 1855 he came out of his seclusion. With the fall of Sebastopol and the end of the Crimean War, Paris society once again opened its doors. Verne went to receptions given by Mme. Gavarni, by the Academician Empis who directed the Théâtre Français, and by M. Pelouse, a director of the Institut Français and director of the state mint – Pelouse's daughter had just become engaged to Verne's friend and doctor, Victor Marie.

At the same time less polite society also returned to normal after the war and the cholera epidemic. Verne began spending half the day and much of the night in cafés and clubs. His father remonstrated with his son about all this socialising: what had it to do with literature. Jules claimed he was gathering material for his comedy.

However Verne's entertainments were of a more basic sort. In a letter to his friend Genevois, Verne admitted that 'all my conquests couldn't care less about me'. He was always welcome in 'the best houses in the rue D'Amboise or the rue Montyon'. These 'best houses' were among the more notorious of the *maisons de tolérance* in the Paris of the period, backing onto the theatrical district. The frustrations of his search for a wife had led him to resort to the more carnal entertainments of the city.

Also about this time he was writing poetry of a kind which would have dismayed his father even more. In Nantes some of Verne's writings had been very free, and had shocked the local literary circle. A piece of his more risqué work has survived in the *Nouveau Parnasse Satyrique*, a set of verses called untranslatably 'Lamentations d'un poil de cul de femme'. Henry Kistemaekers, who included it anonymously in the 1881 edition, added the following note:

This piece was written about 1854 or 1855, the proof of which is the allusion to Russia that is found in it. Which of our writers was then twenty years old and made a journey to the Moon before going around the world? Search in the Vapereau [the French *Who's Who*], in the catalogue of Hetzel, or on the posters of the largest theatre in Paris . . . but if you find out, don't tell the readers of the *Parnasse*.

That, with the references to Verne's greatest literary successes,
is explicit enough. However, Verne was actually twenty in 1848,
the year he came to Paris. So this poem may belong to an earlier
year, though the reference to the Russians seems to date it well
enough:

> Have I not seen all the pricks
> Which had free access to our place,
> Even if they were Russians,
> Especially if they were French.

If this refers to the return of the Russian diplomats after the
Crimean War to Paris, where the peace conference began in
February 1856, then the dating is clear. However this may be,
Verne's private life and subrosa writings were not untypical of the
literary world of his day. (Many other well-known writers also
appear unbuttoned in the *Parnasse*.)

Frequenting brothels and writing obscene verse were perhaps the
results of the deep frustrations of his emotional life, which Verne
longed to bring to a happier consummation than could be found in
the rue Montyon.

Though he knew little or nothing of this aspect of his son's life,
Pierre Verne was still surprised at his son's socialising and
facetious letters. He was still concerned about the course of
Jules's work and criticised the five acts of *Les Heureux du jour* as they
were sent to him. But Jules himself enjoyed his fun and games.

> Saint-Aubin tells me that my sisters are going to M. David's
> ball – but how will they manage to dance before the Ark.
> I'm told that the Vatican has thunderously denounced the
> displaying of ankles. So these little girls are old enough to visit
> the stiffling haunts of society.

'I'm told' indeed, as if the scientist had no time to listen to the
pronouncements of the Vatican on ankles or on other matters.
Once again, beneath the facetious tone, one detects a drifting
away from the respect of the Church which his father had.

> Meanwhile, I've just come from seeing Victor Marie married.
> Everyone is getting married except me. There was a big ball, two

days before the wedding, at the Mint. Then on Easter Thursday, I went to Saint Germain-des-Prés to see the last rites. I was extremely moved when the funeral procession went by. The two vergers in full gala costume struck the church floor with a long series of muffled blows. The father moved foreward, leading the chaste victim to the altar, and there was the husband, then the family filed by, looking solemn as Roman senators, and the organ unleashed its peals of thunder. I was extremely moved – in other words, I nearly choked with laughter, and I haven't stopped laughing yet. I swear that I could never, never, seriously play a part in a ceremony of that sort.

Nearly a month later, on 8 May 1856, Jules wrote to tell his parents that he was going up to Amiens to attend the wedding of his friend Lelarge with Mlle. Aime de Viane. He was planning on staying only two days in Amiens. A week later he wrote to say he was remaining longer and that he had fallen in love again.

At the wedding reception in Amiens Jules had met a young widow who was the sister of the bride. Her maiden name had been Honorine de Fraysse de Viane. She was now Mme. Morel, with two little girls. (Who M. Morel was and what he did is not recorded, except that he had died in 1855.) A week later Jules's mother received a second letter from her son, still in Amiens:

The wedding celebrations are still in progress. I am still in Amiens, the charming solicitations of the de Viane family having forced me to make a much longer stay than I had intended. I shall, in fact spend eight days here in all, in the midst of galas and gallantries, protestations of friendship, tears of joy and pleasure, wedding feasts, conjugal effusions, nuptial emotions, breakfasts lasting an hour and luncheons lasting three, dinners that begin at six and end at eleven in the evening. Ah! I shall be lucky if I don't die of indigestion! But that's not true, for I am in the best of health, I sleep, I eat, I laugh, and moreover I have very distinct views on marriage. I want to get married, I must get married, and it just isn't possible that the woman who is to marry me hasn't yet been born, as Napoleon said.

Reading this his mother must have been surprised at the contrast with his recent letters. What followed made it all clear enough.

The de Vianes are a charming family, made up of a delightful widow who is the sister of the bride, the bride herself who seems very happy, and a young man about my age, who is a stockbroker in Amiens, making a lot of money at it too, and who is certainly the most charming fellow one could hope to meet. The father is an old retired military man, but much more pleasant than the usual run of crusty characters retired from service, and the woman is a woman of great intelligence.

You are not used to see me indulging in such praise of the human race, dear Mama, and natural perspicacity will tell you that there is more here than meets the eye. And indeed, I believe I have fallen in love with the young widow of twenty-six. Oh, why does she have to have two children? I always run up against impossibilities of one sort or another. Please write back to your loving son.

The attraction of Honorine was that she was, like Caroline perhaps, completely feminine, a little silly but quite capable nevertheless. Jules was not looking for intellectual companionship, but for emotional security. Also as a widow, she had none of the simmering flirtatiousness of all those other girls he had fallen for.

Completely set on marriage with this tall, handsome, well-dressed woman, Jules had to think seriously about how he would support her, and the ready-made family he would also acquire.

On his return to Paris he wrote again to Nantes, this time to his father. He did not have to mention the young widow this time.

Young de Viane, whom I wrote to Mama about yesterday, has gone into partnership with one of his friends as an intermediary between investors and shareholders in Amiens and the stockbrokers in Paris. He makes fifty thousand francs a year out of commissions and discounts alone. The point is what he can do in Amiens, I could do even more easily in Paris, by going to the Bourse for no more than two or three hours a day, thus leaving the rest of my time free for literature.

I can't go on living from hand to mouth. To go chasing after every hundred sous may seem funny at twenty. At thirty it is undignified. So what I would like to know is whether you could possibly advance me the sum required to buy a share in a stockbroker's business.

Pierre Verne was surprised and distressed. His son had given up law to pursue literature. Now it seemed he was giving up literature to throw himself into business, moreover into risky speculations on the Bourse. This was not a career that appealed to a provincial lawyer. In the end, of course, he provided the money, after Jules had done his best to defend his way of life.

It's not a question of my giving up literature, for that remains my chosen career, but of pursuing a more lucrative profession at the same time. I want to create a presentable situation for myself. I am tired of living alone. All this merely proves that I have reached the age when one needs, above all, tender companionship and a stable union. At present my heart is a desperate void.

Verne and his old friend Charles Maisonneuve were negotiating with a stock-broker named Eggly to buy into his business. Verne's share was one fortieth, and would cost 50,000 francs. He pleaded with his father for the money, reassuring him about the speculative ventures which formed the financial basis of the economic and industrial expansion of France under Napoleon III.

Finally, I must repeat that, so long as I am a mere supernumerary candidate for fame, I cannot be a candidate for marriage as well, and frankly, I am utterly fed up with my bachelor existence. The same goes for my friends in the *Onze-sans-Femmes* club. In short and although it may strike you as rather comical, coming from me, what I need is to be happy, neither more nor less.

As a preliminary to going into partnership, Jules served a brief apprenticeship with a stock-broker named Giblain. Soon he was prepared to speak again of marrying Honorine.

His parents had, as a matter of course, been making their own enquiries about the family Fraysse de Viane. They had discovered that they were well-connected, that the girl's father was a former captain of cavalry and well thought of in Amiens society. The young widow, who had two children, Suzanne (aged three) and Valentine (aged one), was also well regarded.

Soon Pierre Verne was writing formally, as the old-fashioned etiquette demanded in 1856, to request the hand of Mme. Morel for his son in marriage. These ceremonious exchanges soon arranged everything, though there was a little difficulty over the Morel family's very reasonable concern for the welfare of the two little girls.

For his engagement Jules descended on Amiens and was taken out in local social circles by his new family for a round of gala occasions. But the wedding itself was to be very simple, as he explained to his mother.

Honorine and I have agreed that we should have as little ceremony as possible. She has a few simple pieces of furniture: a sofa, a few armchairs, four ordinary chairs . . . I will buy silver and other things. As soon as I have finished my apprenticeship with Giblain, I shall be in a very good position. Yesterday evening I lost a wonderful opportunity to run off to Brussels with Honorine, and set myself up in magnificent style. I was carrying 500,000 francs ·in bonds in my despatch case, and 95,000 francs in notes, which de Viane had given me for Giblain. However, I decided to be patient. My love to you all, and truly, without illusions or wild fancies, I believe I have really found happiness.

Simplicity was all very well, but his mother was scandalised at the casual way in which he spoke of his present to the bride. Jules had bought her lace, he said, perhaps a piece of intimate lace. His mother felt that his facetious tone was not appropriate for such matters. Jules was beginning to have some difficulty in finding the right tone for his letters to his parents, for he no longer thought quite as they did about many things.

The wedding was in Paris on 10 January 1857. They had told their Paris friends they were marrying in Amiens, those in Amiens that the venue was in Nantes, those in Nantes that it was Paris. The relations at Provins were told it was in the Antipodes!

Thus, we shall not be troubled by having an audience. The mere thought of inviting friends to the marriage service makes my hair stand on end with horror! For heaven's sake, let's have no pomp about it. My sisters will be quite pretty enough if they turn up looking like themselves. After the service, I will take you all off to a good restaurant for a meal, at so much per physiognomy, and that will be that.

Soon, he felt, he would be the happiest man in the world, so long as nothing happened to spoil his chances this time.

Nothing did. Jules and Honorine were married, as required by French law, first at the Mairie of the Third Arrondissement and then at St. Eugène, the sombre church at the end of the Boulevard Poissonière. The bridegroom was well satisfied. But his parents did not care much for the service, or indeed for the reception that followed. The 'Bohemian style' of wedding reception that they had in the restaurant as promised jarred with their provincial tastes. However, when the last course came and the toasts were proposed, Pierre Verne rose and recited the verses he had written for the occasion, and all ended in harmony.

The couple spent their honeymoon in Jules's fifth floor room at 18 Boulevard Poissonière. This too was unconventional, but Honorine does not seem to have minded. A week later they had their wedding photographs taken by the court photographer to send down to Nantes to grace the family album.

The past, whatever it contained, was to be forgotten. Jules took his new wife to the Louvre to show her the Venus de Milo. 'There,' he said, 'is the only woman of whom you need feel jealous.' (Maurice Metral reports another version of this, that the only woman she need be jealous of was his mother – a rich thought for psychoanalysts.) Perhaps Jules really meant this. Then it was off to Provins to stay with his relations.

Married life for the Vernes began in that one room on the Boulevard Poissonière. During the next few years they moved often enough: Boulevard Magenta, Boulevard Montmartre, Passage Saulnier, Carrefour de la Croix Rouge, rue de Sèvres. But always to cramped apartments which inevitably overflowed with books and manuscripts. For during the years from 1857 and 1863, Jules worked away at his writings as well as his stock-broking.

He was becoming very conscientious about gathering facts for his future work. By 1895 he had accumulated over his working life some 25,000 cards which were filed under various categories in a system of pigeon holes. These cards, which would have been valuable for reconstructing his methods of work, have since been destroyed. However in the magazines he wrote for and others which were popular in the period we can track down the original germs of some of his stories.

Later, when discussing individual books, I will give more information about Verne's sources. But here are some examples of what he might have read in the *Musée des Familles*, during these years. In November 1854 the magazine carried an article on contemporary Turkey, from which came some of the details for *Keraban Le Tetu (The Inflexible)*, 1883. In December there was an article about mining from which were derived some of the situations and illustrations for *Les Indes Noires (Black Diamonds)*, 1887. Even more remarkably, in view of the subject of *L'Ile a Helice (Propeller Island)*, was an article in April 1855 about a floating island for 1,500 people with cafés, restaurant, theatre and so on. An article by Guillaume de La Landelle on the sea and ships alludes to the Kraken and the sea-serpent which feature in several of Verne's books. During February and March 1858 there was a series on British India, which gave Verne some of the notions about that country that he used in two or three novels. An article on atmospheric electricity gave him the information about the Aurora that he used in *Captain Hatteras*. The article was by Arthur Mangin, a name we shall meet again, as also La Landelle. The details about coral islands used in *Twenty Thousand Leagues under the Sea* came in part from an article by Bertsch on popular geology in the March 1863 issue. Even more curious is an article by the editor of the *Musée des Familles*, Verne's friend Pitre-Chevalier, in July 1858 about the appearance of Hallet's submarine the *Nautilus* in the Seine.

These notes and clippings which he collected were to give Verne's books a somewhat spurious air of scientific originality. In fact, far from being original in his ideas, he is more often than not brilliantly adapting to fictional purposes someone else's notions. Though he wrote little of consequence during these years, Verne laid very carefully the foundations of his future career by careful study and diligent notetaking.

To achieve all of this large programme of reading and digesting, he would get up at five in the morning, have coffee and work until ten. Then he would take breakfast and go off to the Bourse for the day. He was now established on the Right Bank, but in imagination still hankered after his earlier days on the Left Bank and at the Théâtre Lyrique. But for the present the theatres of the boulevards were abandoned for the duties of the Bourse.

At the Bourse, Verne was having 'more success with his witticisms than with his deals', according to Felix Duquesnel (later a director of the Théâtre Châtelet), who was also a member of the exchange. Verne was one of a small group which included other refugees from the world of the arts. 'Everyone knew our group: Zabbel of the *Charivari*, Gaillardet, Duclerq, the elder Feydeau, and would fling some mocking witticism at us in passing. Verne gave as good as he could, with a ready flow of taunts and irony, sceptical in every respect but one: from his Breton background, he retained a Catholic outlook throughout his life.'

'He was the best among us,' Hector Malot recalled. 'He had a heart of gold.' 'At heart, this gay man-about-town kept his secret well,' Pierre Veron observed. 'When one has the key one can see into him, but nothing will make him expansive about himself' Another business friend, George Le Bastard, also saw him as 'a mixture of coldness and sensibility, of dryness and gentleness. Like tempered steel, he bends for those who are his friends, and remains stiff before others who are strangers; but what really makes him curt and abrupt is his voice, at once vibrant and imperious, and his swiftness of response in conversation.'

Those who remained of the *Onze-sans-Femmes*, although married, still met once a week. This annoyed Honorine naturally enough, but she was mollified by the picnics for the club and their families which Jules organised. But marriage, or the Bourse, could not stand in the way of adventure when it offered.

It was at a meeting of the club to celebrate the rise in stock prices in July 1859 that Aristide Hignard suggested a sea-trip to Verne. His father Alfred Hignard was the Saint-Nazaire agent for a shipping line and had offered him two free berths on one of his ships. He asked his friend Jules to go with him. Verne seized the opportunity at once, calling in on his family at Nantes on his way to join the ship at the mouth of the Loire.

They left at the end of July, bound for Scotland. For Jules, after so many years of dreaming this was his first real voyage. He recorded his impressions in a lightly fictionalised narrative *Voyage en Ecosse*, written after his return, but which was never published. Jules appears as Jacques Laveret, and Hignard as Jonathan Savournan. (This choice of name suggests the closeness of their relationship.)

From Bordeaux they sailed to Liverpool. There they stayed at the Adelphi Hotel. Verne was struck by the wealth of this great port, but also by the obvious poverty which surrounded it and by the free and easy speech and manners of the English in contrast to the more reserved French.

By train they travelled north, a journey which excited Verne very much. 'The fields and farms in England have a green of a peculiar freshness and the eye is aware of a new feeling for colour on looking at them.' But his greatest delight was for the scenery of Scotland, the country of one of his own ancestors and of Sir Walter Scott's novels, where the romance of history was everywhere. His observations filled his letters home and his notebooks. Later much of what he saw was to find its way into *The Green Ray* (1882).

They arrived at Edinburgh in a heavy rain shower. They stayed at Lambert's Hotel, and the next morning set out to explore the city. Their lack of English was a nuisance. It meant they had difficulty getting even breakfast. Later they were guided by a Catholic priest. The poverty of Edinburgh, the 'Auld Reeky' of Scott's novels, surprised them. The scenes along the Cannongate below the Castle would have needed a Delacroix to do them justice.

Later they went out to Portobello, where there was sea-bathing. Whole families spent the day on the beach, but they were surprised to see the men bathing some thirty yards away from the women and young ladies. Such British prudery, they thought. But when they tried to get the proprietor of the bathing-machines to provide them with costumes, they could not make themselves understood. Then they saw wading out of the water in front of them a prize specimen of unclothed British manhood. All was explained. Hesitating no longer, they ran down into the sea as naked as the natives. The water was much colder than it had been at Archachon a few days before. When they came out, they retreated backwards into their box, 'braving the distant laughter of the girls at their modesty and their hasty retreat.'

It was this sort of episode narrated with such light-hearted facetiousness that probably prevented the publication of the book at the time it was written. His later books were to adopt a more 'suitable' tone about such matters.

From Edinburgh, they went to stay at Newhaven, accompanied by Miss Amelia, Hignard's charming cousin by marriage – to whom the heroine of *The Green Ray* owes more than a little. With her they planned their tour of the Highlands. They had invitations to stay in a baronial castle, where they heard Scottish songs sung by Amelia. Crossing the Forth they were caught in a storm, but soon dried out at Oakley Castle. Then on by rail to Glasgow. On the way they passed the mining region at Stirling which made a great impression on Verne. From Glasgow, where the aurora was visible on 30 August, they travelled up Loch Lomond and Loch Katrine, where Jules was to set *Les Indes Noires* (*Black Diamonds*), under the little village of Aberfoyle.

No visit to Scotland would have been complete without a trip to the Hebrides and to Fingal's Cave on Staffa. This scene, as he describes it in *The Green Ray*, impressed Verne as much as it had Mendelssohn.

From this point in the cave there is an admirable vista broadening out into the open sky, and the water filled with clear light, allows one to see every detail of the sea bed. On the side walls, one sees an astonishing play of light and shadows. When a cloud covers the entrance to the cave, everything grows dark, as when a gauze curtain is draped over the theatre proscenium. But everything sparkles and glints gaily with the seven colours of the rainbow whenever the sun breaks through again, reflected off the crystal bottom and glancing upwards in long streaks to the threshold of the central cave. Beyond the waves break at the gigantic arch which forms the opening to the cave: and this frame, black as ebony, throws all the foreground features into full relief. Further out still, the horizon between sea and sky stretches out in all its splendour, with the dim heights of Iona two miles out in the open sea, and the pale silhouette of its ruined monastry . . .

What an enchanted palace this Fingal's Cave is. Who could

be so dull of soul as not to believe that it was created by a god for the sylphs and water-nymphs! And for whom do the wandering winds strike music from this vast aeolian harp? Surely this was the unearthly music that Waverly heard in his dream.

This visit to what was then a temple of romanticism seems to have been crucial in Verne's imaginative development. Images of that watery cavern echo through his work, in *Journey to the Centre of the Earth, The Mysterious Island, Black Diamonds, For the Flag.* The cavern and its mysteries have of course been seen as an image of the womb. More relevantly perhaps Fingal's Cave stands as an image of all that is unknown and mysterious in the natural world.

Fingal's Cave, volcanic in origin, became well known after Thomas Pennant published a description of a visit there with Sir Joseph Banks in 1772. When tourists began going to the Hebrides, Iona and Staffa were the high points of their trip. Felix Mendelssohn was there in 1829, the visit which inspired *Fingal's Cave*, the Hebridean overture to his Scottish symphony. Verne and his friend were merely two in a long series of visitors, though his impressions of what he saw are clearly coloured by the same romantic feelings which were expressed by Sir Walter Scott and epitomised in Macpherson's *Ossian*, the pseudo-Celtic poem which had enjoyed an incredible vogue on the Continent a generation before.

But this was not the only wonder that Verne saw on his trip. They travelled from Edinburgh to London on a Sunday excursion train, which gave Verne the opportunity to see not only the strange customs of the Sabbath, but also to observe the Dickensian characters that crowded onto the train. The industrial regions of the North through which they passed again impressed him greatly, as did London itself. Verne's somewhat mixed feelings about the English clearly date from this visit. He admired their national character and thought they made excellent explorers and scientists, but loathed the pursuit of profit which motivated so many of them.

But it was English wealth which paid for the achievements which Verne admired. The great Blackwall Tunnel for instance. He saw that on his way out to the Isle of Dogs to look at the

Great Eastern, which was being completed. I. K. Brunel's huge ship was one of the wonders of the age, one of those remarkable masterpieces which were decades ahead of their proper time. In spite of its future chequered career the *Great Eastern* was not only the largest ship ever built, but it also incorporated many radical engineering features which Brunel had pioneered. Verne was properly impressed by this great ship (as romantic in its modern way as Fingal's Cave) and surprised his friend Hignard by vowing to sail on her at the earliest date that he could afford the voyage.

But having money to spare for such an adventure would depend on his literary success. During that winter he wrote up his trip as a novel, taking great care with his descriptions. But the book was never published or accepted (and later some of the material was used in *The Green Ray*). Despite this he was certain that success would come, though there were times when he could admit to his father his depression over the difficulties he faced.

> When I say that I am no longer doing anything, my dear father, that is only a manner of speaking; I still go on working, as if in spite of myself, at the ideas that I have in my head. But there are times when I grow discouraged. I can no longer tell whether the inspiration is good or bad. I am still convinced that I will reach my goal in time, but I become frightened, perhaps more than I need be, at seeing myself where I am at thirty-two, when I used to think that at thirty-five I would have an assured place in literature.

He was still working as unprofitably as ever on operettas and plays. In 1860 he produced *Auberge des Ardennes*, with music by Hignard; and *Monsieur le Chimpanze*, with music by Offenbach. Both of these were light, frivolous pieces, with a slight saving grace of social satire. In 1861 came *Onze Jours de Siège*, about a woman who discovers an irregularity in the legal status of her marriage and has to resist her husband's advances for eleven days while her lawyer puts it right. Nothing in the play showed any superiority to the usual run of boulevard theatre fare under the Third Empire.

Three days after this play opened, on 1 June 1861, the Verne family gathered at Provins. In a photograph taken at the time Jules can be seen making the signal of a broker accepting a bid on the Bourse: Honorine had just told the family that she was expecting a baby.

This happy news, however, did not prevent her husband planning yet another cruise with Hignard. This time their destination was Scandinavia. On 15 June they set out in a cargo ship for the coast of Norway. Jules thought he caught a glimpse of Ireland in passing, but the fjords of Norway and the forests of Sweden were more exciting still.

Arriving in Christiana, they set out to see something of the scenery of Norway. In *The Lottery Ticket* (1886) Verne gives a vivid account of the trip to the Falls of Rjukan, based on the notes he made at this time. They took the boat to Drammen, from which they took the stagecoach and kariol cart up country to Dal. There he and Hignard stayed at the local inn which he was to use as the home of Dame Hammer, Hulda and Joel in his novel. But their fictional establishment was far superior to the miserable reality. In his novel Verne mentions the remarks written into the register by previous visitors. The French traveller Leclerq, who also visited Norway, recorded in his account of Dal in 1871 the entry written by Verne. Below Hignard's comment Verne had remarked on a spelling error, and said 'this was a disgrace to the honour of France'. This may have been merely a joke, or possibly an indication that relations between the pair were strained.

Verne in conversation with Adrien Marx, his English translator, told an amusing story about his stay in Stockholm later in the journey. When he was leaving, he wanted to pay his hotel bill. He searched his pocket-book for the draft-at-sight which he had obtained from Rothschilds in Paris. But it was not to be found. There was no doubt about it. He had been robbed.

His landlord looked askance at the excuse, and Verne thought he heard him mutter, 'Adventurer!' Taking his *Swedish Guide*, which he was learning by heart, Verne set off on a round of the banks to warn them against cashing the draft. This took three days. At last he climbed the stairs at the last office, guide book in hand as usual, and began to explain his purpose. The bored clerk casually picked up the guide book and was leafing through it, when a piece of paper used as a bookmark fluttered out. The clerk picked it up. 'Why, here's your draft after all.' Verne returned in triumph to his hotel.

When they reached Denmark, Jules had to leave Hignard in Copenhagen and return to France. Hignard had conceived the idea of an opera based on *Hamlet* and was seeking local colour for it at Elsinore. The French critic Marcel Moré has however drawn attention to the curious fact that from this date Hignard drops out of Verne's life, though he had been one of his oldest and closest friends until the trip to Scandinavia. Was the harshness of the comment in the register at Dal an indication of rising ill-feeling between them? Whatever happened 'Jacques Lavaret' saw little of his 'Jonathan' again.

Jules returned to Paris. He arrived just in time, for his son was born on 3 August 1861. They called him Michel.

Jules was now a father, but as a husband and a family man he was far from a model. On his Scandinavian trip his letters to Honorine contained no messages of tenderness. By temperament he was dry, sharp and explosive. He could stand neither argument nor questions.

One day Honorine received an anonymous letter which said that Jules was having an affair with a girl in a fashionable club. She asked him about this. He took the letter and threw it out of the window, shouting at her that it was monstrous of her to doubt his fidelity, and that even if what the letter said was true, she had no right to meddle in his business.

Honorine said nothing. Deeply hurt, she wrote to her aunt in Amiens.

He is making my life insupportable. I don't know why but the least word annoys him. I tell him that supper is ready, he goes out and eats in a restaurant. I tell him that the little boy has bronchitis, he throws his pen at the wainscotting and says I irritate him, and that in these conditions, he will never write anything again. At night he doesn't sleep. He gets up, talking to himself, mumbling incomprehensible formulas. I am beginning to ask myself if I didn't marry a sick man.

Her aunt's advice nearly overwhelmed her:

It seems that there is a grave sickness in the Verne family. It will be best, my child, if you come back to Amiens and that Jules consults a doctor.

When she told Jules that she might go home, he said she could go 'there or anywhere else . . .' But the next day he became more delicate in his approach. He asked her to forgive him. He had distressed her for the last time. 'I am a miserable type who doesn't know how to do good.'

Whatever the truth about these tensions between Jules and Honorine (for the above is based largely on Maurice Metral alone), there were no more children, and the couple began to sleep in separate beds. If Jules had hoped that the emotional turmoil of his life would end with marriage he was mistaken. All that would ever make him really happy was the literary success that continued to elude him, and the lack of which probably lay behind his irascible outbursts against his wife and family.

He found that he could not work at home with Michel crying. It got on his nerves. He retreated to a new club, the Cercle de la Presse Scientifique, which catered for many kinds of writers. He had joined the club some time before and had made new friends there. Among them was Felix Tournachon, better known in Paris by his pseudonym, Nadar. Nadar was to be an important figure in Verne's life.

Originally Nadar had been an artist, but he had then taken up photography, in which he was one of the really great pioneers: he took photographs of the Paris sewers by electric light, the first aerial photographs, and later in his life, he created the Photo-interview. A Daumier cartoon showed him perilously balanced in the basket of a balloon over Paris with his camera, 'Nadar elevating photography to the height of art'. In 1862 Nadar's current obsession was aeronautic science.

Nadar founded a Society for Aerial Locomotion, with which Verne was also involved, together with Guillaume de La Landelle and others. It was at Nadar's studio that Ponton d'Amencourt demonstrated a working model of a steam helicopter in 1863. In his book *Aviation* (a word he invented) de La Landelle had included a picture of a two-masted helicopter. The debates and disputes over heavier than air and lighter than air flying machines, between visionary helicopters and practical balloons raged intensely among this côterie. Another writer named Duchesne, writing in 1864, criticised these schemes. But Nadar and his friends were enthusiasts. In order to finance their projects, he conceived the idea of a huge balloon to be called *le Géant*.

Balloons had fascinated Verne since at least 1851, and he listened with great interest while his friend outlined his scheme. By this time Verne had read Edgar Allan Poe's story 'A Balloon Hoax' and 'Hans Pfaal' (his edition of Poe is dated 1862), and had been influenced by the American writer's mixture of the fantastic and the commonplace. At this time he was working on an essay about Poe's writing which was later published in the *Musée des Familles* and in 1863 he also published an article on Nadar's project. In October 1863 Nadar's *Géant* finally ascended from the Champ de Mars. But by then Verne himself had made balloons his own imaginative property.

In February 1862, in a letter to his father, Jules had mentioned Poe's story 'A Balloon Hoax'. 'In my own balloon,' he added, 'I'm not going to have any *ducks* [*canards*, a pun] – or drakes for that matter – but human beings. The aircraft will therefore have to be provided with an absolutely infallible mechanism.' The accurate navigation of balloons over long distances was then a great problem.

So while Nadar collected money for his balloon, Verne was drawing up his own account of a balloon flight linked with the exploration of central Africa, at that time another topic of great public interest. There was a superficial similarity between the real and the fictional balloons, for both were made of Lyons silk with a double skin. But the idea of using the prevailing trade winds at different heights for long-distance navigation Verne had picked up from a paper by one of aerostatics' great pioneers, Captain Meusnier.

By May 1862 strawberries were in season. 'Have you any strawberries at Chantenay?' Honorine asked in a letter. 'Jules is eating some now, as he finishes a story about balloons. There are manuscripts everywhere – nothing but manuscripts. Let's hope they don't end up under the cooking pot.'

Some of his old stories had boiled the pot in that way in the past. Discouragement came easily and he expressed himself bitterly to his father that all his ideas seemed to come to nothing. His work had been rejected by many publishers in the past. At first his balloon story suffered a similar fate.

In the summer of 1862 Verne took the manuscript of his new story to François Buloz, the founder of the *Revue des Deux Mondes*. Buloz was impressed enough with the story to accept it for his

journal. But there was one thing to be settled first: how much was
he going to pay, Verne asked. 'Pay you! But you are unknown. It is
as a favour that I am accepting the story, for it is a great honour to
be published in the *Revue*.'

'Pardon me, sir, but my means do not allow me accept such an
honour.'

That autumn he tried a new firm at 18 rue Jacob called Hetzel
and Company.

Hetzel, whose real name was P. J. Stahl, was another of the
generation of 1848, when he had been active in the revolution.
When Napoleon III came to power at the time of the coup
d'état in 1851, he went into exile in Brussels and had only
recently returned to Paris after the amnesty of 1859. He had set
up in publishing once again. Though he brought out George
Sand, Balzac and Stendhal, he was also a publisher of children's
books. He had plans for a magazine which would combine
instruction with entertainment, and was looking for a writer to
produce serials when it started.

When Verne arrived at the shop he was shown into Hetzel's
private room behind the shop, which also served as a bedroom. As
he worked late into the night, Hetzel was in the habit of staying
in bed in the mornings, conducting his business from there. The
room was hung with heavy Flemish tapestries on both the walls
and the floor. Against rich classical scenes of nymphs and
shepherds, Hetzel entertained his visitors. Verne, however,
merely handed over his manuscript and left.

In a fortnight he returned for Hetzel's verdict. Hetzel began
with that well-worn formula of all publishers: 'I am very sorry
that in spite of the great merits of your work, I am unable . . .'
Verne picked up his work and was leaving in chagrin when
Hetzel called him back. Verne had been too hasty. He reassured
Verne that he had all the makings of a great story-teller. He is
said to have pointed out various improvements that might be
made in the manuscript. If Verne could improve the narrative,
making a proper novel from the story, and bring it back as soon
as possible, Hetzel would reconsider it.

Verne left again, at the run. Two weeks later Verne was back
with the revised version of what was now called *Five Weeks in a
Balloon*. This time it was accepted. What the original version was
like – a documentary story, or a purely factual account – we do

not know. But to produce the final draft in two weeks implies either very hard work, or minimal changes of tone and emphasis. In the first flush of his acceptance, Verne outlined to Hetzel the scheme he had long cherished of writing a series of books that would describe the world, known and unknown, and the great scientific achievements of the age. Hetzel realised that he had found not only someone to write his serials, but he had discovered an original genius.

A contract was drawn up which was signed on 23 October 1862. Under this Verne was to be paid 500 francs for the first edition, with different rates for later and illustrated editions. This was not, even at that time, the best of contracts. But doubtless Verne was happy enough to have found a publisher.

This original contract was to be altered later, in Verne's favour each time, according to his family biographers, but in fact, as we shall see, to his disadvantage. Money is the critical key to so much literary activity that the financial side of Verne's life cannot be neglected. In 1862 he was a novice, but that long, imposing procession of works which he had dreamed of as far back as 1854 was taking on substance.

At last Verne was free. He could afford to give up the Bourse and devote himself entirely to his writing, without risking the comfort of his family. His friend Duquesnel recalled vividly over forty years later Verne's speech of farewell to the Bourse. These, he claimed were Verne's very words:

Mes enfants, I am leaving you. I have had an idea, the sort of idea that, according to Girardin, ought to come to every man once a day, but has come to me only once in my life, the sort of idea that should make a man's fortune. I have just written a novel in a new form, one that's entirely my own. If it succeeds, I shall have stumbled upon a gold mine. In that case, I shall go on writing and writing without pause, while you others go on buying shares the day before they drop and selling them the day before they rise. I am leaving the Bourse. Good evening, mes enfants.

What his friends thought of this pretty speech when they heard it did not matter. A few weeks later *Five Weeks in a Balloon* was published and was an immediate success. It was published in time for the New Year of 1863, and was a present to many children, the first of a long series. His first novel had begun its long life both in French and in countless translations. 'An unknown writer,' Duquesnel comments, 'had created the scientific novel.'

Chapter Four

A New Kind of Novel

VERNE CAN REASONABLY BE CALLED THE 'INVENTOR OF SCIENCE fiction', but the great idea of which he spoke when taking leave of his friends on the Bourse had its own prehistory in the creations of earlier writers. Just how original was Jules Verne? And in what way distinctive?

The origins of science fiction have been traced back to the Greeks. Lucian's *True History*, about a voyage to the moon, and *The Birds* by Aristophanes, about an imaginary utopia, are early examples of still popular types of tale. Such imaginary excursions were common enough in the following centuries. But these tales are really only fantasies, and not true science fiction. In turn Swift, Voltaire, Cyrano de Bergerac, even Defoe, used such fantasies to serious or satiric purpose. Yet even when a scientist of the stature of Kepler writes of a moon voyage in his *Somnium*, there is one ingredient of modern science fiction missing: the science.

Science is the essential element that provides the rationale for what would have been only imaginative fantasies in earlier times. But the use of science in fiction had to await the development of the natural sciences during the seventeenth and eighteenth centuries, and among the many imaginary journeys and futuristic tales of the period there are few which make use of real science. Dean Swift's satirical treatment of the Academy of Laputa, where they were trying to get sunlight out of cucumbers (the extraction of vitamin C from vegetable protein as it would now be called) is quite representative of the dismissive attitude to science common to literary men at that time. Even the stories of Edgar Poe are more fantasy than real science, for he deeply mistrusted science. The industrial revolution and with it the rise of modern scientific research during the last century ended all that. The use of an at least adequately researched scientific background seems to me to be the prime element which sets Verne off from earlier writers.

His first novel *Five Weeks in a Balloon* provides a good example of just how Verne was to use contemporary science for his own fictional purposes during his long career. In this novel he adroitly combines mechanics and geography, balloons and African exploration.

Balloons had been a particular interest of Verne's for several years, one he shared with a large number of inventors and adventurers in France and elsewhere. He was a friend of Nadar, as we have seen, and of other enthusiastic aeronauts. Balloons had, of course, originally been a French invention, and the French and Germans were the leading aviation pioneers during the nineteenth century. The hot-air balloon of the Mongolfier brothers and the hydrogen gas balloon of Dr. Charles were both invented in 1783, but it was the gas balloon which was used for the most part during the next century and a half.

The great problem with balloons was that they were difficult to steer over long distances. Usually this was solved by either throwing out sand to rise, or by releasing a little gas to fall, until a wind which took the balloon in the right direction was found. A complex manoeuvre, which was why so many long-distance balloon journeys ended in disaster. Nadar's *Géant*, which had partly inspired Verne's novel, crashed on its first flight across Europe when it went out of control. Verne solved the navigational problems of the *Victoria*, the balloon in his novel, with an ingenious device which heated the hydrogen, thus expanding it and causing the balloon to rise. Several pages are devoted to a detailed 'scientific description' of this device, which seems to have been an invention of Verne himself. If so, it was a lethal one, for he does not seem to have considered just how dangerous it would be if any oxygen leaked into the system. The resulting explosion would have destroyed both the balloon and its unlucky crew. But the semi-technical waffle of his long description was convincing enough for uncritical readers.

The much better idea of using the prevailing trade winds to carry the *Victoria* all the way across Africa, Verne had adapted from an idea of the pioneer balloonist, Captain Meusnier. Strangely enough balloons were little used in this way for exploration; though several attempts were made later to fly over the North Pole. (On one such flight the Swede Andrée and his party perished in 1897; the diary and photographs of the flight recovered later might have been from a novel by Verne.) In Africa Verne's idea of crossing the continent was never taken up. It was not until Anthony Smith (then a *Daily Telegraph* writer and inspired by Verne's novel), took his balloon *Jambo* out to East Africa in 1962 that anyone seems to have actually flown a balloon in Africa at all. Smith was followed by Felix Pole and his expedition over the Sahara with *Daffodil* and *Golden Eagle* in 1972. Both of these men flew over parts of the *Victoria's* route.

In the novel it is the London *Daily Telegraph*, 'a penny paper with a circulation of 140,000 copies, which is not enough to satisfy its millions of readers', which backs the expedition. Dr. Samuel Ferguson, 'the most active and interesting correspondent' of the paper, together with his Scottish friend Dick Kennedy and his manservant Joe, fly from Zanzibar across the sources of the Nile and the forests of the Congo basin to end their flight on the Guinea coast beyond the Sahara.

Basing himself on the latest accounts of central Africa, and gliding swiftly over what were still blanks on the map, Verne's novel brought the whole continent alive in all its variety. When the novel was published early in 1863 Speke and Grant were still out of reach in Africa trying to settle the source of the Nile, which Speke thought he had glimpsed in 1857. They did not reach civilisation until February 1863. Speke had in fact 'settled' the source of the Nile on 28 July 1862 – a month after the fictional Dr. Ferguson had flown over his head. No wonder some early readers were led to think that the book described a real journey. It was as up to date as the next day's paper.

Alan Moorehead remarks in his history of the White Nile that travel books at that time 'had the quality of science fiction'. Reality and imagination cut across each other in strange ways. Looking at the woodcuts by Riou which illustrate the novel it is hard to imagine one is not looking at news pictures from one of the illustrated journals of the day, perhaps *L'Illustration*, the *Illustrated London News*, or *Harper's*. Or indeed at scenes from the books of Burton, Speke or Grant. In fact Riou, who was to serve

Verne very well for many years to come, also did the com-
memorative volume on the opening of the Suez Canal in 1869, so
very often it was the same artist who drew the pictures for the
novels as illustrated the news. Fact and fiction blended in a very
real way.

Verne tried to be careful about the facts for his fictions, and
his African flight was a good example of how he went about his
research. As he pertinently points out, previous travellers had
covered a great deal of ground on foot: only a short distance of
twelve degrees across Africa, between the furthest points of the
expeditions of Dr. Barth and that of John Speke and Richard
Burton, was completely unknown. C. T. Beke's book *The Sources
of the Nile* (1860) and the map of central Africa prepared by
Guillaume Lejean in 1860 provided a basic knowledge of the area.
Much has been made of Verne's description of the fat Negro
women fed on milk at Karagwe, as these did not become
generally known about until the famous description by Speke a
few years later. But in fact Verne would have found them mentioned in Richard Burton's *The Lake Regions of Central Africa* (1860),
which was published in Paris while he was working on his novel.

Why Verne chose Englishmen for his heroes in this novel, as
in many others, is curious. The British were at that time in the
vanguard of exploration, but the French and Germans were not
far behind them. Verne admired the phlegmatic qualities of the
British, which made them ideal characters in his sort of book.
However, being very French in his outlook, Verne did not much
care for the British Empire. In his books the crimes of Imperial
Britain in India, Canada, New Zealand, Ireland and elsewhere
are duly mentioned. We hear little about the French empire,
which was rapidly expanding under Napoleon III, or about events
in Morocco, Madagascar or Indo-China. Verne's anti-imperial
attitudes were of a selective kind.

Dr. Ferguson in the novel sees Africa as the future home of the
European when he has exhausted his own continent. We thus
catch at its very beginnings the scramble for Africa, which was still
a matter of concern for Verne when he published *Le Village
aérien* (1901), in which there is some discussion of an American
colony in the Congo. His novels are spread over such a long life
that we can see in them the developments and changes, not only
of science, but of fashion, politics and history.

Aside from the steering mechanism of the balloon, there are no gross improbabilities in this first novel. Fantasy and speculation are kept well in control. What changes Verne made from the first version is not known, though we do know that he cut out a long digression about Joe's adventures on Hetzel's advice. The changes may well have been matters of editing his longueurs, rather than wholesale rewriting. As it is, the book reads very well, and is still exciting and entertaining, and is one of the few titles out of Verne's sixty odd that has stayed continually in print in both French and English. This in itself is no small achievement when we remember that much of Ballantyne or Mayne Reid are now quite unreadable and unread.

I shall have more to say later about Verne's qualities as a writer, but at the start of his career we should have a look at his literary influences. Defoe, Scott, Fenimore Cooper, Edgar Allan Poe – these writers may seem a strange quartet, but Verne admired them all and continually invoked them. Behind them, however, we can also glimpse the conflicting views of the French tradition of the Encyclopaedists, and the Romantic movement as a whole.

Cooper and Scott were writers of romances, the virtual creators of those two regions of the imagination which fascinated Verne all his life, America and the north of Europe. The virgin American woods of the Leatherstocking tales and the cold misty Highlands of the Waverley novels had been part of his boyhood world. In his own writing he reflects this influence by emphasising the picturesque, but, unlike Scott at least, he has little in the way of love interest. He was a novelist in the Defoe tradition of picaresque adventures, rather than of complicated passions.

As a boy Verne admired Defoe and Wyss; Scott, Cooper and Poe came later. This adventure novel tradition has been neglected, even disparaged by academic literary critics, who believe that the proper role of the novelist is the dissection of emotional and social nuances. But this is not the only role of the novel. The earliest tales were adventures, and genre novels whether of history, adventure or science fiction are still the dominant literary forms. There is still a place for a novel which explores ideas, or environments – in Verne's case the discovery of new lands and the possibilities of a scientific future.

Not that Verne was unimpressed, or uninfluenced, by a certain kind of psychological writing, as his early admiration of Poe shows. Poe had been translated by Baudelaire, beginning in 1854, and the poet's critique of the American writer had been an important event in French literary history. Verne was one of the earliest admirers of Poe. (In translation, of course, as he did not read English.) The edition of Poe in his library was one published by Hetzel in 1862, in a translation by William Hughes. Poe and Baudelaire hardly seem the normal reading of a man of Verne's background. Here again we can see him casting off his father's settled views in favour of the wilder shores of the imagination.

The romantic elements in Poe, the love of the sensational and the macabre, the delight in cryptograms and hidden treasures, the fantastic and suspicious view of science, have struck some as being merely adolescent. Yet the love of the unsolved and the unknown are essential qualities for a scientist. They are not literary virtues, for they often militate against any adult human interest, but they do suggest an affinity between certain sorts of writers and the scientific avant garde. Poe uses scientific ideas, such as hypnosis in 'The Facts in the Case of M. Valdemar', to the bizarre ends of his private imagination. But the science is still there.

Verne also delighted in mysteries, treasures, cryptograms and bizarre scientific details. But for the most part his use of science was always more realistic, more closely based on documentary sources than Poe's flights of imagination. Nevertheless the influence of the American was there: the balloon in his novel is named for one in Poe's 'Hans Pfall'. In an essay on Poe written during 1862, while he was working on the book, Verne outlines what he saw as Poe's virtues and defects. (One of the stories which interested him was 'Three Sundays in a Week', about gaining a day by going east around the world, a fact he was to recall much later.) The materialism of the American troubled his still basically Catholic outlook. But the Goncourt brothers, after reading the first volume of Baudelaire's versions of Poe, in 1856 had been impressed enough to extrapolate from Poe the germs of the novel of the future. This they saw as 'analytic fantasy', 'something monomaniacal', the 'basis of the novel transferred from the heart to the head'.

Verne was the first writer to fill these terms. His kind of adventure-cum-science novel did away with the need for emotional interest. The excitement came from mere facts in themselves. His novels were, for Verne, a means of escape from the emotional turmoil of his own life into something at once serene and exciting. Work on his novels insulated him from the demands of his wife and family. Their content took him completely away from the drab everyday bourgeois existence he led with Honorine, into exotic vistas of the imagination, where the dramas of the mind were played out by dauntless heroes.

The influence of science on Verne seems suddenly to well up in 1862. He had always been interested in travel and the sea. Geography was the one science in which he was an expert of standing. (He was to become member 710 of the Société de Géographie in 1865.) For the other natural sciences he relied on the advice of friends, or on his extensive reading in journals and papers. He rarely went back to original research for his ideas. His early writing career had been imitative, an attempt to write popular plays in the popular style of the boulevard theatres. This was not his métier. The discovery of this new form of novel enabled him to combine his love of facts with a vivid imaginative treatment. He was able to evade the sad fate of a fourth-rate playwright to become an excellent story-teller and to escape into the career of a scientific prophet.

'The scientific romance': this was the genre that Verne can justly claim to have invented. The elements had existed in writers before him, but in his long series of novels beginning with *Five Weeks in a Balloon* he bridged the gap between the romantics and the modern movement, between the age of balloons and the aeroplane, and helped to establish science fiction as a major form of fiction in the twentieth century.

Chapter Five

Journey to the
Centre of the Earth

With his first book Verne became a prominent novelist rather than a fourth-rate playwright. His success was still only in France. Universal fame was yet to come. But now he had found his way. He had arrived. He was, as he had hoped when he came to Paris, established by the age of thirty-five.

In September 1863 he moved to a house in the respectable Paris suburb of Auteuil, 39 rue La Fontaine, an indication of increased prosperity. During the year he had been working on a new novel dealing with the adventures of a British expedition in the Arctic, which was in two parts, *The English at the North Pole* and *The Desert of Ice*. The first part he took to the printer himself in September, but revisions continued as the book began to appear in serial form in *Le Magasin d'Education et de Récréation*, which was edited by Hetzel, Jean Macé and Verne. Verne signed a second contract covering this novel, and two others which he planned to write, a history of exploration and the story of a journey round the world. This last was the germ of *Captain Grant's Children*, not to be completed in fact until 1866.

In the story of the English at the North Pole, Verne once again based himself very closely on actual reports. Several Polar explorers have admitted that nothing could be more realistic than his descriptions both of life aboard ship and of the hardships and wonders of the northern seas. Now in a new novel, to be called *A Journey to the Centre of the Earth*, Verne set out to explore a realm of pure imagination, a poetic elaboration of the prosaic facts of scientific geology.

During the winter of 1863–64 Verne came to know Charles Sainte-Claire Deville, a geographer who had explored the volcanoes

81

of Teneriffe and Stromboli. From his conversations with Deville, Verne had conceived a new story about a journey to the centre of the earth.

Also behind his new novel were the more extraordinary theories of John Cleves Symmes, United States Infantry, that the earth was actually hollow and open at the Poles. As one of Verne's characters, a certain Dr. Clawbonny, remarks:

> In recent times it has even been suggested that there are great chasms at the Poles; it is through these that there emerges the light which forms the Aurora, and you can get down through them into the interior of the earth.

That was Symmes's idea. He thought that inside the hollow earth there were five concentric spheres, all with openings several thousand miles in diameter at the Poles. The idea of the origin of the Aurora was from the astronomer Edmund Halley, who had published an essay on the topic in 1692. In a far more elaborate form, Symmes had been lecturing on his theory since 1818. It had been the subject of a book in 1816 by James MacBride, and in 1838 an American expedition had gone to the Antarctic after efforts by one of Symmes's admirers in Congress to have the Poles properly explored.

Verne was familiar with this expedition, and combining it with his friend's idea that the volcanos of Europe might be connected by passages through the earth, he began work on a story about a journey to the interior of the earth which begins in Iceland. Symmes's theory had already inspired one novel, by a pseudonymous writer named Captain Seaborn (perhaps hiding Symmes himself), whose *Symzonia* had appeared in 1820. Poe's long story *The Narrative of Arthur Gordon Pym* (which Verne greatly admired) was also derived, although with more imaginative substance, from the same source.

Seaborn and Poe had looked south; Verne looked north again. His novel describes how the Danish Professor Lidenbrock and his nephew Axel travel from Copenhagen (drawn from Verne's memories of his own visit) to Iceland in search of an opening down into the secret interior of the earth. Lidenbrock has discovered a manuscript note in code in an old Icelandic volume, which he decodes with Axel's unwitting aid:

Descend into the crater of Sneffels Jokul over which the shadow of Scataris falls before the kalends of July, bold traveller, and you will reach the centre of the earth. I have done this. Arne Saknussemm.

This person, the well-informed Lidenbrock tells Axel, was a sixteenth-century Icelandic alchemist, who had been condemned as a heretic. Aroused by this message from the past, the two of them set off to follow Arne with the aid of an Icelandic guide down into the bowels of the earth.

Once again Verne took trouble over his research. Drawing on an account of Iceland written in 1857 by Charles Edmond, he has Lidenbrock and Axel meet real people and scholars in Iceland, including a Dr. Friderickson and a Dr. Hjaltalin (one of the few men ever actually to have examined a dead lake monster). This gave rise to a legend that Verne had corresponded with Friderickson: this was not so, he had merely done his research well. Some of the names he uses are slightly deformed, not to disguise them, but simply because Verne was often unable to read his own notes.

The book was planned as a geological epic. From our point of view this seems a strange interest for Verne. For many religious people at the time, Catholic as well as Protestant, the findings of modern geology which questioned the account of the Creation of the World in *Genesis* were anathema. Verne seems to have had few qualms about this. A scientific work such as Sir Charles Lyell's *Principles of Geology* (1830–33), which Darwin had taken with him on his momentous voyage around the world in the *Beagle*, had shaken many beliefs. Darwin's *Origin of Species* had appeared in London in 1859. In 1863, while Verne was working on his novel, a French translation was published in Paris. The great debate on the antiquity of the world and of man had entered its final stage. As Bishop Wilberforce had expressed it a few years before, one was either on the side of the apes or the angels. Verne, it seems, was on the side of the apes.

The novel was right up to date. For the new illustrated edition published in 1867, Verne included the very latest details about the discovery of fossil men. For, of course, the explorers find their own prehistoric skull in a cavern by the underground Lidenbrock Sea. The professor outlines for his companions the recent controversies, and suggests that perhaps man might well be over 100,000 years old. (Recent discoveries in Africa in 1975 have pushed back the horizon of man's appearance to three million years ago.)

As if to complicate the issue, however, there is also a strange vision of a giant man-like creature, driving a herd of mammoths. What Verne intended this to be is a puzzle, for it was not until this century that Von Königswald discovered in a Chinese drug shop the teeth of Gigantopithecus, a twelve-foot high creature which it is thought may lie behind the reports of the Abominable Snowman.

But perhaps the most impressive part of the book is Axel's dream, a vision of the earth's past history which unites the scientific outlook with romantic feeling into one great prose poem:

Now, however, my imagination carried me away among the wonderful hypotheses of palaeontology, and I had a prehistoric daydream. . . . The whole of this fossil world came to life again in my imagination. I went back to the scriptural periods of creation, long before the birth of man, when the unfinished world was not yet ready for him. Then my dream took me even further back into the ages before the appearance of living creatures. The mammals disappeared, then the birds, then the reptiles of the Secondary Period, and finally, the fishes, crustaceans, molluscs, and articulated creatures. The zoophytes of the transitional period returned to nothingness in their turn. The whole of life was concentrated in me, and my heart was the only one beating in that depopulated world. There were no more seasons or climates; the heat of the globe steadily increased and neutralised that of the sun. The vegetation grew to gigantic proportions, and I passed like a ghost among arborescent ferns, treading uncertainly in iridescent marl and mottled stone; I leaned against the trunks of huge conifers; I lay down in the shade of sphenophylas, asterophyllas, and lycopods a hundred feet high.

Centuries passed like days. I went back through the long series of terrestrial changes. The plants disappeared; the granite rocks softened; solid matter turned to liquid under the action of intense heat; water covered the surface of the globe, boiling and volatilising; steam enveloped the earth, which gradually turned into a gaseous mass, white-hot, as big and bright as the sun.

In the centre of this nebula, which was fourteen hundred times as large as the globe it would one day form, I was carried through interplanetary space. My body was volatilised in its turn and mingled like an imponderable atom with the vast vapours tracing their flaming orbits through infinity.

Even now this is a remarkable vision of the evolution of the earth: in 1863 it would have been extraordinary. That Verne had no qualms about accepting so easily both the great age of the universe and of man seems remarkable, and a comment on the increasingly relaxed nature of the religious faith which his family insisted that he maintained all his life.

When he revised the book in 1867 and included fresh details about fossil finds, Verne had been living in a little port at the mouth of the Somme for a couple of years. A former customs official for the area based on Abbeville had been the famous anthropologist Boucher de Crèvecoeur de Perthes. As he died only in 1868, it is quite possible that Verne may have met him, and that part of the inspiration behind his ideas derived from this great man who had laboured all his life against prejudice to prove the antiquity of man.

Also the controversy over the fossil jaw-bone found at Abbeville (it was a fake) made Verne's work very topical. Prehistoric exhibits had been very prominent at the Paris Exhibition of 1867, and Verne may well have seen them. Indeed the very word 'prehistory' itself became widely current for the first time that year.

The summer of 1864 Verne and his family spent at Chantenay with his parents. There he worked on his serial about polar exploration and completed his new novel during August and September. His mother had been very impressed by the reviews of his first book and welcomed him eagerly to the family reunion. His brother Paul was marrying Mlle. Meslier de Montauran that year. His three sisters were by now married themselves: Anna to Ange Ducrest de Villeneuve in 1858; Mathilde to Victor Fleury in 1860, and Marie to Léon Guillon in 1861. The house at Chantenay now rang with shouts of romping grandchildren. The evenings of that hot summer were gay and animated, with Jules being his old facetious self.

This provincial and settled background makes a strange contrast to the new worlds which Jules was creating in his imagination. His mother reproved him, as she always had, for his ribaldry, his father for his lack of polite restraint. Yet the implications of his fictional adventures were more shocking (or should have been) from a Catholic point of view. The start of this holiday had been marred by an attack of facial paralysis, his fourth, for which he had received electric shock treatment – the very latest thing at that time. This crisis was a small indication that, in spite of his gay manner with his family, he was working under great emotional and nervous strain to produce his visionary masterpieces.

Chapter Six

Astronauts by Gaslight

IN HIS NEXT BOOK, PREPARED IN 1864, VERNE WAS CARRIED away by the dream of interplanetary flight. *De la Terre à la Lune* is often said to have been suggested to him by Poe's story of Hans Pfall's journey to the moon by balloon, which was, of course, a hoax. But ideas about space travel and stories of space journeys, what we now think of as almost the essential matter of modern science fiction, were actually commoner than is now supposed.

In 1865, the year in which Verne's novel was published, there was *Voyage à Venus* by Achille Eyraud; *Voyage à la Lune* by Alexandre Dumas père; *Un Habitant de la planète Mars* by Henri de Parville; and two anonymous works, *Voyage à la Lune* in French, and *The History of a Voyage to the Moon*. The French astronomer Camille Flammarion also published that year his *Mondes imaginaires et mondes réels*, one of a series he was writing about popular astronomy. This book was a survey of all previous imaginative works dealing with astronomy, astronomical ideas, plurality of worlds, the habitability of other planets and attempts at interplanetary communications. All of this was in one year. Verne was not alone then in his speculations, but it is significant that he is the only one of these writers who is still read today.

Most of these other books are now of little interest. However Achille Eyraud's book, though of no literary value, made little stir at the time and had only one printing, is important, according to the German rocket expert Willy Ley, 'in signifying a change in attitude'. The author actually describes a spaceship, which is moreover powered by a reaction motor. This engine is not a rocket, though he uses a firework to explain the principle of reaction, but is worked on water. However Eyraud makes an

87

error when he suggests preventing the loss of the ejected water by having it collected in a container behind. This would not have worked, though it was seriously put forward as a possibility as late as 1927 by an Austrian engineer, Franz Abdon Ulinski.

Two of the other stories are very alike; the anonymous *Voyage à la Lune* and de Parville's story both begin with the discovery of a message in a meteor. De Parville was interested in the possibility of intelligent life on other planets, but the moon story was an account of a trip to the moon with the aid of an anti-gravity substance.

Whether Verne read any of these rival works is not known, but he was certainly well aware of the problems involved in trying to reach the moon and did his best to solve them. Mysterious anti-gravity devices were not for him! In his novel Eyraud had described a reaction motor, and modern research has followed him. But Verne, who had been impressed by the rapid improvements made in large scale artillery during the American Civil War, settled instead on a gigantic gun.

From the Earth to the Moon was set in post-bellum America. The Gun Club of Baltimore, a group of irascible enthusiasts and retired artillery men, most of them lacking limbs, have grown bored with peace. Their president Impey Barbicane suggests that they attempt something altogether new: shooting a projectile at the moon. Greeted with enthusiasm, the scheme rapidly gets under way.

In writing this book Verne had his calculations carefully checked over by his mathematical cousin, Henri Garcet. There was the muzzle velocity needed for a projectile to escape from the gravitational pull of the earth. Then there was the problem of the gun. The giant cannon was to be cast in the ground, the shell was to be of aluminium (then a rare and expensive metal). The site selected by the Gun Club after some controversy was at Stone Hill in Florida, almost on the same latitude as Cape Kennedy. This was only one of the many ways in which the novel prefigures the American space programme.

When all the preparations for the firing are nearly complete, the Gun Club receives a strange telegram. From Paris an adventurer wires his offer to travel in the shell. His name is Michel Ardan, a name which everyone in Paris would have recognised as an anagram of Nadar. Verne gives a pen-portrait of his friend, and the illustrator of the novel modelled Ardan on photos of Nadar. Thus Verne paid an oblique compliment to his friend's enthusiasm for aeronautics.

The shell is redesigned as a spacecraft with padded walls, in which Ardan will travel to the moon with Barbicane and his rival in gunnery expertise, Nicholl. The book ends with the firing of the gun and the attempts to track its flight with a giant telescope, whose twenty-inch mirror rivalled that of Mount Palomar. Would the three space travellers be heard from again? Would they be able to communicate with the earth?

Verne's readers had to wait until the publication of the sequel, *Autour de la Lune* (*Around the Moon*) in 1870. This novel described the experiences of the three adventurers in the capsule, including the strange weightless conditions of outer space but neglecting, unfortunately, the initial shock of the firing, the sudden acceleration of which would certainly have crushed them to pulp. Much of the book is taken up with mathematical and astronomical speculations. Deflected from their course by passing too close to the earth's second moon (an improbable fiction convenient for Verne's purposes), they pass around the back of the moon.

The mysterious dark side of the moon is invisible so we learn nothing about that, except for the intense cold they suffer when cut off from the rays of the sun. Firing auxiliary rockets, they break out of orbit round the moon and fall back to earth, splashing down in the Pacific Ocean off the Mexican coast. The capsule is retrieved from the sea bed by a ship of the American Navy. Inside the padded shell the three heroes of the hour are found calmly playing bridge.

These novels presaged the realities of space travel in a remarkable way. The location of the launch site, the shape of the capsule, the weightlessness of space, the use of rockets to alter orbit,the splash down at sea which the Americans were to use in preference to the ground landings of the Russians. However they are also riddled with errors which many critics have since delighted to point out, trying to illustrate that Verne was a fool. Admittedly certain other details, such as the relative comfort of the launch, the opening of the capsule in space to throw out the dead dog, the restriction of weightlessness to a midpoint rather than the whole flight, the capsule's survival intact after a fiery re-entry, are open to criticism. Nevertheless Verne created the idea of space travel as a real possibility in many people's minds. And he rightly emphasised that the problem was basically one of reaching the right escape velocity.

Perhaps because 1865 was such a fruitful year for space fiction, it was a long time before writers returned to the theme. Verne himself, in his 1877 novel *Hector Servadac*, which described a journey round the solar system, extended the idea of space travel. Many others followed him in the 1880s and 1890s.

But at least the idea, the dream of space flight was kept alive by his books. The schemes of the Russian genius Konstantin Tsiolkovsky and the original researches of the American Robert Godard grew out of his novels. Even today, looking at the illustrations, one has the sense of seeing astronauts certainly, but 'astronauts by gaslight' as the novelist William Golding has recently described them in a felicitous phrase.

These were then, for all their errors and naïvetés, prophetic novels of the first order. Already Verne had seen one clear function of science fiction, the creation of possible futures.

Chapter Seven

Captain Hatteras and Captain Grant

IN HIS NOVELS VERNE ALSO EXPLORED MORE MUNDANE AREAS than the interior of the earth or the dark side of the moon. His first novels had been science fiction of a recognisable kind. But geographical adventure and the romance of the real world was to be his main forte in the years to come. Two early novels were good examples of this other kind of fiction he wrote. In *Voyages et Aventures du Capitaine Hatteras* and *Les Enfants du Capitaine Grant* he explored two contrasting parts of the real world which fascinated him: the North Pole and the Antipodes.

The Adventures of Captain Hatteras was first published as a book in 1866, and in an illustrated edition, the first one to appear in fact, the next year. It had been begun as a serial in 1866, but as Verne had a habit of setting his novels in the year that he began them, it may have been sketched out in 1861, the year it opens with the start of a mysterious expedition from Liverpool.

When the ship is at sea it is revealed that her captain is the notorious explorer Hatteras and her destination the Arctic. Her command and destination had been kept a secret for fear that no sailors would sign on with such a well-known fanatic for the frozen north.

Arctic exploration had a long history in England and Holland going back to the sixteenth century. Early in the nineteenth century the British Navy had led the way in the exploration of the Arctic, and Verne's novel was particularly indebted to Sir John Ross's *Second Voyage in Search of a North-West Passage* (1835). It was on this voyage which began in 1829 that the Northern Magnetic Pole was discovered. The course followed by Hatteras was that of Ross, though Verne has him abandon the search for the North-West Passage and turn to the North Pole. Verne had read the theories about there being an open sea around the Pole, which had been reported by Dr. Hayes in 1861. He thought that active volcanoes might be the explanation for this.

But it was the loss of Sir John Franklin and the ships *Erebus* and *Terror* in 1845, while trying to find a North-West Passage, which focused the attention of the world on the bleak northern reaches of Canada during the 1850s. Expedition after expedition went out in search of Franklin and finally in 1855 the pathetic remains of the last of the survivors of his party were found.

Verne had been enthralled by the search for a North-West Passage ever since he had heard the tales of Chateaubriand. But after 1855 popular interest shifted from seeking the fabled northern route to the Orient, towards exploration of the Arctic islands and, of course, the discovery of the North Pole.

Thus Verne's novel in which the determined Hatteras leads his reluctant crew towards the North Pole came at an opportune time. Verne was able to rehearse much of what had already been discovered and to make use of some of the popular Polar theories. These included not only the idea of an open sea at the Pole, but also Captain Symmes's notion of a large opening there into the interiors of the earth. Mount Hatteras, the volcano they discover at the Pole, reflects this idea. For the details of his book he relied on Sir John Ross, on Edward Parry who had tried to reach the Pole overland in 1827 and on the American Kane who had tried to make his way into the 'open sea' in 1853–55.

The adventures of Captain Hatteras end on the sombre note of madness. For on reaching the Pole, he climbs the volcano and nearly dies there. He is rescued, but has lost his reason. Confined in a mental home in Liverpool, he is observed following the same walk every day, still travelling obsessively northwards.

This novel was Verne's first extended narrative, running to two large volumes. *The Children of Captain Grant*, which also appeared as a book in 1867, was even longer, running to three volumes. Verne was now completely confident of his ability to carry the interest of his readers through such vast works. Both books, which sold over 37,000 copies in the ordinary edition by the time of his death, were among his most popular books. Hatteras seems to have been more popular in France, while the adventures of

Captain Grant's children appeal more in Anglo-Saxon countries, being one of the Verne stories filmed by Disney.

Though it describes a circumnavigation of the Southern Hemisphere, the story of the search for the vanished Captain Grant might have been suggested to Verne by the searches for Sir John Franklin. A message from Captain Grant is picked up in a bottle off Scotland. The sea, however, has got at it, so that the only clear detail, even though it is written in several languages, is that he was lost along the 37th line of latitude. This was a device which enabled Verne to take his characters not only across South America, but also through New Zealand and Australia, the new worlds of the Antipodes.

Captain Grant, whose name he borrowed from the famous African explorer, had disappeared while searching for somewhere to found a Scottish colony. This was not such a strange idea. There had been an ill-fated Scottish colony in Darien in the seventeenth century. And for modern Scottish nationalists the hope of a New Caledonia overseas would have been attractive: after all the Welsh were well established in Patagonia. Certainly the opening of the novel expresses some far from admiring thoughts on the English treatment of the Scots. Verne's sympathies were often with the underdogs of history.

But soon this is all forgotten, as the children set out on a yacht belonging to Lord Glenarvan to find their father. Among the passengers is a French geographer named Paganal (a name borrowed by Verne from a French historian whose books were once used in schools), who provides a certain amount of light relief in the course of the novel. He is supposed to be the secretary of the Société de Géographie in Paris – of which Verne had become member 710 in 1865.

Failing to find the Captain in South America, the party set out by way of Tristan da Cunha for Australia. But there is no trace of him either there or in New Zealand. Returning home, Lord Glenarvan stops off at Maria Theresa Island in the Pacific and, in the dark, the children hear a cry which they say is their father. The others say this is impossible. But the next day they rescue Captain Grant and his two men, the only survivors of his expedition.

This colourful novel became very popular, and was staged in 1878, in a much adapted version. The characters of the resourceful

Robert Grant and of the absent-minded Paganal became part of French folklore. Yet aside from them, the real interest of the novel is in the varied countries through which they travel, and on which Paganal always has something apposite to say. Into this armchair geographer turned traveller Verne may have put something of himself. He was an armchair expert himself. But he also harboured longings to escape to sea on just such a yacht as the *Duncan*.

'My story,' says Captain Grant, 'is that of all Robinsons thrown up on an island who . . . feel the struggle for existence pressing on them.' The use of this Darwinian phrase is striking, making it clear that Verne was influenced by the current debate about evolution at a very basic level.

With the publication of these books Verne's continuing popularity was assured. He was not a one-book author. In December 1865 he had signed a third contract with Hetzel. His earlier contracts had been for individual books, and two of them had even been published without a contract. The new contract was to run from 1 January 1866 to 31 December 1871. During those six years Hetzel was to receive from Verne three volumes a year, similar to those already published. (These books were often to be one book in three volumes, as *The Children of Captain Grant* had been.)

A strange clause, article 4, described the illustrations which were to be such a feature of Verne's books as being 'without value'. Verne indeed had few rights in the more lavish illustrated editions of his books. The woodcuts were of course an intrinsic part of the popular appeal of his books, and Hetzel was to make a fortune selling them for foreign editions. An element of commercial sharp practice can be seen here. But even if he was being deprived of his full rights in his own work, Verne was at least being paid for his own convenience a generous monthly stipend of 740 francs.

Verne's family biographers have almost made a legend out of the happy relationship which existed between Verne and his exclusive publisher Hetzel. Mme. Allotte de la Fuÿe says, for instance, that Hetzel cancelled and renewed the contract on five occasions without being asked to, 'each time to the greater advantage of the novelist'. The records of the firm preserved in the Bibliothèque Nationale show otherwise. Hetzel, as we shall see, was to make a fortune out of Verne. He was sharp enough to realise his firm had a hot property in Verne's imaginary voyages, and was determined like all publishers to turn it to his greatest advantage. Verne was content to be published.

Despite his success, which was now assured, Verne was still short of money. During the summer of 1865 to the end of 1866, while he was completing *The Children of Captain Grant*, he was forced of necessity to take on other work as well: household expenses still outran his income. He undertook the editing of the *Géographie illustrée de la France et de ses Colonies*, which meant a great deal of tedious work as well as long journeys through France. As he explained in a letter to his parents in January 1866:

I am working like a galley-slave on an *Illustrated Geography* of France, which is coming out in ten-centime parts. Théophile Lavellée, who had started the work for Hetzel is dying, and I have taken it over. It will mean an advance on my contract, which Hetzel is going to alter further to my advantage as soon as he has arranged his capital. I hope at the same time, to be able to write the first volume of the *Voyage under the Oceans*, the outline of which is completely finished, and which will be really marvellous, but I musn't lose a minute. For the rest, I rarely visit Eggly and I never set foot on the Bourse. Heaven be praised! Your very affectionate son, who is working like a beast of burden and whose head is going to burst.

This work exhausted him eventually. He felt he needed a change of air from Paris. In March 1865 he and Honorine together with Michel (Honorine's daughters stayed in Paris) moved to the little fishing village at the mouth of the Somme called Le Crotoy. They had spent a holiday there the summer before and Verne had loved the place. They rented a house overlooking the little port. The house had two storeys, a garden and pavilion. Behind them were the sand dunes, the haunts of teal and other wild birds. Verne converted the pavilion into a work room which he called 'La Solitude', which allowed him to joke about working in 'solitude'. The burden of his work made him bad tempered, a veritable 'beast of the Somme'. Here his imagination was now completely absorbed in his latest vision – of a voyage under the oceans of the world.

At Crotoy he bought a converted fishing boat which he named after his son, and after the patron saint of the Channel, *St. Michel*. She was to be the first in a series of boats which grew grander and grander with his increasing prosperity. The first boat, however, was a small cramped craft which Verne himself commanded, dressed in a fisherman's jersey. He had two old sailors for his crew, Alexandre Lelong and Alfred Berlot. Berlot was a deep-sea sailor of some experience, and told tall tales of brushes with real cannibals. Sailing was Verne's only escape from work. When he lay stretched out prone on the deck, Honorine would twit him. 'However do you manage to write such beautiful things, my poor boy, when you never look at the sky . . . except with your bottom.'

His hack work for Hetzel brought a few thousand francs which helped them survive. It also provided the wherewithal for Jules and his brother Paul to take a trip to America on the *Great Eastern*. Having been a failure as a passenger ship after her launching, she had been converted for laying cables. The cable between Europe and America completed, she had laid one to India. Now she had been taken over by a French company to carry freight and passengers once again across the Atlantic. The Verne brothers sailed on her first trip under this new ownership.

They arrived early in Liverpool so that they could observe all the preparations for departure. Jules, who planned to write up the trip as a book, kept detailed notes. When they boarded the ship the conversion of the cabins was still being finished and departure was delayed. When they finally did leave, a sailor was killed in an accident and his body had to be taken ashore while the boat was moving down the Mersey. Once at sea, the weather was the worst which Paul recalled seeing in all his years as a professional seaman.

They stopped in at Cobh in Cork, and Verne caught a brief glimpse of the Irish coast. They passed Fasnet and were on their way. The crossing took fourteen days rather than the ten intended. Jules enjoyed himself immensely, observing the working of the ship and the strange goings-on of the passengers. There was a Mormon missionary aboard, but his lecture about the delights of life in Utah had to be cancelled as the good ladies on board did not want their husbands to hear about polygamy. The Sabbath was kept with proper English solemnity which amused Verne, though he was less amused at an American preacher who seemed to think that the United States were paradise.

But when he and Paul arrived in New York, Verne found himself very impressed with the New World. They docked on 9 April and had a week to spend before the ship returned to Europe, or 192 hours as he calculated. They planned to spend the time on a trip up New York State along the Hudson to see the Mohawk Valley, Lake Erie and Niagara, 'and all the country which Cooper has made so familiar'.

In New York city they stayed in a Fifth Avenue hotel and walked along Broadway in the evening. They saw a play at the Barnum Theatre called *New York Streets*, which featured a real fire and a fire brigade. The next morning they collected their mail and called on the French consul, before taking the steamer *St. John* up the Hudson to Albany in the evening. This was a paddle steamer of huge size which impressed Verne with its elaborate decorations. The boat carried 4,000 passengers, which included 1,500 emigrants on their way west.

The ship arrived late in Albany and the early train had left, so they had time to look around the state capital, the sights of which included a remarkable fossil museum. At once they caught the train to Niagara. Verne was amused to see that it was without any station barrier or ticket collector; one just climbed aboard the train stopped in the middle of the street. The train was fast and comfortable. Refreshment buffet, bookstalls, everything was at hand for the traveller. The train passed through the Mohawk Valley, and they caught a glimpse of Lake Ontario on the horizon. This was the land of Fenimore Cooper, but 'this theatre of the grand period of Leather Stocking, formerly wild country, is now civilised'. Here was clear evidence of the progress of the nineteenth century.

They changed trains at Rochester, and at two o'clock in the morning arrived at the village of Niagara Falls, where they stayed at a hotel called Cataract House.

Niagara Falls separated the United States from Canada: 'its right bank is American and its left English; on one side policemen, on the other not the shadow of one'.

The next morning they set out to visit the Falls. They crossed a bridge to Goat Island from which the full splendour of the Falls could be seen. They then climbed up Terrapin Tower, which looked right down into the waterfall.

> The tower is in the midst of the cataract. From its summit the eye plunges into the depths of the abyss, and peers into the very jaws of the ice-monsters, as they swallowed the torrent. One feels the trembling of the rock which supports it, but can hear nothing except the roar of the surging water. The spray rises to the top of the monument, and by the sun shining on the vaporised water, forms splendid rainbows.

They found that because of rock falls they were unable to visit the Grotto of Winds, which was hollowed out behind the central Fall.

After dinner they returned once again to the Terrapin Tower to watch the sunset over the Falls.

> The last rays of the setting sun had disappeared behind the grey hills, and the moon shed her soft clear light over the landscape. The shadow of the tower stretched across the abyss; further down the stream the water glided silently along, crowned with a light mist. The Canadian shore, already plunged in darkness, contrasted vividly with the moon-lit banks of Goat Island, and the village of Niagara Falls. Below us, the gulf, magnified by the uncertain light, looked like a bottomless abyss, in which roared the formidable torrent. What an effect! What artist could ever depict such a scene, either with pen or paint-brush? For some minutes a moving light appeared on the horizon; it was the headlight of a train crossing the Niagara bridge about two miles away. Here we remained silent and motionless on the top of the tower until midnight, leaning over the waters which possessed such a fascination. Once, when the moon-beams caught the liquid dust at a certain angle, I had a glimpse of a milky band of transparent ribbon trembling in the shadows. It was a lunar rainbow, a pale irradiation of the queen of the night, whose soft light was refracted through the mist of the cataract.

The Niagara Falls made an overwhelming impression on Verne, and despite what he says here, he himself described them in two of his later books: in *Family without a Name*, the young lovers are swept to their deaths in their boat over the Falls, while in *The Master of the World* Robur escapes from his police pursuers by launching the *Terror* from the top of the cataract.

Verne also recalled that Blondin, the French acrobat, had crossed the Falls on a tight rope with a friend on his back. The next day they saw the site of this exploit when they went over to the Canadian shore. There, dressed in waterproofs, they were able to walk behind the cascading waters, another exciting scene.

They went on by train to Buffalo, where they walked down to look at Lake Erie, which Verne was to recall in *The Master of the World*, finding it nearly frozen over. Then back to Albany and New York City. There they had a few final hours of sightseeing before going back aboard the *Great Eastern*. Twelve days later they reached Brest.

The two brothers were popular passengers. On the way out Paul had been much in demand at the piano, as Verne noted in the novel he based on the trip. Paul was asked one night to play the French national anthem. He started into the first bars of *Partant pour la Syrie*, but his audience demanded the 'real' anthem of France, the *Marseillaise*, which the obedient pianist provided 'with a compliance which betokened a musical facility rather than political convictions' for the song by Rouget de L'Ile was then considered far too revolutionary.

As they approached Brest at the end of the voyage, Verne was offering a toast at dinner. A heavy swell upset them all, rolling them backwards to end up improbably at the foot of the 'throne' in the first class toilets. This was not one of the ship board experiences included in his novel of the cruise. Learning by the failure of his Scottish book, Jules provided a plot this time, a sensational affair of separated lovers, a wicked husband, a mad woman, a duel and death by lightning! The melodramatic story line contrasts oddly with his scientific enthusiasm for the wonders of the 'floating city', as he called the *Great Eastern* in the book, and the marvels of the New World. America had captured his imagination and he was to set some of his later and best-known books there.

At Brest the brothers were met by their brother-in-law Du Crest de Villeneuve, who was a commander at the French naval base there. The Guillons also came over from Nantes to hear about their trip and were entertained by Jules's racy stories. While relating the misadventure of the toilet, Jules threw a carafe out of the window in his excitement. His brother-in-law was horrified. Being deaf, he had been unable to hear the anecdote and thought this behaviour very shocking.

While on the *Great Eastern* Jules had talked to some of the crew who had helped to lay the Atlantic telegraph cable. Their stories, as well as his own experiences at sea, provided more material for his new novel about a voyage beneath the oceans. His Atlantic crossing had increased his longing to explore the secrets of the sea.

Chapter Eight

Twenty Thousand Leagues under the Sea

VERNE BEGAN WRITING THE FIRST DRAFT OF HIS NEW NOVEL IN the spring of 1867. A synopsis had been drawn up in 1865, but pressure of work had prevented him doing anything on the book. Much of the work was now done on the *St. Michel*, which he had rigged up as a floating study. He worked with Victor Hugo's novel *The Toilers of the Sea* propped up by his lamp as a source of inspiration.

The original idea for the book may have come from George Sand. Verne, or perhaps Hetzel who was her friend and publisher, had sent her copies of his first two books. She knew about his projected series of scientific romances. The ones sent her pleased her very much.

I have only one regret that I have finished them and have not another ten volumes to read. I hope you will take us soon into the depths of the sea and that you will make your characters travel in one of those submersible boats which your imagination and knowledge will make perfect.

That was something which previous experimenters had been unable to do. The submarine had a long and complicated history, but up till then it had been for the most part one of failure. That man might one day travel under water had struck many people in the past from Alexander the Great to Leonardo. The first working submersible was built about 1620 by Cornelius van Drebel, a Dutchman living in England, who plied the Thames in his invention between London and Greenwich.

Other early efforts were by John Day in 1772, David Bushnell in

1776, and Robert Fulton who built his *Nautilus* in 1800. Both
Bushnell and Fulton, who were Americans, tried to interest the
government of revolutionary France in their inventions. But being
ahead of their time, they had no success. Fulton's other ideas, for
mines and steamboats, were also premature.

So it was not until 1839 that the idea of the submarine was
taken up again, this time in Germany by Wilhelm Bauer. His
Fire-Diver was the second submarine, after Bushnell's, to act in
war. The boat sank however, and Bauer and his crew had to make
the first submarine escape in history. Bauer tried to interest the
British in his invention, then the Americans, finally going to
Russia with it. But there he achieved nothing. All the same, his
new submarine the *Sea-Devil* had an observation dome and air-
lock fourteen years before Verne's *Nautilus*.

Submarines had been used in the American Civil War. One had
been built by an engineer originally from Nantes named Brutus
Villeroi, who may possibly have been a teacher of the young
Verne. Villeroi had experimented with a submarine at Noirmoutier
on 12 August 1832. His experiments were described the *Annales
de la Société royale et académique de Nantes* later that year.

This was not Verne's only source of information about submarines. His friend Pitre-Chevalier had described the appearance
of Hallet's submarine in the Seine in 1858; and Verne himself
may have seen it there. Nearer home he may have heard about the
Amiens inventor, Jean Baptiste Petit, who was drowned while
experimenting with a submarine between Saint Valéry and Le
Crotoy in 1834 when the boat sank. At Le Tréport about 1865
he made the acquaintance of a local inventor Jacques-François
Conseil, who had been working on a steam-driven salvage
submarine for several years. In 1858, accompanied by four
members of the Académie Universelle des Arts et Manufactures,
he had made a half-hour dive in this boat. Conseil received no
official encouragement, his only reward being the pleasure of
having Verne give his name to Professor Aronnax's servant in
the novel. The professor, as the illustrations to the novel show,
was modelled on Verne himself.

But the submarine in the novel had an even more immediate
source. By 1869, the year *Twenty Thousand Leagues Under the Sea*
was published, at least twenty-five authenticated crew-carrying
submarines had been built and dived successfully. In these

researches France played a leading role, and she was to lead the world in practical submarine building in the second half of the century. In 1858 the Ministry of Marine invited shipbuilders to tender for the building of a submarine from the designs of a Capitaine de Vaisseau, Simeon Bourgois. The tender of M. Charles-Marie Brun was accepted and work was begun on the boat at the Rochefort naval yard. The submarine, called *Le Plongeur*, was launched in 1863. This was the first submarine ever to be built with the resources and skills of a well-developed shipbuilding industry behind her.

Le Plongeur was huge in comparison with the boats that had gone before. She was 140 feet long, 20 feet in beam and 10 feet deep, displacing 410 tons. She was the largest submarine ever to be built before the present century. She had to be this great size because she was driven by an 80 H.P. compressed-air engine, and the tanks containing the 'fuel' took up most of the space inside the boat. The crew of twelve were amidships with the controls. The air was vented inside the vessel to pressurise the hull.

In 1865 *Le Plongeur* began her trials at Rochefort. On her first run one of the glass windows in the conning tower caved in and the boat was flooded. She was raised, and modified in the autumn to put to sea again. There was a great deal of difficulty in handling the submarine in 'zero buoyancy' and the boat would plunge up and down alarmingly as she moved through the water. A vertical propeller was added and more trials were made. But the difficulty of keeping a steady depth line was not overcome.

As a weapon of war, *Le Plongeur* was of little use, especially as her only armament was a mine attached to a spar on the nose. The lack of a useable weapon led the Ministry to abandon the trials (the Whitehead torpedo was only then being developed in Trieste).

A large model of *Le Plongeur* (now in the Musée de la Marine) was displayed at the Paris Exhibition in 1867, where Verne was able to see it for himself. This submarine was the direct inspiration of his own *Nautilus*, which he was able to perfect in his imagination. The electric engines were his idea – though a professor of science had recently built a model electric submarine, it was not until 1881 that the Frenchman Goubet constructed the first practical electrically driven submarine. Riou, Verne's illustrator, based his drawings of the *Nautilus* on the model of *Le Plongeur*, even down to including the compressed-air tanks, which were redundant in an electric boat. Verne himself is not explicit about how the engines work: as Captain Nemo, the commander of the *Nautilus*, says, 'My electricity is not like everyone else's.' Nemo seems also to have invented a superior system of controls as well, but for attack the *Nautilus* simply used a ram: one shudders to think what Nemo might have done with Whitehead torpedoes.

If submarines were not new, neither were novels about them original. An under-sea novel, *Voyage au fond de la mer*, by Captain Merobert was published in 1845. In October 1867 while Verne was working on his own novel, the *Petit Journal* began a serial called 'The extraordinary adventurers of Doctor Trinitus'. The author was Aristide Roger, a name which hid the identity of Dr. Jules Rengade, a member of the Amiens academy. Dr. Trinitus commands a submarine eight metres long called *L'Eclair* which is powered by electricity, which he uses for wreck-hunting in the Coral Sea and which is itself wrecked on the shores of the New Hebrides.

The novel appeared as *Voyage sous les Flots* in 1868, and was republished in 1890 with a note drawing attention to the parallel with Verne's novel which did not appear until 1870. But Verne himself had hastened to escape the charge of plagiarism, by writing to the editor of the *Petit Journal*. He pointed out that he himself was working on a novel then called *Voyage sous les Eaux*, but that work on the illustrated geography of France had prevented him completing it. His novel had already been announced by Hetzel in the *Magasin d'Education et de Récréation*. He hoped he had prevented any unpleasant comparisons being drawn between the two books. And perhaps he had, for the adventures of Dr. Trinitus are now quite forgotten, while the *Nautilus* continues its own extraordinary voyage.

The under water world which Captain Nemo made his own was a quite unknown realm. In 1869 oceanography was hardly even a science. The wonders of the ocean which Verne makes such dramatic use of may seem small beer in these days of Jacques Cousteau in colour on television. But when the novel was written they were as strange as the far side of the moon. Arthur Mangin in his book *Les Mystères de l'Ocean* (1864) was one of the few writers who attempted a description of this new world, and Verne drew heavily on him for his scientific information. In 1873 Sir Charles Wyville Thomson wrote:

Every gap in the noble little army of martyrs striving to extend the boundaries of knowledge in the wilds of Australia, on the Zambesi, or towards the North or South Pole, was struggled for by earnest volunteers, and still the great oceans slumbering beneath the moon covered a region apparently as inaccessible to man as the 'mare serenitatis'.

This could almost be Verne speaking, for a similar feeling inspired him in writing his novel.

The difficulty was one of access. This problem had been partly solved by another French invention, the first semi-independent compressed-air diving dress with a face mask which Benoit Rouquayrol and Auguste Denayrouze had brought out in 1865. This was called the 'aerophore'. The diver wore an air reservoir strapped to his back into which air was forced by a pipe from the surface. On the tank was a regulator which released air at the hypostatic pressure the diver required for his depth. Also he could disconnect the pipe and walk around freely for short periods on the air in the reservoir. This device was the direct ancestor of the modern aqua-lung and of the first fully independent lung invented by Denayrouze in 1875.

Nemo tells Aronnax that he has perfected the Denayrouze-Rouquayrol system by providing his divers with a copper helmet to withstand high pressures. Here Verne has made a classic error, for if the pressure of the water on the head is less than the pressure on the body, the result will be a rush of blood to the head and a fatal haemorrhage. Verne was a clever story-teller, but no scientist.

France had a tradition of diving naturalists, beginning in 1844 with Professor Henri Milne-Edwards, the first scientist to dive under the sea. 'My worthy master,' Professor Aronnax calls him. In the novel Aronnax photographs the underwater world with the help of arc lights – a feat that did not become a practicality until Louis Boutin took the first underwater pictures in 1897.

The two great pioneers of the oceans, Forbes and Maury, were only recently dead. Forbes had explored the world of the sea shore and the depths of the Mediterranean. Maury, an American naval officer, was most famous for discovering the Gulf Stream, and for his idea that the oceans, like the body, had a system of circulation. Beyond that the oceans were scarcely plumbed, the sea floor unknown. Verne's novel is an imaginative extension of man's knowledge of the oceans a century ago, and so little have we progressed that *Twenty Thousand Leagues Under the Sea* still remains his most prophetic book.

The novel opens topically enough. The year is 1866. There has been a spate of mysterious encounters at sea with what might be a moving reef or a huge animal. These echo the reports which were then current about sea monsters; Verne mentions the well-known sighting of a sea-serpent from the *Castilian* in 1857. A ship is equipped by the United States government to pursue this mysterious object. Professor Aronnax of the Paris Museum of Natural History is invited to join the expedition, together with his assistant Conseil and a Canadian whaler, Ned Land. They come upon the object and their ship is sunk. The three heroes of the book find themselves aboard a great submarine, the captives of Captain Nemo.

On this super-vessel they set out on a long cruise around the world under the oceans. Verne gives haunting descriptions of under-water life, of submarine forests and the coral kingdoms of the sea-bed. From these hidden resources Nemo has gathered not only everything he needs to live on, but also inestimable wealth, in pearls as well as in treasure from wrecked ships, such as those in Vigo Bay. Some of this wealth he is using to finance liberation movements, such as the one in Crete against the Turks. At Varikoro in the South Pacific the submarine comes upon the remains of the expedition of La Perouse, the French Captain Cook, who was lost in 1728. And in the Atlantic they glimpse from the viewing window the ruins of Atlantis. The journey is not without danger, as when the submarine gets stuck under the ice shelf of the Antarctic, after surfacing at the South Pole. (The idea that there was an open sea at the South Pole was a contemporary one, which was mistaken of course, but there was an echo of Nemo's feat when the USS *Nautilus* surfaced at the North Pole in 1955.)

A vivid chapter of the novel is devoted to the giant octopus, in which Verne mobilised a great deal of mistaken learning. Indeed, much of the information which Professor Aronnax provides his friends with is a jumble of facts and names which is often totally inaccurate. In Hugo's novel about the Channel Islands, *The Toilers of the Sea*, the hero fights with an octopus. This scene, despite its popularity, was scientific nonsense. The octopus is in fact a quite harmless creature, as are the squids. The giant squid is a different matter. For many centuries there had been legends about a many-tentacled creature which was capable of sinking ships. Few people gave these any credit, though the naturalists Erik Pontoppidan and Denys de Monfort collected some convincing evidence. Then in November 1861 the French naval vessel *Alecton* encountered a 'giant octopus' near Teneriffe, which was harpooned and nearly hauled aboard. The creature – which was in fact a giant squid – broke away and they were left with a piece of the tail weighing forty pounds. The commander of the boat, Lieutenant Bouyer, reported that it was about 15 to 18 feet long. This report created a sensation and was sceptically received in some quarters. But when a whole series of these creatures, which were then found to be squids rather than octopuses, were washed up on the Newfoundland coast over a decade later, scientists everywhere admitted the existence of what is now known as Architeuthis. At present the record size for one of these monsters, and they may well come larger, is held by one stranded at Thimble Thickle, Newfoundland, in 1871, which was over 35 feet long!

The *Alecton* incident had made a great stir, and no book about the sea would have been complete without the appearance of such a monster. But Verne, like Hugo and many others since, was confused about squids and octopuses. In the novel's illustrations his 'giant octopus' is given the appearance of a giant squid, based on the one seen by Bouyer.

The bloody encounter with this monster is one of the great set-pieces of the novel. Another is the scene which ends part one, the funeral of the dead sailor in a coral graveyard, a scene which deliberately echoes one of Chateaubriand's great description passages, the burial of the heroine in the virgin forest in his Indian tale, *Atala*.

But the mystery of underwater life is only one theme of the novel. The real mystery centres on the creator of the *Nautilus*, Captain Nemo himself. His motto is painted on the stern of the boat: *Mobile in Mobilis* around a capital N. That monogram would have reminded every French reader of one thing only, the arms of Napoleon. But Nemo is clearly not French.

The decorations in his cabin, his age, his hatred of imperial navies, all suggest not merely an anarchist but also a man of 1848. The portrait of Daniel O'Connell he possesses along with other national leaders identifies him with the European nationalist movements of the period. But his origins remain a mystery to Professor Aronnax to the very end.

The name of the submarine was taken from Robert Fulton's boat built in 1800, which was offered to Napoleon. As Bernard Heuvelmans, the Belgian zoologist, observes, 'Fulton was an idealist with utopian ideas: he thought it was possible to put an end to all wars by making them insupportable by means of his redoubtable weapon of the deeps'. Clearly Fulton served as one model for the characteristics of Captain Nemo. Fulton had as his motto Libertas maris, terrarum felicitas, and it is easy to see in him the original of the haughty and antisocial commander of the *Nautilus*.

But as Verne's correspondence with Hetzel makes clear, there was initially more to Nemo's character than the published text made clear. Verne had conceived Nemo at first as a Polish patriot, violently anti-Russian because his family had been murdered by the Russians during the rebellion of 1863. But because of the delicate political and diplomatic situation between Russia and France, Verne was persuaded to tone this down and to make Nemo's hatred of tyranny less particular. This is more effective than his first idea would have been, for Nemo can now prowl through the sea as a lone wolf, seeking fearful vengeance for unnamed horrors.

Verne took many details for Nemo from the character of Colonel Charras, who had been a friend of Hetzel and involved in the events of 1848. It has also been claimed that the research scientist aspect of Nemo's character was suggested to Verne by Albert I of Monaco, who was one of the great oceanographers of the last century. His complex origins notwithstanding, Nemo remains a strange and mysterious invention. Though Aronnax and the others speculate about him they learn little about his past, though Nemo does show the professor the manuscript of a book about his researches at sea which includes an account of his life. The details of this remain unrevealed, however.

At the end of the novel Nemo disappears with his submarine into the Maelstrom off the Lofoten Islands (borrowed from Poe perhaps). Professor Aronnax and the others survive and wonder if Nemo does too. Has his vengeful heart been influenced into the ways of science by the sights of the oceans?

Will the waves one day wash up on the shore his manuscript, containing the story of his life? Shall I ever know what his real name was? Will the nationality of the last ship he sank give us a clue to the nationality of Captain Nemo?

We are not told the nationality of that ship, but after he has sunk it Captain Nemo falls on his knees in his cabin before the portrait of a young woman with two children. Later as they make their escape from the doomed submarine, Aronnax hears Nemo's last words: 'Almighty God! Enough, enough.'

So the enigma of Captain Nemo remained a secret for five years, until the publication of *The Mysterious Island* in 1875. Here Verne with his passion for sequels was to give an account of Nemo's past which would conflict rather with his earlier picture of the captain of the *Nautilus*.

Chapter Nine

The Coastguard at Crotoy

IN DECEMBER 1868 VERNE GAVE THE FINISHED MANUSCRIPT OF *Twenty Thousand Leagues Under the Sea* to Hetzel. His publisher was delighted with the new book, and persuaded Verne himself to come up to Paris to sit for Riou who was collaborating with another artist, de Neuville, over the illustrations for the deluxe edition. Arms akimbo, Verne impersonated Professor Aronnax staring out to sea to catch a glimpse of his mysterious quarry.

The first volume of the novel was published on 28 October 1869, and the second in June 1870. The outbreak of the war with Prussia postponed the appearance of the illustrated edition until the end of 1871. But the novel had been recognised almost at once as being Verne's best book so far.

Early in 1870 Ferdinand de Lesseps, who was a great admirer of Verne's books, solicited the Legion of Honour for the writer. Hetzel obtained the support of his friend the influential critic Jean-Jacques Weiss. The Interior Minister Ollivier accepted the nomination, and the decree lacked only the royal signature when the war with Prussia broke out on 19 July 1870. In the crisis which followed the defeat at Sedan, Ollivier fell from office. However three days beforehand, he had sent the decree to the Empress Regent for signature. It was one of the last signed by Eugénie in those chaotic days of defeat before the Third Republic came into being.

Verne went home to Chantenay to celebrate with his family. His father was very gratified about the public recognition. But forty-eight hours after he arrived there, Jules' mobilisation orders came through. He was too old to serve in the ranks, but the army sent him back to Crotoy to set up a coastguard unit there. His father and sisters saw him off from the door of the little house. 'Goodbye, my son, my first born!' 'Goodbye, Papa,' Jules called back as he walked down the hill. It was the last time he saw his father alive.

The next day Pierre Verne wrote to a friend who had congratulated him on his son's decoration. 'I am happy that Jules' success rests on such a solid foundation. He is gaining innumerable readers, but what does it profit a man if he gain the whole world and lose his own soul?'

Meanwhile Jules had arrived back at Crotoy after making a detour through Brittany and Normandy. He was under orders to defend the Bay of the Somme against the Prussians. To do this he had his own boat, twelve veterans of the Crimean War, three flintlocks, and an artillery piece of such ridiculous dimensions that he nicknamed it 'The Poodle'. Its shells were about as effective as the old cannon-balls which had been chained up in the town square at Crotoy since 1419.

Though he took the *St. Michel* out on patrol in the bay and along the coast, Verne was careful not to go very far. If he even went as far as Ostend he might be interned, should Belgium declare war on France. The Prussian advance brought with it rumours of burning and pillaging. He felt his wife and family would be safer in a city, so he sent them to live with her people in Amiens where he rented a house. As Honorine made clear in a letter to Hetzel thanking him for his efforts to obtain Jules's decoration, things were at this time a little strained between them. Perhaps the separation was for the good. He believed that peace was near, but it would be better if his children did not have to witness the disasters of war.

If we get out of it with paying two milliard francs indemnity and seeing the fortresses in Alsace and Lorraine dismantled, we shall have got off lightly. After that, we shall have a civil war, but it will be a minor matter by comparison. The militia will keep these ranters under control. The Republic is the only government that has the right to take ruthless measures against the extremists, since it is the government that the majority of the herd have chosen. In spite of everything, I have settled down to work again, and in this month of solitude I have written almost a volume.

This new book was *Aventures de trois Russes et trois Anglais dans l'Afrique australe*, translated as *Measuring a Meridian*. This dealt with the efforts of the six geographers to measure an arc of the meridian in the favourable conditions of the Kalahari Desert. The actual geodesic task involved in making an exact triangulation was explained by means of a diagram 'borrowed from Professor Garcet's lessons in cosmography'. Such a task had been attempted by Nicolas de La Caille in South Africa in 1739, and Verne drew on his experiences and on those of Sir George Everest (after whom he named one of his characters) who had completed measuring the Meridional Arc of India in 1841, and after whom the mountain is called. He also made use of the experiences of the French astronomer François Arago, who had completed the measurement of an arc in Spain in 1806.

During their work his astronomers hear that the Crimean War has broken out. But they complete their work in peace and harmony. Returning to Europe they learn that the siege of Sevastopol is still going on. One of the Englishmen turns to his Russian colleagues: 'We have fulfilled our task in complete mutual understanding – a task which will win us the esteem of all learned Europe. In addition, through working together, we have come to look upon each other as lifelong friends. But until Sevastopol has fallen into our hands, I feel we must once more regard ourselves as enemies.' The Russians reply that they were about to make the same suggestion.

This contempt for the divisions arising out of wars between nations singles Verne out amid the patriotic enthusiasm with which France had entered the war. As a citizen he was prepared to do his bit by defending Crotoy, but he was not enthusiastic about warfare, and had never been. He had seen the great Krupp cannons at the Universal Exhibition in 1867, and had realised that these great monsters made war a very different business indeed from the romantic affair that many people imagined it was.

The Prussians, with the help of Krupp armaments, took Alsace and Lorraine. On 2 September Sedan surrendered and the Emperor was captured. The road to Paris was open. On 4

Jules and Honorine at home in Amiens.

Jules Verne's only son, Michel, as a young man.

Jules Verne in the garden of the house in rue Charles Dubois, Amiens.

Jules Verne (foreground), with Honorine and Follette, the dog, outside the house in rue Charles Dubois, Amiens.

Verne's study-bedroom.

Captain Nemo by N. C. Wyeth, the well-known American illustrator of children's books.

Phileas Fogg, hero of *Around the World in Eighty Days* (woodcut illustration from the original French edition of 1872).

Inset: the real Mr. Fogg: W. Perry Fogg, author of *Around the World*.

A scene from *Six Weeks in a Balloon* capturing the spirit of liberating adventure characteristic of Verne's novel.

Conseil's design for a submarine, Verne's initial impetus for *Twenty Thousand Leagues Under the Sea*. Verne named Professor Aronnax's servant after the submarine's inventor.

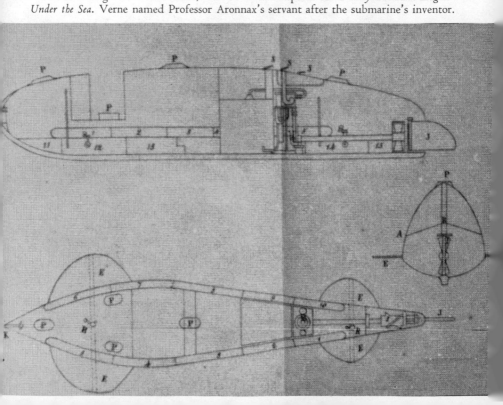

Verne seated in his library.

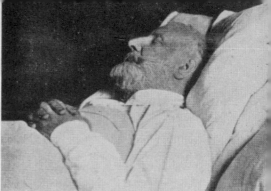

Verne at 25 years of age (*left*)
and on his deathbed (*above*).

The last journey: Verne's coffin is placed in the funeral carriage.

September in Paris Gambetta and others declared a new Republic and set up a national defence force. But the new government was unable to get any foreign aid and the Prussians closed in on the capital. The government retreated to Tours. From 18 September 1870 to 28 January 1871 Paris was under siege.

During these months, when the city's starving population was reduced to eating the animals in the zoo, there were some Vernian adventures with balloons. This was the first 'air-lift' in history. Some 66 balloons left Paris during the siege, 58 of them landing in friendly territory, carrying pigeons, dogs and letters. The dogs and pigeons were to carry replies back into the city. Most of the balloons were piloted by sailors, for there were naturally few professional aeronauts in Paris. The last of these to escape was Gaston Tissandier, flying in *Le Celeste* on 30 September: we shall hear of him again. One of the later balloons flew 600 miles to Königsberg in Norway, while another made one of the fastest balloon journeys on record flying 3,132 kilometres in 14 hours and 40 minutes at a speed of 95 miles an hour. These events were to be recalled by Verne when he was writing *The Mysterious Island* a few years later.

Verne himself was far removed from all of this at Crotoy. Early in December he paid a three-day visit to his family in Amiens, but then returned to his post at Crotoy. With winter closing in Verne began work on another book *Pays des Fourrures*, translated as *The Fur Country*. This was set in the Canadian wilderness on the edge of the Polar seas in the year 1859. The novel was an escape from the more pressing events of 1870 perhaps, the story of a Hudson Bay Company trading post which is thought to be built on solid ground, but is in fact standing on part of the ice-cap. The ice-cap calves and, perched on a shrinking iceberg, the post is carried away to the south through the Bering Strait to melt in the warm waters of the Pacific. The novel might almost be a parable of how precarious civilisation really is.

Floating ice-islands such as he imagined have been used in recent years by both the Soviets and the Americans in the exploration of the Arctic. The Russian writer Ivan Papanin gives a vivid description of life 'aboard' an ice-island which almost rivals Verne.

On 28 January 1871 the armistice was signed. The fighting ceased and Paris was occupied by the Prussian army. At the palace of Versailles the German Empire was proclaimed. Verne left Crotoy and hurried down to the capital. He was grieved to learn that his old friend Henri Garcet, who had stayed at the Lycée Henri IV during the siege, had died, worn out by the fearful privations of those long months when people had been reduced to eating rats from the sewers.

At Hetzel's establishment he found that his old friend had gone to Monte Carlo. He had remained in Paris also during the siege, but the humiliations of the Peace Treaty, the annexations of Alsace and Lorraine and the declaration of the German Empire had been a bitter series of blows. He had gone south to rest, but while he was there the city had been taken over by the Commune on 18 March. Verne arrived in Paris at this moment to find that the civil war which he had predicted had broken out. Confusion reigned everywhere. Hetzel's printing works was deserted as the typographers had all joined the ranks of the insurgents.

The Commune came to an end in the Week of Blood, when the forces of the provisional government entered the city and fought the insurgents from barricade to barricade. Meanwhile the settlement with the Germans went ahead.

For Verne, as for many others, these were desperate times. He had four manuscripts ready (three novels and a story, *Dr. Ox's Experiment*), but all his savings were gone and there was little hope of the books being printed at once. In April his parents asked him to come to Chantenay. He sent his family but did not go himself. He would go back to Paris, for he was worried about his literary position. He might even have to go back to the Bourse to earn a living.

As for public matters, I very much fear that Thiers may not have the strength needed to build a government on the ruins of the Commune. The Versailles Assembly seems to be completely lacking in political sense and does nothing except pass petty minded laws. Nevertheless, it does seem that the only thing that can save France at the moment is the Republic. I have just made a fourth trip to Paris. I was there three weeks ago, and was able to leave after getting a pass from the Communard Prefecture of Police, which started off: 'We, civil delegates . . .' and went on in the same vein. What a horrible and grotesque farce.

In Paris he was staying with his brother Paul and his wife at their apartment in the rue Tronchet. He went back to the Bourse during the summer of 1871. But his renewed commercial career was short-lived. The book trade began to revive after the war, and already his imagination was developing a new idea. Some time about now he picked up from Cook's Travel Agency around the corner on the Place de la Madeleine a promotion leaflet about a planned trip around the world.

In my moments of leisure I am writing the account of a journey accomplished with the maximum speed possible now. As for the illustrated books you asked me for, my dear father; *A Floating City* has not yet been published, nor has the illustrated *Around the Moon* appeared yet. Henri Garcet would have been interested in Bayard's and Neuville's drawings for *Around the Moon*. They are excellent. One of my friends, Bechenec [of the *Onze sans Femmes* dinners], has lost his reason as a result of the war. Poor devil! They say there's no hope for him. It is curious and impressive to see how life begins to reassert itself among the ruins. Do you know the macabre drawing by Daumier in the *Charivari*?

This engraving had shown Death disguised as a shepherd playing his pipes of Pan among the flowers of a meadow watered by the Seine, every flower a skull.

On 3 November 1871 death struck elsewhere. Pierre Verne was paralysed and died within a few hours in the presence of his wife, Paul and the three girls. Jules came home only in time to see his father laid out on his death bed. In the course of a funeral address a friend repeated his father's remarks about his son's success. Jules was touched. The stern judge of all his actions was dead, happy with the thought of his son's career, but a little doubtful about his beliefs.

Science was undermining orthodox religion, and Jules could not cultivate his interests without perhaps becoming aware of the distance that was growing between the religious and the scientific view. There is evidence of this in his light-hearted novella *Dr. Ox's Experiment*, which was published in 1872.

In a passage in *Around the Moon*, after the astronauts have recovered from the toxic effects of breathing in pure oxygen by error, Verne had speculated on the social effects which an oxygen *regime* might have. If a whole nation could be saturated with the gas 'what a supplement of life it would receive'.

This was the idea he developed a little later in *Dr. Ox*. A sleepy Flemish town has new lighting installed by the mysterious doctor and his assistant Ygene. As the pipes spread through the town curious things begin to happen. The whole population changes over night, and is suffused with energy. While they are preparing for a war, the gas works explodes, and things return to normal. Dr. Ox vanishes.

The mystery is explained: instead of gas, Dr. Ox was pumping oxygen into the houses and streets of the town. And, although pure oxygen would have been fatal in the long run, at the start it exalted and excited the citizens.

These ideas about the physiological action of oxygen Verne derived from the recent researches of Paul Bert, a stout Burgundian anti-clerical. He was to publish his magnum opus *La Pression Barométrique* in 1878, but already his work was well known. 'Are virtue, courage, talent, wit, imagination – are all these qualities or faculties only a question of oxygen?' That was Dr. Ox's theory, and also the theory of Paul Bert. 'For ourselves, we utterly reject it,' says Verne. But the doubt was there. Were personal qualities, the moral views his father admired, merely a matter of organic physiology? Verne was perplexed. And even today the physical basis of personality is a matter of deep dispute.

Perhaps Pierre Verne had some reason to die doubting the nature of his son's beliefs, however much his work was honoured.

A further honour came the next year. In August 1872 the Académie Français crowned his works. Fifteen years before Jules had refused to bow and scrape for such an honour, despite his father's wishes. Now, his father sadly no longer there to enjoy it, the success had come. And on the great day, when M. Patin was extolling the virtues of Verne's work, there was a great round of applause. 'It was an historic event,' his brother wrote to their mother, 'and would certainly have made father very proud and happy.'

But despite such recognition, Verne was leaving Paris for good. To please Honorine he had decided they should settle permanently in Amiens. It was, so he told his old business colleague and fellow-writer, Charles Wallut, a sober, well-policed, even-tempered city, its people friendly and literate. He had accepted membership of the Amiens Academy. He was near enough to Paris, yet away from its noise and agitation. 'And, when all is said and done, I still have the *St. Michel* moored at Crotoy.'

Chapter Ten

The Feat of Phileas Fogg

AFTER MOVING TO AMIENS VERNE MAY HAVE BEEN REMOVED from the hectic activity of Paris, but this change of pace marked a turn in his career. Success, both critically and financially, was now his. In the next few years, however, he was to become universally famous, a household name.

Much of this was due to one novel. His son-in-law Colonel de Francy recalled that on the evening of their wedding settlement, 10 November 1872, Verne read out to his family passages from 'his masterpiece, *Around the World in Eighty Days*'.

While I myself would dispute its status as his masterpiece, this was the novel that finally made Verne's fortune, not as a book but as a play. Out of the sixty-odd books which he wrote, this is the one that everyone remembers, if only on account of David Niven in the amusing film version made by Mike Todd. In terms of mere sales it was his most popular book, for at the time of his death the ordinary French edition had sold 108,000 copies.

Serialised in *Le Temps* before publication, the novel made a sensation from the beginning, and was reprinted as it appeared in a Philadelphia paper. The travels of Phileas Fogg and his servant Passepartout enthralled the world. So great was the impression they made that the origins of the novel have become obscured. Yet they are almost as curious as the novel itself.

Verne's own version has already been mentioned. During the summer of 1871, while he was working in Paris on the Bourse, he had chanced to read a promotional leaflet issued by Thomas Cook's travel agency. This pointed out that with all the facilities of modern travel it was now possible to go right around the world in ease. The idea took hold of his imagination. A race around the world against time. Soon he had his characters in mind. He cut figures of them out of cardboard and, stuck in with pins, was marking their route around the world as he wrote . . . Such was Verne's version, as set down by his family biographers. But there was much more to the background of the book and the character of Phileas Fogg, as I have recently discovered.

The schedule of eighty days had been published by the *Magasin pittoresque* in March 1870. This, with a couple of emendations, is the time table which appears in the novel, supposedly from a London paper. Verne was a reader of the *Magasin*, and had doubtless cut out the piece, which was brought back to his mind by the leaflet from Cook's. What the leaflet dealt with was the first *tourist* trip around the world which Thomas Cook was planning for the autumn of 1872. But there was even more than this to the origins of the novel: there was, in fact, a man who claimed to be Phileas Fogg.

This was George Francis Train, a wealthy Boston businessman. The heir to a shipping fortune – he had himself set up routes between Liverpool and Australia – Train was the complete eccentric. His trip around the world in 1870 was only one of his bizarre adventures. He had just completed work on his brainchild the Union Pacific Railroad, and he thought he needed a change of pace. A rapid trip around the world, going westward, suggested itself.

He took seven days to reach San Francisco from New York. He left for the Orient and arrived in Japan twenty-five days later. There he surprised the Japanese by joining them in a public bath – in the nude. On he went through Hong Kong, Saigon, and Singapore, to reach Marseilles by way of the Suez Canal. An ardent democrat, his fame had preceded him to France, and the local Commune called on him to lead them. Train had been involved with Irish Fenians, Australian republicans and American radicals. Nevertheless he refused. But in the troubles that followed he wrapped himself in the Tricolour and called on the soldiers of the Provisional Government to shoot on their country's flag – if they dared. He was arrested and jailed in Lyons, but was released through the intervention of Dumas, and taken to meet the republican politician Gambetta at Tours. Gambetta helped him on his way out of the country by laying on a private train to take him to England. From Liverpool he took the boat to New

York and reached home (discounting his days in jail) eighty days after he had left.

Train was an inspired self-publicist, but he was later to complain in his memoirs about his forgotten role in literary history. 'Remember Jules Verne's *Around the World in Eighty Days*. He stole my thunder. I'm Phileas Fogg.' Verne had probably heard about Train from his old friend Dumas.

But Train was not entirely right. For the original of Mr. Fogg was *Mr. Fogg*. William Perry Fogg, that is. Another American businessman, from Cleveland, Ohio, W. P. Fogg, was the author of a book published in 1872 called *Round the World*. In 1869 he had crossed the United States to California, and sailed from San Francisco to Japan. He was one of the first foreigners to enter the country after the end of the civil wars. He then went on through China, India and Egypt, and spent a year in Europe before returning home in 1871. His book about his travels consisted of the letters he had written for the *Cleveland Leader* while on his tour. As with Train, Verne never admitted to any knowledge of this man. In an interview with a British journalist in 1903 Verne did admit that he set great store by the names of his characters, 'and when I found "Fogg" I was very pleased and proud. And it was very popular. It was considered a real *trouvaille*.' But he did not say how he found it. Neither is it on record what the original Mr. Fogg thought about being made a character in a novel.

Train arrived home on 14 October 1870. Phileas Fogg set out on his (albeit fictitious) journey on 2 October 1872, returning on 21 December 1872. This was about the same time that Verne completed the novel. That same month, unaware of the fiction he had inspired, Thomas Cook was organising the first tourist trip around the world. His party of ten tourists (four were British, and four American, with a Greek and a Russian) left London in September 1872, returning 222 days later. Also conscious of the value of publicity, Cook sent a series of letters to the London *Times* describing their adventures. These were later issued as a small book, now so rare that even the British Library does not have a copy.

Whether as a rash adventure or a sober tourist trip, a journey round the world was in fact an easy enough matter. Verne, taking hints from these and other excursions, provided more thrills for his heroes. The key to the book was the famous time-table.

This was accurate enough, for the opening of the Suez Canal in 1869, and the completion of the last section of the trans-Indian Peninsular Railway in March 1870, made possible a trip of about the time that Fogg took. In 1956 G. B. Young, writing an introduction for the book, had a travel agency calculate what it would then take to do the same journey. As against 80 days in 1872, in 1956 it would have taken 58 days.

Inspired by his novel, valiant efforts were made during Verne's lifetime to break the round the world record. The first trip was made by Nellie Bly, an American journalist working for the New York *World* in 1889–90, who took 72 days, 6 hours, 11 mins, and 14 secs. She was followed by Elizabeth Bisland, another journalist, who thought the whole thing very easy, but took 73 days in 1891. The indefatigable Mr. Train made another two trips, sponsored this time, of 67 days in 1890, and 60 days in 1892. Nellie Bly called on Verne in Amiens, as did Gaston Stiegler, a French journalist, who did the trip in 1901. These efforts amused Verne, who mildly satirised them in *Claudius Bombarnac*, with the German Baron Weisschnitzerdörfer who is trying to go around the world in 39 days. What with missing his boats and trains he takes instead 187 days!

The last attempt of which there is any record was made by the American writer S. J. Perelman in 1972. But his account of his misadventures would put anyone else off the idea of following him. Perelman had worked on the screen play of the Mike Todd film, but on rereading the novel years later, he was surprised on the very first page to discover that Verne was *wrong*. In spite of the convincing apparatus of research the novel manages to suggest, Perelman became convinced that the book was hokum.

For the opening chapter Verne had drawn on his own memories of London, and on an article by Francis Wey about the English at home, in which there was a description of the Reform Club. But this Perelman realised, as a member of the club, was completely wrong in every detail. Nor was that all.

Mr. Fogg we are told lives in number 7 Savile Row, but this was not the house in which Sheridan died as Verne claims: that was number 17. The distance between the house and the Reform Club, duly paced out by Perelman with a pedometer, was also wrong. His researches into Verne's inaccuracies took him off on his own demented trip around the world.

Verne did make mistakes, and sometimes these were brought to his attention. In the original edition of the book the newspaper in the first chapter that carries the time-table was the *Daily Telegraph*. But an irate member of the Reform pointed out to Verne that the conservative political tone of that paper made it unwelcome in the more liberal atmosphere of the club. Verne duly changed the paper to the *Daily Chronicle*.

Verne was exact enough about such details as names and places, which were easy enough to look up in a gazeteer, but he easily missed the substance of foreign life. In Britain, for example, Fogg sits down to a very substantial luncheon at the time of the French *déjeuner*, and dines at an incredibly early hour. He then starts to play whist at seven, which would be a more appropriate hour for dinner. And so on through the book. The account of the law court at Calcutta is grotesque, with Judge Obadiah and Oysterpuf the recorder as stage Englishmen, the products of Verne's national bias. As Arthur Ropes pointed out in 1904: 'Too obviously, the author knew nothing about Indian magistrates and procedures, and had not time to find out; he therefore filled the gap with a farcical distortion of something he had read about legal proceedings in England.'

In the American chapters too there is a great deal of caricature, what with the bizarre election in California and the long aside on the Mormons, about whom Verne like most Europeans was very curious. Here too his haste in constructing the novel shows, with the rescue of Passepartout taking place off-stage, simply from the need to speed Fogg and his party on towards London.

One curious point about Aouda. She is the widow of the rajah of Bundlekund, a real place through which the railway did indeed pass. But that is where Prince Dakkar came from. Is Mrs. Fogg Captain Nemo's daughter-in-law?

The point of the novel, that Fogg has gained a day in going east, was known to Verne from Poe's story, 'Three Sundays in a Week'. Verne was later to read a paper on the subject to the Société de Géographie in Paris, of which he was now a leading light. It was in their library that he did much of his research when he was in Paris.

In 1872 the idea of a swift trip around the world was still a novelty. Crossing the Atlantic had become easy enough with the introduction of regular steamships. With the completion of the great transcontinental railroads, the Union Pacific and the Canadian Pacific, the western ports of the American coast were only a week away from New York, the Orient less than a month.

But beyond these routes, travel was still difficult, whatever Thomas Cook might say to encourage tourists. The rapid improvements even in the previous decade were radically affecting people's lives. Canada, the United States, and Australia were now the goals of poor Europeans anxious to build new lives away from the social and political constraints of Europe. Verne's novel dramatised the speed with which they could now travel. But he was not as yet interested in why people, as opposed to explorers, travelled to remote lands. The thing itself fascinated him, not the reasons behind it; exploration rather than empire interested him.

Around the World easily lent itself to dramatisation. Even before the serialisation had ended in *Le Temps*, the dramatist Edouard Cadol approached Verne for permission to adapt the novel for the stage. Verne signed a contract with Cadol, and the adaption was duly completed, but Cadol was unable to find a producer for his competent but unremarkable version. Time passed. Then in January 1874 the directors of the Porte Saint-Martin Theatre suggested to Verne that D'Ennery adapt it. D'Ennery was a talented adapter of novels and a clever dramatist of the popular kind. A new plot was made and went into production. The play opened on 7 November 1874 and was an instant critical success.

A columnist in *Le Figaro* wrote that '*Around the World* has put all Paris in a holiday mood, and when the theatre opens its doors, the Boulevard Saint-Martin presents a curious and joyful spectacle.' He also reported that the box-office takings were another reason for joy. 'Yesterday it was 8,037 francs, and in a fortnight, it had amounted to 254,019 francs.' These kind of takings continued for two years. In the entrance to the theatre a transparent globe was set up on which the progress of Fogg and company was marked at every interval. Verne was caricatured in *Le Charivari* as an acrobat juggling the earth on his feet before an enraptured crowd; and in *L'Eclipse* turning the globe on a handle like a chicken on a spit. Mr. Fogg's real feat was not his rapid transit of the world, but the making of Verne's fortune.

In adapting the novel D'Ennery had taken every excuse to provide spectacular stage effects, such as snakes for a cave scene in Malaya, and the greatest triumph of all, a real elephant. The one in the Paris zoo having been eaten during the siege, this was the first chance that many Parisians had had for a long time of seeing such an exotic sight. They were delighted with the play.

But during the rehearsals for the spectacular Verne had been beset with doubts. After all, Dumas had failed in the theatre. He asked his old friend Felix Duquesnel what he thought: 'Between ourselves, a success?' 'No,' answered Duquesnel, 'a fortune.' And he was right. A fortune it was, for Verne, D'Ennery and the producers. And even for Edouard Cadol. For he had registered the title with the Society of Authors, and under French law he had priority in it. After a law suit, the others had to buy him off with a quarter of the play's royalties. Even today his heirs still hold these rights.

Later the play was produced in many other places, adding to Verne's fortune. Much more recently, in 1956, the film version was also an immense success, partly due to its numerous stars and the novelty of the wide-screen. But little effort was really made to achieve any truly spectacular effects, and the camera-work was uninspired. The balloon-flight was borrowed, of course, from Verne's first novel. And, for me at least, despite the acting of David Niven and Robert Newton, the film was a disappointment.

Success took other forms as well. On 17 May 1875 Verne signed another contract with Hetzel, which, simply renewed in 1889, was to stand for the rest of his life. This was drawn up to allow Verne to take advantage of the great vogue his work was enjoying since the publication of *Around the World in Eighty Days*. From that date it was agreed that he would be paid not a fixed monthly sum, but a royalty on the number of copies sold. But other clauses of the agreement still deprived Verne of money from the illustrations, and from the illustrated volumes (which outsold the ordinary editions) until 1882. Though Hetzel died in 1886, the contract continued. And when Verne renewed it, it was through loyalty to his old friend.

Charles-Noël Martin, having studied closely the Hetzel papers in the Bibliothèque Nationale, in 1971 went into the matter of how much money was being made from Verne's books.

A calculation, based on all the new facts, shows that Jules Verne made, from his rights as an author with Hetzel, in forty years, a million francs in that period, which is equal to four million francs today. Hetzel himself made well over twenty million francs in present day terms [two thousand million to those numerous French people who think in old francs]. Who made the fortune of whom?

In sterling, that would be about £10,000 a year for Verne, as against £50,000 a year for Hetzel.

One source of revenue was the sale of foreign rights. These were the special concern of Hetzel's son, Jules, who was to take over the business when he died. There were, of course, in those days before the Berne Convention, pirated editions. But reputable foreign publishers would bring out an 'author's illustrated edition'. Verne received something from these sales, but the money from the valuable illustrations was Hetzel's alone. The sale of the cuts in Russia, Spain and England for five of the early books, which cost 3,370 francs 96 centimes to make, brought Hetzel 8,776 francs 7 centimes. An account for 1870, the year *Twenty Thousand Leagues Under the Sea* was published, shows that the author was paid on all his works 7,666 francs 70 centimes. Hetzel in the same year made 64,429 francs 54 centimes from the same book. Such were the rewards, to author and publisher, of imaginative genius.

Verne was happy to be translated as this made him known all over the world. In England *Five Weeks in a Balloon* appeared in 1870; *Journey to the Centre of the Earth* in 1872; and *From the Earth to the Moon* in 1873. This was a good year for Verne's name in England, for in 1873, no less than four titles were published in different editions. In 1874 five titles appeared. Many of these translations were merely anonymous hackwork. But a regular translator of many of his later books was W. H. G. Kingston, the editor of the *Boy's Own Paper*, where they were serialised before appearing in volume form.

Some of his translators committed awful butcheries on Verne's stories and language. Whole sections were cut out, lengthy additions were made, the sense of whole episodes altered. As he was only a 'children's writer' no one cared what they did with him. Edward Roth, the American translator of some of the novels, claimed to have rewritten Verne as he would have written if he were an American. It is a minor miracle that Verne's reputation survived all this. But survive it did. His English publishers Sampson Low and Marston had his books in print continuously up to the 1920s.

If *Around the World in Eighty Days* was Verne's most successful novel, his masterpiece was *The Mysterious Island*, which was published in 1875, after many years of preparation. He had been working on the novel since 1871, and in many ways this 'scientific Robinsonade' was the epitome of Verne's life's work.

The book begins in America, for Verne a country of infinite possibilities. Five Union prisoners escape from Richmond during the last months of the Civil War by balloon (echoes here of the escapes from Paris in 1870). A storm carries them across the American continent to be wrecked on a desert island in the Pacific. Equipped only with the barest of essentials, they set about colonising Lincoln Island, as they call it, building a new life for themselves. They are a mixed group, an engineer Cyrus Harding, a newspaper man Gideon Spillet, a sailor, Harding's Negro servant, and a boy. The novel was planned by Verne as the ultimate version of the island theme as used by Defoe and Wyss: from one stray seed they are able to grow an entire crop of corn. Slowly they recreate man's discovery of all the arts and sciences. The book is a parable of man's resourcefulness in the face of adversity, and is optimistic about man's future. These men are a success.

Many of the events since their arrival on the island, however, had seemed strange and almost supernatural to them. But finally they discover the secret of the island. The mysteries were all the work of Captain Nemo, the genius of the island, who has been watching paternally over their welfare. On his death bed he tells the colonists the strange story of his life. In the five years since finishing *Twenty Thousand Leagues Under the Sea* Verne had rethought his ideas about Nemo. Nemo tells Cyrus Harding and the other colonists of Lincoln Island about himself on his death bed aboard the submarine in the cavern under the island. This was his story:

Captain Nemo was an Indian, the Prince Dakkar, son of the Rajah of the then independent territory of Bundlekund in central India. When he was ten, his father had sent him to be educated in Europe, in the hope that with his talents and knowledge he might one day take a leading part 'in raising his long degraded and heathen country to a level with the nations of Europe'.

For twenty years Prince Dakkar travelled and studied and prepared himself. He went all over Europe. His rank and fortune caused him to be everywhere sought after as a social lion. But the pleasures of the world had no attraction for him. 'Though young and possessed of every personal advantage, he was grave – sombre even – devoured by an unquenchable thirst for knowledge, and cherishing in the depths of his heart the hope that he might become a great and powerful ruler of a free and enlightened people.'

Though he might have seemed a cosmopolitan dilettante, Prince Dakkar was a deeply learned scientist and a cultivated artist. 'This artist, this philosopher, this man was, however, still cherishing the hope instilled into him in his earliest days.'

Prince Dakkar returned to Bundlekund in the year 1849. Verne appreciated the benefits of colonialism in raising the Indians out of anarchy and warfare and establishing peace and prosperity in India. There the Prince married and had two children. Then in 1856 he became involved in the Indian Mutiny.

Dakkar saw in the Mutiny the opportunity of realising his own ambitions for his country. He joined the other chiefs and princes and fought bravely against the British. But in the end the bloody mutiny was put down and the rebels were defeated.

British rule in India had never faced such a threat before. If the rebels had received help from outside (the Russians were busy in this way) their influence and supremacy in Asia would have been broken. The name of Prince Dakkar was well known. He had fought openly. A price was set on his head.

'Civilisation never recedes,' Verne comments, 'the law of necessity ever forces it onwards.' The sepoys had failed to restore the old ways in India. British rule resumed.

Prince Dakkar, unable to find the death he courted in battle, returned to the mountains of Bundlekund. There, alone in the world, overcome by disappointment at the destruction of all his vain hopes and the slaughter of his family, a prey to profound disgust for all human beings, filled with hatred of the civilised world, he realised the remains of his fortune, assembled some score of his most faithful companions, and one day disappeared.

Where then, did he seek the liberty denied him on the inhabited earth? Under the waves, in the depths of the ocean, where none could follow. Prince Dakkar became Captain Nemo. The warrior became the man of science.

On a desert island in the Pacific he established a shipyard, and there he constructed a submarine from his own designs. By methods 'which will at some future day be revealed' he rendered subservient the illimitable forces of electricity and discovered the secret of generating power from the sea directly. Electricity was used in the submarine for power, lighting and heating.

The sea with its countless treasures, its myriads of fish, its numberless wrecks, its enormous mammals, and not only all that nature supplied but also all that man had lost in its depths, sufficed for every want of the prince and his crew. Never again would he have communication with the land. He named his submarine the *Nautilus*, called himself simply Nemo, and disappeared beneath the seas.

During many years this strange man visited every ocean, from pole to pole, gathering incalculable treasures. The millions lost in Vigo Bay in 1702 by the galleons of Spain furnished him with inexhaustible riches which he devoted, always anonymously, in favour of those nations who fought for the independence of their country.

In November 1866, Nemo picked up Aronnax and his two companions, and they sailed with him for seven months until 22 June 1867, when they escaped and the *Nautilus* was engulfed in the whirlpool. Nemo escaped and continued to travel the oceans.

He was now sixty years old. Altogether alone now aboard his ship, he navigated the *Nautilus* towards one of those submarine caverns which had served him as harbours in the past. There he was living when the fugitives from the American civil war were cast up on the shore. (The dates here are of course quite inconsistent. Verne does not seem to mind.)

With the entrance to the cavern now blocked, Nemo was unable to escape. He remained, and though hidden, observed the efforts of the castaways to establish themselves on the island, helping them as he could. Thus the seemingly supernatural events that had puzzled the castaways were explained. They had learned the secret of the mysterious island.

Now that they knew his history, Nemo demanded their judgment. Cyrus Harding answered for them all.

'Sir, your error was in supposing that the past can be resuscitated, and in contending against the inevitable progress. It is one of those errors which some admire, others blame; which God alone can judge. He who is mistaken in an action which he sincerely believes to be right may be an enemy, but retains our esteem. Your error is one that we may admire, and your name has nothing to fear from the judgments of history, which does not condemn heroic folly, but its results.'

But Nemo still wondered if he was wrong or right. 'All great actions return to God, from whom they are derived. Captain Nemo, we whom you have succoured shall ever mourn your loss.'

So Nemo died. Leaving the castaways two chests with a fortune in diamonds and pearls, he asked only to be buried in his boat. He passed away with 'My God and my country' on his lips. The castaways left the submarine after opening the sea-cocks to let it flood. The *Nautilus* sank slowly beneath the waters of the cavern.

But the colonists were yet able to follow its descent through the waves. The powerful light it gave forth lighted up the translucent water, while the cavern became gradually obscure. At length this vast effusion of electric light faded away, and soon after the *Nautilus*, now the tomb of Captain Nemo, reposed in its ocean bed.

The enigmatic figure of Captain Nemo contrasts with that of his unwarlike creator. Can this romantic figure of violence and vengeance, this courageous explorer of worlds unknown, be a reflection of the secret heart of Jules Verne himself? The answer may well be yes.

By 1875 Verne was universally famous as a writer. The volumes of Hetzel's series *Les Voyages extraordinaires* were established as seasonal presents in France, and translations were also popular Christmas presents in England and America. 'Vernian' was already an adjective with an accepted meaning.

But success on this scale brought its own problems. Fame and fortune brought those anxious to seize a little of each. Verne had readily changed real people into fictitious characters, now he found that rumour had turned him into a fictional figure, a renegade Polish Jew.

In Chapter One I mentioned the anxiety of the Verne family

over proving that Jules Verne was really French. This was due to
an absurd rumour that he was in fact of Polish origin. This
bizarre episode is worth describing, even if it digresses a little
from the main narrative. For though the legend has been laid long
since, again and again it has been revived as a sensational press
story.

In July 1875 Verne received a letter in Polish from a man
named Olscievitcz, claiming he was his brother. Thinking this
was some kind of silly joke, Verne ignored the letter. Then a
second arrived, to be followed by a dark stranger, who accused the
author of not being what he claimed to be. The stranger was a
Polish journalist who was after the truth.

> Sir, I know all about you. You are a Polish Jew, born at Plock.
> Your real name is Olscievitcz, from *alscha*, meaning an alder,
> which you have Frenchified as Verne, an old French word
> which means alder. You abjured your religion at rome, in 1861,
> before the Fathers of the Resurrection, in order to marry the
> Polish princess Kryzanowska. Fr. Semenenko was your confessor.
> But the engagement was broken off, and the Vatican obtained
> for you from the French government a post in the Ministry of
> the Interior. You are totally integrated in France and having
> become the great writer you are, have always taken care to hide
> your origins.

Verne was astonished. The story was quite absurd. But in a
mischievous mood, he put the stranger right on a couple of points.
The lady's name was Crashovitz, and he had eloped with her, but
after a lovers' quarrel she had drowned herself in Lake Leman.
'But keep quiet about all of this,' he added. 'I prefer to pass as a
Christian even though . . .'

He made a snipping motion with his fingers, leaving the
stranger to infer that he had been properly circumcised.

Verne may have been amused, for he told his family about the
stranger's tale and about his witty retort. However the matter
worried him, and he wrote to Hetzel to ask what he should do.
His vulgarity had been misplaced, for soon the joke backfired.
The story was published, and for the next twenty-five years went
the rounds of many newspapers. After Verne's death in 1905 a
Fr. Smolikowski wrote about the supposed Jewish-Polish origins

of the late French author in a Polish paper. The St. Petersburg paper *Krasianin* also published the claim. It was refuted by Georges Montogueil in *L'Eclair* in 1905 but that did not kill the legend. Nor did it make any difference that Canon Duville in Nantes produced documents on Verne's lineage; or that Raymond Joëssel, a director of the Audincourt foundry and a family friend, published extracts from the parish registers in Nantes and Provins in *L'Intransigeant* in 1924. The next year a Paris paper was still asking 'Was Jules Verne French?'

In fact it was not until 1928, after the story had been written up again in *Giornale d'Italia* (10 and 13 April), that the Italian critic Edmondo Marcucci investigated the background to the affair, and laid the rumour for good. It was the Fathers of the Resurrection who provided the clue.

The Congregation of the Resurrection was founded in Paris in 1836, by among others, Fr. Pierre Semenenko (1814–86), inspired by the Polish Catholic tradition. Their headquarters was in Rome in the Via San Sebastianello. Fr. Semenenko, like many other exiles, was fond of reunions with his own countrymen, and he kept in touch with a wide circle of fellow Poles. Among these was a man named Olscievitcz, who had abandoned his Hebrew faith, and on going to live in France had adopted the name Julien de Verne.

He had a brother in Poland named Hermann, and it was he who had written to Verne in 1875 claiming him as his long lost brother. In 1928 Polish papers taking up the 'Jules Verne affair' tracked down letters in French between the two brothers and other letters in Polish to Fr. Semenenko. The curious coincidence of the names was enough to convince both the priest and the brother in Poland that Verne was in fact a Polish Jew.

When Fr. Smolikowski had written the matter up in 1905, his superior in Rome had suspected that there was some confusion. But the superior was then a young man and he had not insisted on Fr. Smolikowski publishing a retraction. In 1928, after Marcucci had written making enquiries about the affair, he admitted this to him. The results of the professor's researches were published in the *Bulletin* of the Jules Verne society, and the legend died.

Charles Lemire, the first biographer of Verne and a close friend of the family, writing in 1908, was indignant that anyone could believe that Verne was Jewish. Verne's grandson, however, thinks the confusion illustrates the ecumenical nature of Verne's talent. Verne, he says, was not himself anti-semitic.

Yet the anti-semiticism is quite explicit in an early work of Verne's, *Martin Paz* (1852). And then there is the unpleasant portrait of the Jewish pedlar Isac Hakhabut in *Hector Servadac* (1877), written shortly after the visit from the Polish journalist. This character upset the Chief Rabbi of Paris, Ladoc Kahn, so much that he wrote protesting to Hetzel (3 June 1877). Hetzel asked Verne to come up to Paris from Nantes where he was staying at the time to discuss the matter. The French editions were not changed as a result, but in the American adaption by Edward Roth (which in many other ways also bears little resemblance to the original) the character of the Jew is exonerated before the end of the novel.

The Rabbi's complaint does not seem to have affected Verne's opinions very much. For in *The Carpathian Castle* (1892) Verne makes it clear that Jonas, the Jewish innkeeper of The King Mathias, is exceptional. 'His fellows in religion, his brethren by profession – for they are all innkeepers, selling drinks and groceries – carry on the trade of money lenders with a bitterness that is not promising for the Roumanian peasant. Gradually the land is passing from the native to the foreigner. Jews are becoming the proprietors of the finest farms mortgaged to their advantage, and if the Promised Land is not to be that of Israel, it may one day make its appearance on the maps of Transylvanian geography.'

The small village merchant who gains an economic hold over the local peasantry – what in Ireland was called a 'gombeen man' – has always been deeply resented. Verne, however, here suggests a motive for anti-semitism which was to grow far stronger in the years after World War One. In France such attitudes flourished at the time of the Dreyfus affair. But as the British historian of the Third Republic, Guy Chapman, points out, there were very few Jews in France, and most of them were concentrated in Paris as financiers and stock-brokers – in Verne's other profession in fact. Such anti-semitism as did exist in France was found in the same class. But as many of the wealthy families were connected by marriage with Jewish families, such prejudice was more of a 'conversational paradox' than a reality. Verne then was no more, or no less, anti-semitic than any other professional Frenchman of his class and time.

Meanwhile Verne went from success to success. The publication of *The Mysterious Island* in 1875 marked the high point of his career. The next year saw the publication of *Michel Strogoff*, which was an even greater success. This colourful tale of a courier of the Czar in Central Asia was very popular with his readers, combining as it did exciting adventures with a tragic though happily concluded love story. It was also adapted for the stage, once again by D'Ennery. When it was produced on an extraordinarily lavish scale in 1880 it was an instant hit. 'It's Strogoff,' became the catch-cry of the season for anything spectacular and colourful. The play ran on and off with *Around the World* at the Chatelet for nearly fifty years until 1925 – which must be some kind of theatrical record. It was then transferred to the much smaller theatre at Porte Saint-Martin, where it was a commercial disaster and soon folded, much to the chagrin of the Verne heirs.

In 1877 *Dr. Ox* was produced as a comic opera with music by Offenbach at the Théâtre de Variétés. The words were written by Philippe Gillé, Verne's old friend who had followed him as secretary at the Théâtre Lyrique in 1854.

Verne decided to mark his financial and social success by buying yet another new boat for himself, and by giving an immense fancy dress ball at Amiens.

As he explained to Hetzel, he gave the ball so as to open the doors of provincial society to Honorine and the children. They had now been married for twenty years, and the early, tempestuous years were over. The move to Amiens had made things even more settled, as had the calming effect of his success on Verne's temperament. Three hundred invitations were sent out, and two hundred people accepted. At the last moment there was a crisis. Honorine, who had been seriously ill, had a relapse and was only saved by a blood transfusion, the very latest thing in medical treatment which had been introduced the year before. The ball, however, went ahead as planned, but Honorine did not attend.

On 2 April the Salon Saint-Denis in Amiens was the venue. Among the vast throng was Nadar, Michel Ardan in person, who arrived in a mock-up of the spacecraft from Verne's moon-flight novels. The theme of the ball was the extraordinary voyages themselves, with other guests got-up in appropriate costumes. Part of the evening's entertainment was a performance of *Les Compagnons de la Marjolaine* which Verne had himself written back in 1855.

The whole affair, including the elaborate costumes, was designed by Gedeon Baril. The party cost Verne some 4,000 francs, the costumes and toiletries some 10,000 francs. A costly affair indeed, but one which seems to have had the desired effect of making the Verne family conspicuous in Amiens society.

That Honorine came very close to death at the time made something of a mockery of such grand social flattery. But she did not die. She recovered, and the domestic life of the Vernes resumed its accustomed course.

Chapter Eleven

The Bourgeois Façade: Jules Verne at Home

VERNE THE WRITER WAS A FAMOUS PUBLIC FIGURE. VERNE THE family man was silent and reclusive. By now his son was grown up, and Honorine's daughters were married. But the family life of the Vernes had been a troubled one.

The early years of their marriage had been unsettled, with Jules moody and gay by turns. There is some evidence, quoted by Maurice Metral, of an affair, and that Honorine was worried and unhappy. But by 1877 Jules was a successful writer and a wealthy man, and fame and wealth cure many troubles. True he had a bohemian past and radical friends in Paris. But at home in Amiens Jules and Honorine erected between themselves and the world outside a carefully correct bourgeois façade.

What secrets did it hide? Few, if any at all, if we are to believe the family biographers. But nevertheless, all was not completely serene in the Verne home.

In Amiens Honorine saw no reason why she should not enjoy the fruits of their position in society. In Paris, living in poverty, she must have felt a little lost. Moving back to Amiens made her a big fish in a little pond. This pleased her. Local affairs, local gossip, and local charities became her routine way of life.

Yet even after five years in Amiens, living in a pleasant house in the rue Charles Dubois, their social life was limited. French society, especially provincial society, was rigid and conventional. Proust, an instinctive authority on such matters, notes 'that middle-class people in those days took an almost Hindu view of society, which they held to consist of sharply defined castes, so that everyone at his birth found himself called to that station in life which his parents already occupied, and nothing, except the

chance of a brilliant career or a good marriage, could extract you
from that station or admit you to a superior caste.'

The son of a lawyer, and a stock-broker by profession, Verne
was a respectable person by caste. But few writers lived outside of
Paris, except for those driven into political exile. A creative
artist might feel terribly out of things in a city of 80,000 souls
intent on trade and the velvet industry, social life and mother
church. Some might well be anxious to meet the famous author,
but not his wife or family. Hence the eventual need for the
extravagant ball to break down this reserve and bring some
reciprocal invitations for Honorine and the children.

With the two girls now married (Valentine to a wounded
veteran of the Franco-Prussian war, Colonel de Francy; Suzanne
to an Amiens man named Lefèvre), the excitement of new friends
would be largely for Honorine's benefit. As for Jules, he was not
too reluctant to settle in Amiens, dull though the town might
seem to those in Paris. Domestic routine had its uses if he were to
write his books. But Amiens had few attractions for him. For
many years it was his custom to spend several days a week in
Paris, staying with Hetzel, at the Hôtel de Louvre or with other
friends. He had a safety valve in being able to escape into his
research at the Geographical Society, and in meeting his intellectual friends. Because of this there may have been even more
need for Honorine to occupy herself in Amiens.

Did Honorine really understand what went on in the imagination of her husband? It does not seem likely. From all accounts,
both from family biographers and from visitors, such as the
English writer Maria Belloc Lownes, who sought out the great
man at home, she appears for what she was, a contented middle-
class wife, just the sort of woman one would expect to go with
the sober black suit and discreet ribbon of the Legion of Honour
that her husband wore. Her life had no secrets. She was placid,
steady and unimaginative.

Honorine loved to entertain. When admirers arrived she would
go up and knock on his study door. 'Jules, for pity's sake, do
come down, you're wanted in the drawing room. There are people
here from Paris and Carpentras and Philadelphia.' But he would
reply: 'What's the use. You will be able to talk much better if I
am not there. I seem to have a knack of killing all conversation
dead.'

All too often this was quite true. In 1881 to celebrate the 100th performance of *Michel Strogoff*, an Amiens hostess asked the Vernes to dinner. Verne was seated beside the most beautiful woman present that evening. But he said hardly a word, and pretended not to recognise the significance of the set-piece in the centre of the table, which showed the Russian fortress which his hero had saved.

Was this bad manners, or tension? Perhaps a little of both. Certainly he was always under some strain. Much of the tension in his life arose from the troublesome behaviour of his son Michel. Born in 1861, the boy had been a difficult child. Honorine was doting and indulgent, Jules remote and uninvolved. What had been pranks in childhood, became more serious in his teens. The Vernes tried a school at Abbeville, then a sanatorium, then yet another boarding school in Nantes (where Jules rented a house during term time), and finally jail. They even took the extraordinary step of taking Michel before a magistrate, who was empowered to lock him up for a corrective period in prison. This was an extreme resort. Finally he was sent to sea as an apprentice officer on a sailing ship. This was supposed to be a punishment, but instead the boy loved every moment of the voyage. The ship, the *Assomption*, was bound for India by way of the Cape of Good Hope and the French islands in the Indian Ocean, Reunion and Mauritius. Michel was seeing the sights that his father only dreamed of.

The French critic Hervé de Ranville recalls how he was in Mauritius at the time, and how the rumour ran that Jules Verne's son had landed. 'A slim, fair-haired young man admitted that he was indeed the novelist's son. That night a planter gave a dinner for two hundred people on the island at which Verne and his son and his heroes were all toasted in turn. But whether this was really Jules Verne's son or some young naval officer only too delighted to lend himself to a hoax, I am unable to say.'

On his arrival in Calcutta in November 1878, Michel wrote his father a long letter full of conceit and self-satisfaction such as only a seventeen-year-old can write. His father was not amused. It was, he told Hetzel, 'the most horrible letter a father could get'. He thought Michel was a disgrace with no respect for anything decent. Michel naturally enough began living down to his father's opinion of him.

He returned home in July 1879, and began to live as wildly as ever. Even allowing for 'a touch of madness' Verne thought he was a complete delinquent. In December Michel left home, took lodgings in the town, and fell in love with a young actress at the municipal theatre. His father was opposed to the affair and to marriage. So at the end of March 1880 Michel ran away with his young star, and married the girl despite his father's objections. Jules, through Hetzel, arranged for a thousand francs a month to be paid to Michel from his royalties. This was a comfortable income at that period. The couple moved on to Nîmes, where their marriage began to break up, and where Michel became involved with a sixteen-year-old music student. Late in 1883 he ran away with her. Verne sheltered Michel's wife, whom he was now surprised to find was a very nice girl. But his initial opposition had driven Michel into a marriage which the boy could not now endure.

Meanwhile, Michel was behaving as if he had already obtained a divorce and remarried, for his new girl Jeanne had two boys by him, eleven months apart. Verne by now was paying an allowance to Michel and another to his abandoned wife. In the end the actress gave Michel his divorce and he married Jeanne. Verne found he had to accept things as they were, as Honorine wisely suggested he should.

Michel now went into business for himself, making bicycles. But this was a disaster, and his father had to pay off his debts when the company folded. For a few years he had difficulty keeping any job, but slowly under the influence of Jeanne he settled down. Though the couple were associated with the artistic crowd who used the *Chat Noir* club in Paris, Michel eventually ceased to be a bohemian and became prosperous. He was involved with the preparations for the Universal Exhibition in Paris in 1900 – 'Michel's Exhibition', as his mother called it. Later he was involved in mining operations in the Balkans, and he and his wife went around in fashionable society.

The reformed family man that Michel eventually became impressed his father, and the two became reconciled. Michel came down frequently to Amiens and even helped his father with his literary work. Whether he did more than help over some items is a question we shall look into a little later.

Michel and Jeanne had three sons: George, Michel and Jean,

the last of whom is still alive, and is the author of the second family biography of Jules Verne. Jean Jules-Verne is a retired lawyer, the family tradition reasserting itself after two generations.

Honorine's two girls took a very proper attitude to Michel and his wife. Brahmin-like, they too took a Hindu view of society, and looked upon their half-brother as an 'untouchable'. In June 1893 the Lefèvres refused to see Michel and Jeanne when they visited Amiens, and the de Francys too were not above trying to discredit Michel, as Jean Jules-Verne was pained to discover from a letter among the papers of Mme. Allotte de la Fuÿe. These petty feuds are, so he claims, the only family secret behind the bourgeois façade. He is glad to have aired them. But these feelings of hate and jealousy cannot have endeared family life to the aging Verne.

If there were other secrets Jules Verne kept them to himself. In 1898 he burned a large part of his personal papers, manuscripts and account books. Some parts of his life he seems to have been determined to destroy for ever.

The great mansion on the rue Charles Dubois to which they moved in 1882, and where most of his later work was done, was the house where many of his visitors came to see him. He lived and worked in spartan simplicity, Honorine in comfortable state. The contrast was very marked.

Downstairs in her domain were large reception rooms, furnished in the heavy, ornate style of the period. Upstairs on the second floor was Verne's library, with a well-used collection of books for his research, as well as editions of his books in many languages, including Arabic and Japanese. Here also were his reference notes, 25,000 of them, carefully pigeon-holed on one part of the wall, according to subject. These notes collected over the course of his working life were the solid foundations of his novels. The library included his favourite poets Homer and Virgil, as well as Montaigne, Shakespeare, Scott, Fenimore Cooper and Dickens, who was a special love, and an author he thought comparable to Balzac. Surprisingly Sterne was another writer he read and admired.

Beyond the library was his workroom-cum-bedroom, 'a tiny cell-like chamber', according to Mrs. Belloc Lownes. In front of one window, looking out towards Amiens cathedral, was his plain wooden work table. No ornaments, except two busts, of Molière and Shakespeare, and a few pictures including a water-colour of the *St. Michel*.

Here Verne slept and worked. He would rise at five, so that by eleven his actual writing, proof-reading and research were over for the day. Every night he would be in bed by eight or half-past eight, to rise again at five. Between pauses in his work, by glancing up, he could see the dawn breaking over the tall spire of the cathedral.

His was a solitary, almost hermit-like existence. The contrast between her world and his was the contrast between the stolid bourgeois life of Amiens, and the restless world-roaming imagination the house harboured. The contrast suggests that behind the secrets of the bourgeois façade of their lives, there lay the even more secret heart of Jules Verne.

Chapter Twelve

'Freedom, Music and the Sea'

THAT SECRET HEART, WHICH VERNE WAS SO CAREFUL TO HIDE, had its own private passions, pains and hopes. After his death his nephew Maurice said that, 'At heart my uncle had only three passions: freedom, music and the sea.' Verne's three loves were a romantic trinity which he shared with his own great creation Captain Nemo.

Writers may well feel a sense of identification with their characters just as their readers do. But these three passions are pagan, sensual pleasures. Suitable enough for the renegade commander of the *Nautilus*, but hardly for the son of a respectable provincial lawyer.

Besides, his family insist that Verne lived and died 'a good Catholic'. Now Catholicism, despite what is often said about it, is admittedly a flexible faith for those who hold it. It has been a refuge for both the puritan and the libertine, for Mauriac and Wilde. But Verne's books, which should be a clear guide to his mental outlook, are not really religious. What then does this suggest about Verne himself? Was he in fact what his family said he was? Or was he, like Captain Nemo, a pantheistic agnostic?

His family have always gone to great pains to describe Verne as a Breton Catholic. As we have seen, his claim to be a Breton is tenuous. So I think is the claim that he was a Catholic. As his religious opinions would have an important bearing on his work, this is a matter worth settling. As a young man in Paris Verne had discussed with his father various religious matters, including the painful one of the spiritual destiny of his agnostic friend. The son was already haunted by doubts his father had never known. The religious references in his books are perfunctory, and providence and chance rather than Almighty God preside over the destiny of his characters. The name of Christ is never uttered.

Halfway through his career as a writer we may safely say that Verne had ceased to be a Catholic in any sense which his father would have recognised. But like many cradle Catholics he kept up a certain social appearance to please his wife. Later, however, he even gave up going to Mass on Sundays, and she had to go alone.

And this was only in his middle years. His final position was to be very different, almost certainly closer to the agnosticism of his own strange hero the Kaw-Djer in his 1909 story, *The Survivors of the Jonathan*. This would be the result of a general disillusionment with mankind, and because of other unhappy events: the loss of a loved one, an attempt on his life, increasing ill health. The brisk optimism of his earlier books was to become a dark and sinister pessimism about man and his future.

So Verne seems to have broken with the religion of his father. And also, because his father had been a lawyer who worshipped law and order, he himself tended towards anarchy, the denial of law and order, in favour of an ideal and perfect personal freedom.

Freedom was very dear to Verne. He had escaped from Nantes and become a writer, so gaining his own freedom. Liberty was the great Liberal watchword of the nineteenth century, the cry of those who put up the barricades in Paris, marched in their red shirts on Rome, who ached from Mayo to Minsk for an end to imperial tyranny, from Africa to Alabama for an end to slavery.

But what did 'la liberté' mean to Verne? Political freedom of a certain kind. His books consistently support national movements for freedom in a liberal way. Yet in his home town his political ideas were more mixed. Political parties he had little time for. Hence perhaps his admiration for the Anarchists among whom were the geographers Prince Petr Kropotkin and his friend Elisée Reclus. They were men of far greater honour than many who took part in the politics of the Second Empire or Third Republic.

Verne had won his own personal freedom at some cost. The office in Nantes would have been an easier option than his garret in the Boulevard Poissonière. Yet when his son Michel also struggled to escape from parental control he was shocked. Freedom of that perfect, anarchist kind was to be found only in art, in his writing, in music and in the sea.

Music was an early passion. Even when penniless in Paris, he acquired a piano to play. Though few of his admirers have made much of his musical tastes, his novels show music and musicians as a continuing interest.

He had composed music and songs when he was young, though not with any great success. Most of his songs were written and published between 1850 and 1857 with music by his friend Hignard. In 1870 they also wrote the words and music for *Les Clarions de l'armée*, as a patriotic gesture.

Early in his life Verne had been an admirer of Wagner, an early one in fact. He refers to him in *The Children of Captain Grant* (1868) as an 'incomparable genius'. Wagner's music was also in the collection of Captain Nemo – was perhaps even played on that extraordinary organ. At a later date, though, Verne came to identify Wagner with the militant Teutonic spirit of German nationalism, so that his name does not appear in the list of great musicians in *Propeller Island* (1895) which is given by Calistes Munbar.

Verne much enjoyed opera both in Paris and in the local theatre at Amiens. From Stendhal, whom he also admired greatly, he had come to appreciate Rossini, while the fictional opera *Orlando* by Arconti in *The Carpathian Castle* (1892), in which La Stilla dies while singing, has been identified by Marcel Moré as Verdi's *Otello*, a study in jealousy which is appropriate to the theme of Verne's book.

Music was one way to freedom for Verne. But the great way was the sea. Since his earliest childhood the sea had dominated his imagination, his day dreams and his novels. His brother Paul had been lucky enough to go to sea as a sailor – he himself made some long voyages – but for the most part he was able only to travel the oceans in his imagination. His heart went with every departing ship he saw.

The sea as a symbol in Verne's novels is very potent. In *The Children of Captain Grant* the sea is the traditional enemy that wrecks their father and imperils them in their search for him. But in the saga of Captain Nemo the sea has become the great saviour the source of heat, light and energy, a dispenser of infinite bounty. In *The Chancellor* (1875) the sea becomes again the great enemy that reduces the survivors to cannibalism. This contrast continues through the novels, until in *The Invasion of the Sea* (1905), in which the ocean floods into the North African desert, the sea at once destroys and revives.

As we shall see in a later chapter, *Mathias Sandorf* (1885), with its great yacht, was directly inspired by Verne's own voyages. And certainly much of what Verne felt about the sea is put into the mouth of Captain Nemo:

The sea is everything. Its breath is pure and healthy. Here man is never lonely, for on all sides he feels life astir. The sea does not belong to despots. Upon its surface men can still make unjust laws, tear one another to pieces, wage wars of terrestrial horror. But at thirty feet their reign ceases, their influence is quenched, and their power disappears. Ah, sir, live – live in the bosom of the oceans. There alone I recognise no master! There I am free.

The quest of the masterless man for a perfect freedom would fascinate Verne to the end of his creative life. For Verne the anarchist war-cry 'No god, no master' echoed in the loneliness of his own heart. In 1875 he might be uncertain of his faith; by 1905 he had surely become the Kaw-Djer, the remote, lonely, unbelieving anarchist hero of his last novel. No god, no master: in the quiet of his cell-like chamber, Verne plotted the only real freedom an artist ever knows, the freedom to create.

Chapter Thirteen

Imaginary Journeys

IN THE 1870S VERNE WAS AT THE HEIGHT OF HIS FAME AND popularity as a writer. So great was his appeal that in Russia, Italy and Spain, his name was used to sell the work of other inferior writers. The appearance of each new volume in the series *Les Voyages extraordinaire* was an event of the year which his countless readers in Europe and America looked forward to eagerly.

Yet there is no escaping the fact that after *The Mysterious Island* and the death of Captain Nemo, Verne's novels show a falling off in quality. Quantity was well maintained according to his contract, and a book or two a year continued to appear right up to the time of his death. But rarely did they rise to the great imaginative heights of the earlier books. For the most part their titles are unfamiliar, and some of the later ones were not even translated, despite the appeal of the author's name. In terms of sales Verne reached a high point with *Around the World in Eighty Days*, which sold 108,000 copies during his life in the ordinary French edition. With *Tribulations of a Chinaman* in 1879 his sales fell to 28,000 and they never again rose above this. At the time of his death a later novel such as *The Aerial Village* was completely sold out at only 6,000 copies. From being a phenomenal bestseller, Verne had sunk to being on a level with run-of-the-mill sensationalists.

In this chapter I will have something to say about each of the books that appeared between 1875 and 1885, up to *Robur the Conqueror* in fact, a novel better known in English as *The Clipper of the Clouds*, some seventeen novels in all.

The first of these, *The Chancellor* (1875), was possibly written a little earlier, as the story is set in 1869. A story of shipwreck and cannibalism, it has been well described as 'the grimmest story Verne wrote'. The sources of the novel were in the disastrous voyage of the *Sarah Sands* which blew up off the African coast on the way to India in 1857; the open boat voyage of the *Bounty* survivors under Captain Bligh; and the painting *The Raft of the Medusa* by Géricault. This picture, one of the great master-pieces of French neo-classicism, had its origin in the terrible fate of a ship-load of colonists for Senegal who were reduced to cannibalism after their boat was wrecked on the African coast. In Verne's novel after a series of unfortunate disasters – the cargo of cotton goes on fire – the survivors of *The Chancellor* are also reduced to cannibalism. This is hardly the ordinary material of a 'juvenile novel', and one wonders if Verne himself did not often wish that his talents as a novelist could not be stretched to deeper levels of experience than an adventure story would allow.

His next book *Michel Strogoff* (1876) also had its share of horrors, but these were a real part of the book's background, the Russian imperial adventure in Central Asia. At the moment this is the only colonial empire which still exists, all the others having ended in liberation. Verne's story is set at the moment of greatest expansion by the Russians. Some of the local colour was personally provided by the anarchist Prince Kropotkin. The book was read in manuscript by Turgenev, and the Russian ambassador in Paris Count Orloff, for fear it might offend the Russian government.

Written with an eye to eventual dramatisation, this melodrama was unlikely to have offended anyone, except perhaps the Tartars who are the villains of the novel. The play was eventually written by D'Ennery once again (after Verne's old friend Felix Duquesnel had refused to do it), was staged at the Chatelet in 1880 and was, as has already been described, the great success of the season.

The next novel published in 1877 had no dramatic potential, but was a return to the science fiction of the earlier books. *Hector Servadac* was originally to have been called *A Journey Round the Solar System*, which would have been a better title. In translation it appeared as *Off on a Comet*. A comet strikes the earth and carries away part of Algeria into space. The alterations of gravity and climate are amusingly described. As a reflection of contemporary knowledge the book is of great interest. Verne's novel was a fictional counterpart to the more sober works of an astronomer such as his friend Camille Flammarion. As a scientific fantasy it was a return to the spirit of his first triumphs.

The same year also saw the publication of a novel inspired by his Scottish journeys. *Black Diamonds* is the strange story of a coal mine under Loch Katrine, the biggest in the world, and of the child who lives in its depths, unaware of daylight. As a parable of the new industrial age and its consequences, the book is chilling, the illustrations recalling Doré's engravings for Dante's infernal visions.

A Captain at Fifteen (1878) was probably written in 1873, the year in which it is set. This Marryat-like tale of a boy who takes command of a party of survivors after a shipwreck on the Angolan coast and leads them to safety is a somewhat tedious story, interesting however for Verne's views on the effects of slavery, white traders and alcohol in undermining the morale of the Africans. Verne's hatred of slavery is made explicit.

The Tribulations of a Chinaman in China (1879) is a light-hearted affair centering around the arrangements by Kin-Fo to have himself murdered in the hopes of adding some excitement to his life, as well as providing for the widow he plans to marry. Verne had a touching habit of providing his heroes with young widows whenever some love interest was needed. Much of the local colour was taken from the reports of the French explorer Père David.

Far more serious in its intentions was the other book he published in 1879, *The Begum's Fortune.* A French scientist, Dr. Sarrasin, an authority on hygiene, inherits through the Indian marriage of a relative the fabulous fortune of the world's wealthiest man, the Begum of the title.

Another claimant, a sinister German scientist called Professor Schultz, appears. After legal wranglings (which consume a mere million pounds of the fortune) the two divide twenty million pounds between them.

Sarrasin uses his money to found a utopia in Oregon called Frankville – at this date the American West was still a land of infinite possibilities. The regime of the city was taken by Verne from a lecture by the great British authority on social hygiene Dr. Richardson, published in 1876 as *Hygiea, a City of Health.*

Schultz follows him to America and founds another town some

thirty miles away called Stahlstadt, Steel State. Whereas the first city is dedicated to peace and progress, Stahlstadt is a military city from which Schultz plans the conquest of the world. His first aim is, however, the destruction of Frankville. The means of conquest was Schultz's secret weapon, a giant cannon – inspired by those great guns which Krupp had made for the Franco-Prussian war in 1870, which were to be so much improved by 1914.

The great cannon is fired, but due to errors in the calculations of the trajectory, its shell overshoots Frankville, and goes into orbit around the world. (In point of fact the shell would have been destroyed on firing. But once again Verne connected space satellites with guns rather than with rockets. Even so he was not the first with the idea. Eight years earlier E. E. Hale had described an artificial satellite in his novel *The Brick Moon* (1870); and his was in fact the first fictional space station.)

The struggle between the two cities continues, ending in the eventual triumph of Frankville. Clearly influenced by the events of the Franco-Prussian war, the novel forecast the fascist manifestations of the present century only too clearly. Whether Verne was being too optimistic in his hopes for the eventual triumph of good over evil is another question.

India had provided the fortune for his two cities, and India was the setting for *The Steam House* (1880). The novel deals with the aftermath of the Indian Mutiny, an event which still fascinated Verne. A real character of history who disappeared after the Mutiny, Nana Sahib, plots more treason against the British in the background, whilst Colonel Munro and his friends travel across the jungle in the steam-driven vehicle of the title, which is drawn by a mechanical elephant. This machine is said to have owed its inception to the steam-car invented by Verne's friend Dr. Conseil, which Verne had seen at Le Tréport.

In 1881 Verne published *La Jangada*, the story of a voyage down the Amazon on a giant raft, a veritable man-made island, which was large enough to carry a church and houses. This story, in the second part of which a cryptogram plays an important part in saving a condemned man's life, was a romance in which most of Verne's best features as a writer were displayed. In this it was quite unlike *School for Robinsons* (also 1881), which was a silly and facetious satire on the whole desert-island genre.

The Green Ray (1882) made more use of the Scottish scenes which

Verne had revisited in 1879. The 'green ray' of the title is sometimes seen, according to legend, at the last moments of the
sunset, flashing up from the horizon. Whoever sees it makes no
mistakes in love. The two uncles of the young heroine have
selected a cold-hearted scientist as her suitor. But the girl refuses
to marry at all until she has seen the green ray, and so has her own
way in love at last, marrying the dashing young man who rescues
her from death in Fingal's Cave.

Kereban the Inflexible (1883) was an adventure story planned to
illustrate the geography of the Black Sea, the Crimea and the
Ottoman Empire. The book was dramatised, but otherwise was
of little interest. The Aegean was the background to *Archipelago
on Fire* (1884), which deals with the aftermath of the Greek revolt
against the Turks. The efforts to put down piracy in the Greek
Islands after Navarino is the theme of the novel. Verne had earlier
been attracted to the national struggle in Greece – Captain Nemo
aids the Cretans in their fight for freedom.

The same year also saw the publication of *Star of the South*, a
story of the South African diamond fields and efforts to make
artificial diamonds. The plot was the work of André Laurie, but
Verne in rewriting the story made it completely his own.
Attempts at such modern alchemy have recently been successful,
but during the nineteenth century were on the fringe of scientific
possibility. In 1880 a Glasgow chemist J. B. Hannay made small
crystals from a mixture of paraffin, bone oil and lithicum heated
at red heat in sealed wrought-iron tubes. These were examined by
Story-Maskelyne of the British Museum and were said to be
diamonds, and this was confirmed in 1943. But other efforts to
make diamonds were either frauds or failures, until General
Electric made the modern breakthrough in the manufacture of
industrial diamonds in 1955.

The book also dealt with the British imperial adventure in
South Africa and the treatment of the Boers. Though he admired
British energy and enterprise, Verne did not always find their
deeds wholly admirable.

Mathias Sandorf (1885) was conceived as a tribute to his old
mentor Dumas père and was dedicated to Dumas fils. This was to
be the 'Monte Cristo' of the *Strange Journeys*. Sandorf is a
Hungarian patriot imprisoned for fomenting a revolt against the
Austrians. He escapes and under the name of Dr. Antekirrt,

acquires great wealth and an island fortress off the coast of Tripoli. As a scientist and a doctor he combines the talents of East and West. Verne's own yacht appears as Dr. Antekirrt's boat, and that character himself was inspired by Verne's friend Prince Louis Salvador, owner of a large estate in the Balearics. Much of the earlier background of the book, and even some of the events and descriptions, down to the figure of Sandorf, were taken from the books of Charles Yriarte, an exile from Dalmatia, who lived in Paris.

The Lottery Ticket (1886), which mentions the resistance of the Norwegians to Swedish rule, involved a ticket which was to save a poor family from ruin. The village background, which was very detailed in its account of Dal, was based on Verne's visit to Norway and his own stay in that little village.

In 1885 Verne published a novel which was written in collaboration with Pascal Grousset, another man of 1848, who for political reasons had to write as André Laurie. Laurie had provided the ideas for both *The Begum's Fortune* and *Star of the South*. *The Salvage of the Cynthia* was the only time Verne actually collaborated with another writer on the writing of a novel. His friend Laurie had been a leader of the Commune in 1871 and a radical socialist deputy. The melodramatic plot concerned a young man's search for his real identity and was fitted out by Verne with geographical details of great authenticity. The boy in the novel actually manages a feat which has never been achieved by anyone, the complete circumnavigation of the North Pole.

These books had been very mixed in their plots and their quality. The theme of liberty which runs through many of them was continued in such books as *The Road to France* (1887), *North Against South* (written in 1881) and *Family Without a Name* (1889). But the great masterpiece of the period, which rises above them all in both plot and imaginative quality, was *Robur the Conqueror* (1886), a visionary novel of aerial adventure.

The ideas in his novels were often brilliant, the treatment sometimes sketchy and finished in haste. This was a defect of much of Verne's later work, but as is often the case in science fiction, it was the matter and not the manner that counted with readers.

The inspiration for the new novel went back to the earliest days of his career, when he had been intimate with Nadar. At a meeting in Nadar's studio on 30 July 1863, Nadar advocated heavier than air machines as the real solution to the problem of flight. On display was a model helicopter run on steam built by Ponton d'Amencourt. This model was not a success, but other clockwork ones built the same year worked quite well. The notion of the helicopter was an old one: Leonardo da Vinci had sketched one. But it was not until the nineteenth century that any real attempt was made to build one that would fly.

In 1863 Nadar also founded a society to promote the cause of heavier than air machines. He also started a journal which ran for only five issues called *L'Aeronaute*. (Later it was revived.)

The words 'aviation' and 'aviator' were coined in 1862 by Gabriel La Landelle, who was another of this group. He designed a fantasy helicopter in 1863, and it was this machine, with its long body and row of counter-revolving propellers that lay behind Verne's design of the *Albatross*, as Robur's flying machine is called in the novel.

More immediately there had been a series of experiments with models in the 1870s: by Pomes and de la Panze (1871); Melikoff (1877); and Castel (1878) and Forlanini (1877). These efforts had come to nothing. But the idea of a heavier than air machine was topical when Verne began his novel. In 1888 Dieuaide published in Paris a *Tableau d'Aviation*, a large chart showing over fifty heavier than air designs from Leonardo to date. This chart was very popular and influential. Scientific works by L. P. Mouillard and M. A. Goupil also appeared at this time.

Even more topical was the opening of the novel, in which a mysterious flying object is seen in several parts of the world. Nowadays we would call this a flying saucer, but a century ago it could only have been some kind of balloon. The book opens at Niagara Falls: actually in September 1880 the New York newspapers had been full of stories about an unknown object which was seen moving through the sky in several places, especially around St. Louis and Louisville, Kentucky. Charles Fort, who collected these and other accounts of mysterious flying objects, commented: 'Unless an inventor of this earth was more self-effacing than the biographies of inventors indicate, no inhabitant of this earth succeeded in making a dirigible aerial contrivance, in the year 1880, then keeping quiet about it.'

Certainly Verne's inventor has no intention of keeping quiet about his flying machine. At the Weldon Institute of Philadelphia the members are arguing about the construction of an 'aerostat', that is a dirigible lighter than air balloon, when a stranger appears and grandly informs them that only an 'aeronef', a heavier than air machine, would solve the problems of flight. The stranger is Robur, and later he kidnaps the leading members of the Institute and takes them on a flight around the world on his flying machine. This part of the novel is too like the adventures and behaviour of Captain Nemo to be really convincing. After flights over Africa, the Far East and the Antarctic, the novel reaches its climax at an air meeting, where the *Albatross* challenges the *Go-Ahead*, a dirigible balloon. This machine was based on those built by Krebs and by the Tissadier brothers, and was as up to date as it could be made. But the *Albatross* conquers all. After this display Robur vanishes, leaving unanswered the mystery of his identity. He is, Verne tells us, the science of the future. But he disappears taking his secrets with him, though with a promise to return. 'To the *Albatross* is reserved the conquest of the air.'

Robur is a peculiar figure. He lacks something of the mystery and romance that surrounded Captain Nemo. But in his ruthless pursuit of his own ends, he does indeed foreshadow the popular idea of the scientist in the twentieth century, toiling to perfect the radiation bomb or biological weapons. Robur identifies himself with the science of the future. If so, one feels, God help the future.

Verne's imaginary journeys were supplemented by books describing the discovery of the world (1878–80), of which the part about Columbus and America was issued as a separate volume (1883). With his *Geography of France* this work was his contribution to the science he had loved since childhood. These literary journeys in fiction and fact were also supplemented by his own cruises aboard his yacht, the *St. Michel*.

Chapter Fourteen

The Captain of the
St. Michel

FOR VERNE, AS FOR CAPTAIN NEMO, THE SEA WAS AN ESCAPE: from his family, from Amiens, from writing, even from mere society. On his yachts, a series of three all called *St. Michel*, he was his own captain. He sailed on a series of long cruises and saw a little of the world through which his imagination roamed so freely.

The first *St. Michel* was the converted fishing boat already mentioned which Verne bought at Crotoy in 1868. In this small boat his voyages were limited to cruises along the Channel coasts and the river Seine.

After the great success of the stage version of *Around the World in Eighty Days*, he bought the second *St. Michel*. Though this was a larger boat, she did not fulfil Verne's ambitions as a captain, even if she were elegant and finely designed.

The third in the series was bought in 1877, and was a magnificent yacht in the grand tradition of the period. The boat had been built in 1876 for the Angevin nobleman the Marquis de Preaulx at the Nantes yard of Jollet and Babin. This extravagant gentleman seems to have made only one cruise on the boat before he brought it back to the yard and ordered an even larger boat. Verne, who was in Nantes at the time, learned that the boat was up for sale. He called on the Marquis and was shown over the craft. The deal was settled the same day, and Verne bought the boat for 60,000 francs.

He engaged a crew. As captain there was Ollive of Trentemoult-les-Nantes, and four deck hands, four engine hands and a cook. Babin refitted the boat for Verne, and when finished she was very impressive.

Paul Verne, in a memoir of one of his cruises with his brother, which was published as an annex to *The Giant Raft* in 1881, waxed lyrical over the third *St. Michel*.

The boat had sails just in case the engines broke down.

But the engines, capable of developing a hundred horsepower, designed by the Normand engineering works at Le Havre and built at the Jollet and Babin shipyards, are absolutely perfect. As to the interior arrangements of the yacht, it is laid out as follows: at the stern, there is a saloon, panelled in mahogany, with seats which also serve as bunks, and from there one passes into the bedroom, furnished in pale oak. The engine room and boilers occupy the central part of the ship. In the fore part of the ship is the dining saloon, from which a curved companion-way leads up to the captain's cabin and the steward's pantry. Farther on, there is the galley and the crew's quarters, containing six seaman's bunks. In short, nothing could be more gracious than this yacht, with its tall masts, it's black hull relieved by a fine gold stripe at the water-line, and the general elegance of its outline from mast-tip to stern-post.

In Verne's imagination this elegant craft was transformed into the *Ferrato*, the magnificent yacht of the mysterious Dr. Antekirrt, which he describes in *Mathias Sandorf* (1885):

The *Ferrato*, built in France at the Loire shipyards, was a superb vessel. In every detail it bore the mark of an extreme elegance: in the whiteness of its decks of Canadian pine, in the teak hatches and skylights, the brass fitments gleaming like gold, the neatness of the rigging, the halyards colourfully contrasting with the gunmetal grey of the stays and guyropes, the ornamentation of the rudder, the gleaming black of the hull, set off by a fine gold thread running from prow to poop.

'Inside' – but there Verne's imagination fitted out the fictional boat in a style that far surpassed the elegance of his own *St. Michel*.

After a few trial runs, the first proper cruise on the new boat was made in 1878. Starting from Nantes at the end of May with his brother Paul, Hetzel junior, who was thirty, and the young lawyer and deputy Raoul Duval from Rouen.

Duval, a Bonapartist, was one of Verne's close friends, and an enthusiast for Volapuk, the universal language which Johann Martin Schleyer invented in 1879. Duval was an internationalist and an influence on Verne, who became a partisan of Esperanto a decade later when it was introduced by Zamenhof, as a more logical artificial language.

Their first call was at Vigo, where Captain Nemo had recovered the treasure in the sunken galleons a year ahead of the real-life French divers. The local paper at Vigo, *La Concordia* noted Verne's visit on 3 June 1878. Then on to Lisbon, Cadiz and so to Africa. At Tangiers M. de Vernouillet and the Italian Minister, Signor Scovazzo, organised a boar hunt so that the author might see a little of the country.

Then through the Pillars of Hercules and past Gibraltar to Tetuan in Spanish Morocco. On to Mostaganem, where George Alotte de la Fuÿe, at that time a captain of Spahis stationed at Oran, took his cousin to see the Bay of Azer. George was the original of Captain Hector Servadac, and had provided Verne with background material on Algeria for his novel two years before. Verne was fascinated to see the scenery which he had only imagined in his novel. In Algiers Verne gave a lavish dinner on board the *St. Michel*, with the finest wines, for the local dignitaries and their wives. For a time the solitary Verne became a socialite.

They landed in France at Sete, leaving Captain Ollive to take the boat back to Nantes, while they returned home by train. So as to have the boat nearer to Amiens, Verne brought it round to Le Tréport on the Channel. There in 1880 he became friendly with the Orléans family, the pretenders to the throne of France. The Comte and Comtesse de Paris asked him to visit them, and Verne presented the Comte with one of several manuscripts of *Twenty Thousand Leagues Under the Sea*. Verne was also friendly with the Duc de Montpensier and the Comte d'Eu, who was seen as a future ruler of Brazil, after his father-in-law Don Pedro. Verne thought the Orléans family were 'very nice people' and 'very open-minded'.

But mostly Verne was a solitary, with little time for the lighter side of life. On one cruise the *St. Michel* was at Cowes during the Regatta. The Royal Yacht Squadron sent Verne an invitation to attend a reception for the Prince of Wales. Verne left Cowes at once. As he told his son-in-law, if he could not get any peace, he would have the boat registered in the name of his crew. 'What do I care about the King of England,' he exclaimed confusedly.

It was from Le Tréport that Verne began his second long cruise on the *St. Michel* in 1879. This time he went north and took with him Hetzel junior and Raoul Duval, to see Norway, Scotland and Ireland. Though he was to write accounts of his other cruises, Verne wrote nothing directly about this trip. However, much that he saw went into his novels. *Black Diamonds* had been published in 1877 and had drawn on his first trip to Scotland. Now he saw the sights which were to reappear in *The Green Ray* (1882), set in the Hebrides; *A Lottery Ticket* (1886) set in Norway; and Ireland, then beset by the troubles of the Land War with its evictions and boycotts, was to be the setting for *Foundling Mick* (1893).

A third cruise in 1880 took them to the Baltic, along the North Sea coast, through the Eider and the Kiel Canal. This was the voyage described by Paul Verne in his memoir *From Rotterdam to Copenhagen on Board the St. Michel*. At Kiel Harbour Verne had a chance to see for himself the growing navy of the German Empire. The pleasures of the little villages and of Copenhagen itself were slightly reduced by these sombre sights, which made many people in England and France uneasy for a continuing peace.

It was a few years before Verne ventured on another long cruise, but when he set out in 1884, it was with the hope of collecting material for a novel set in the Mediterranean. This was to be the most spectacular of his voyages.

In the spring Honorine, Michel and an old friend of Verne, Robert Godefroy, a lawyer who was later to be prefect of Haute-Savoie in 1905, had gone out to Algeria, where they were staying with friends named Lelarge, at whose wedding Jules had met Honorine, who was Mme. Lelarge's sister.

Jules was to join them there. On 13 May together with his brother Paul, and Paul's son, Gaston, he set off in the *St. Michel*. His nephew had the idea of keeping a log of their journey in a cheap school copy book. His jottings allow us a glimpse of the novelist at large, even though Gaston seems jealous of the welcome which his uncle received everywhere.

On 18 May the *St. Michel* arrived at Vigo. The daughters of the French Consul 'looked on Uncle Jules as if he were a demi-god'. This was the beginning of his triumphant progress.

In Lisbon, Hetzel's agent in Portugal, M. Coradsi, gave a delightful luncheon in my uncle's honour. All the cultivated society of Lisbon were there. In the evening, there was a splendid supper given by the Portuguese Minister for the Navy. At dessert, Jules Verne was presented with his own works in Portuguese, stacked on a plate of Majorcan workmanship, decorated with crustaceans and shellfish, which he was to take away as a souvenir.

Gaston was sent back to the boat with the plate while his father and uncle Jules went for a ramble with a young Parisian actress they had met who was on tour in Lisbon.

At Gibraltar, 25 May. The 'Lobsters' give Jules Verne a wonderful reception! Their officers carry him off in triumph to their mess. There, they drink punch, applaud loudly, drink more punch. On his return, Uncle asserts that 'he can no longer stand upright on his Pillars of Hercules!'

Two days later they arrived at Oran, and met up again with the rest of the family at the Lelarges'. The Oran Geographical Society gave a reception for Verne: more toasts were drunk. (His impressions of Oran were later used in *Clovis Dardentor*, 1896.)

On 29 May they arrived in Algiers. There Honorine's eldest daughter and her husband were stationed with the Army. He and his family were waiting on the quay, together with a large curious crowd. But Verne raised the gangway as soon as his relatives were aboard, for fear the crowd would also storm aboard.

The company of George Francy and Maurice his brother, who was an archaeologist working at Tebessa, roused Verne into good form. His Rabelaisian witticisms were lost on his young nephew however, as his diary is discreet about them.

10 June. Anchored at Bône. A businessman, M. Papier, and his wife, a former dressmaker from Paris, managed to slip aboard the *Saint Michel*. They beg me to introduce them to 'Monsieur Jules Verne', whom they adore without ever having met. Effusive greetings. 'I did my best to be nice to them,' remarks Uncle. 'After all, I didn't want to rumple the *papers!*'

On they went to Tunis, but the sea was very rough. A liner had just sunk near Bône with all hands. Honorine was terrified. She wanted them to continue the journey by land, which would be far safer. Captain Ollive could bring the boat on later to La Goulette. Verne gave in. They went ashore.

The railway between Algiers and Tunis was unfinished. There was no track between Souk-Aras and Gardimaou. So they had to do the hundred kilometres in a battered carriage.

At Gardimaou, however, they found that the French agent had worked a wonder. The private train of the Bey of Tunis was waiting for them. And the Bey himself, with drums and dancers, to welcome the genius of the sea and air, as he effusively hailed him.

At Carthage, two of Verne's friends held a reception for him. He visited the ruins of the ancient city and also the tomb of St. Louis, to which they were guided by the head of the White Fathers, Fr. Delattre.

Meanwhile the *St. Michel* had arrived at La Goulette. From there they sailed for Malta. But the weather worsened. After the Gulf of Tunis and even before rounding Cape Bon, the boat had to seek shelter in a small bay, Sidi Yussef. Here they were in the real desert, no water, nothing but sand.

> Uncle thought we would be shipwrecked. He was delighted. We went for a swim, and he performed a fierce war dance round an imaginary stake. Michel, who was on board, fired a rifle. Somewhere out of sight, Arabs, thinking themselves attacked, replied with rifle shots. Perhaps they were Senussi.

(There were no Senussi in Tunisia, but they had appeared in *Mathias Sandorf*.)

But no Arabs appeared, so after this single brush with romance, they started the next day to try and reach Malta. The storm seemed to have abated, but as they crossed the open sea, the storm grew worse. Robert Godefroy heard Verne sternly invoking his patron saint: 'Saint Michel-du-Peril-en-Mer, come to the rescue'. But neither the archangel nor a pilot appeared, even after the captain had hoisted a distress signal. Approaching Gozo, the light from its lighthouse vanished. For a while it seemed as if the boat might really be wrecked. At the dawn the wind was still strong. The *St. Michel* might well have gone down. But at the last moment the pilot came out, and Captain Ollive was able to bring them safely into Valletta twenty minutes later.

In Malta Verne and his party were again made much of by the British garrison. The governor, Lord Simmonds, showed him the sights of the little island, the chapel of the Knights of Malta and the picturesque quarter of Manderaggio, where the poorer Maltese lived.

A cosmopolitan population swarms about the port, and in the narrow streets, old women squat in their little shops with the sharp profiles of witches.

However, letters from France reminded Verne that he had better not delay too long in returning home. He had planned to visit the sea coast of the Adriatic to gather more material for his novel about the Mediterranean, the book that later became *Mathias Sandorf*. He had begun work on the book in 1883 and it was largely completed. But not so complete that he could not include a storm at sea which damages Dr. Antekirrt's yacht, which is repaired in Malta by the same yard which did such a swift job of repairing the *St. Michel*.

Instead of heading east, they sailed for Catania. From there they made a brief visit to Mount Etna. On then to Naples and Civitaveccia, where Stendhal had once been the French consul. Originally they had intended to make for Genoa, but Honorine had been very shaken by the crossing to Malta. Captain Ollive could bring the boat home. She wanted to return to France by land. She had had quite enough of the sea. Jules, ready enough to see more of Italy, gave in to her whim. From Naples they took the train north to Rome.

They arrived there on 4 July, and Verne solicited an audience for himself and his family with the Pope. In the Vatican these things are not hastily arranged. Meanwhile the social round was as hectic as ever, with a gala performance of *La Favourite* at the Humberto Theatre, which Verne and his wife attended as the guests of the Prefect of Rome and his wife. This was followed by a reception at the Farnese Palace.

On 7 July their audience with the Pope was granted. Verne and his party had the privilege of a private audience lasting an hour. According to Maurice Metral, Verne told the Pope: 'The man that I am now thinks always of the boy I was. It is for him that I write, for him that I imagine.' 'I am not unaware of the scientific value of your works,' His Holiness said. 'But what I esteem in them most of all is their purity, their moral value and their spirituality.' This was a remarkable tribute, for though Leo XIII had established an observatory in the Vatican, written a poem in Latin on 'The Art of Photography', and was concerned with social justice, he was notable for his resistance to the modern world in many of its manifestations.

The whole family were naturally very impressed by their audience with the ageing yet vital Pope. 'It was a vision of On-High,' Gaston noted in his diary. 'Even my uncle was in tears.' From which we may perhaps deduce that his uncle was not often moved by religious feelings.

The party passed through Florence unnoticed. This did not suit Honorine. And even when her husband signed the hotel register in Venice as 'Prudent Allotte', she gave him away and more civic receptions followed. The manager of their hotel scurried about arranging decorations and a fireworks display. In the evening banners were strung up with *Eviva Giulio Verne* on them, and lanterns lined the balconies.

A young girl presented Paul Verne with a laurel wreath, mistaking him for his famous brother. Jules had gone to bed early, leaving the rest of his family to enjoy the evening with its illuminations and fireworks. Honorine, who was enjoying these social events enormously, was as delighted as the young people with their reception. But when they came back to the hotel, Jules was snoring away pretending to be asleep. When they gave him the laurel wreath, he draped it over the chamber-pot, popularly called a 'Jules'. 'How gracefully Italy paid homage to artists in those days,' Mme. Allotte de la Fuÿe comments, but of course she does not mention the chamber-pot.

But there was one encounter in Venice which Verne valued. The next day he had a caller at the Hotel Oriental, the Austrian Duke Louis Salvador of Tuscany, the brother of the Archduke John Salvator who had disappeared in such mysterious circumstances after the Mayerling affair, and was later drowned in South America living under the name of John Orth.

Louis Salvator was himself an interesting character. He had an estate on Minorca, and brought with him his books about the

Balearics as a present. He wanted Verne to visit him there, and to sail on his magnificent yacht the *Nixe*, on an oceanographical expedition. Verne declined, but he was to correspond with the prince for many years to come. And also is there perhaps a little of Louis Salvator in the character of Dr. Antekirrt and his island kingdom of Antekirrta in the novel published a year later.

On the way back to France, Verne passed through Milan, where he is said to have gone out of his way to Brera to examine the notes and sketches of Leonardo da Vinci for a flying machine. In a letter to Hetzel (25 February 1885) he talked about his new novel, which would deal with neither space nor infinity. 'We maintain ourselves very modestly in the air and we cannot escape from it. Therefore it will be called *The Conquest of the Air*, the true title, though it belongs to a pamphlet which I have and which is well known.' This was the book which was to become *Robur the Conqueror*, and the inspiration behind his flying machine did indeed owe something to Leonardo.

By 18 July 1884 Verne was back in Paris, and showing Hetzel the final version of *Mathias Sandorf*, which had gained a great deal in local colour during his cruise, even down to the storm. In the pictures for the novel which Bennet was doing, the young Sandorf was based on Hetzel himself, while the Dr. Antekirrt whom he becomes was drawn from his dead friend Jacques Bixio who had died in 1865. The book itself was published at the end of 1885.

This was perhaps the peak of his commercial success. He was not to know that the decline was setting in, and that his sales and revenues would fall. Feeling confident for the future, Jules and Honorine gave another great fancy dress ball on 8 March 1885.

This time the venue was their own house in the rue Charles Dubois. A vast billboard over the entrance announced 'The Great World Tour Inn – Food, Drink, Dancing, Free of Charge'.

The couple presided over a great stew-pot wearing cooks' hats and aprons, but in fact more elaborate fare awaited the best society of Amiens inside the house. This was catered for by a man named Sibert, who had married a former singer from the Théâtre Lyrique, Mlle. Larsennat. She had known Jules in his early days as the half-starved secretary of the theatre. What a long way he had come since then. How prosperous he now seemed.

Perhaps this was even then an illusion. In February 1886

Verne was in Nantes trying to sell the *St. Michel*. This sale was to be explained by his poor health at a later date. But there is now no doubt about the date of the sale, for the actual bill of sale still exists. The Prince of Montenegro had been interested in acquiring the boat, and Verne sold it to him through a M. Martial Noe of Nantes. The boat had been bought at a time of exceptional affluence, but the maintainance of such a craft was very expensive. By now both the hull and the engines needed attention as the craft was nearly ten years old. The *St. Michel* had cost him 60,000 francs. He sold it for 23,000 francs.

His days as a deep-sea sailor were over. A month after he sold the boat, his own life was very nearly ended by one of his closest sailing companions.

Chapter Fifteen

A Shot in the Dark

On 9 March 1886, Jules Verne was returning to his house in the rue Charles Dubois at half-past six. He had spent the day as usual: after his morning's work, he had lunched and then gone down to the library at the Société Industrielle where he had read the papers. Then he had taken a turn around the town, stopping in at his club and at a café for a soft drink.

On this evening, as he was opening the door in the great iron gate to his house, there was a shot. A revolver bullet struck the stone step two centimetres from the ground.

Turning round to see who was responsible for this unpleasant joke, Verne saw on his left a youth pointing a revolver at him. There was a second shot, which hit him in the foot, where it joins the tibia. Though badly wounded, Verne threw himself after the youth, shouting 'Arretez-le.'

A neighbour M. Gustave Frézon, who happened to be passing at that moment with his family, did not hesitate to come to the rescue. In a moment the would-be assassin was arrested and disarmed.

Verne recognised him now – it was his nephew Gaston Verne, Paul's son. The boy had been not only his companion on his cruises but had also been very fond of his uncle. Subsequently Gaston had joined the diplomatic service, and hard work had led to a nervous breakdown. He had been ill for several months, but had seemed to improve. His father Paul had allowed him to leave Blois to attend a wedding in Paris. But Gaston had travelled on to Amiens. He had spent the day wandering around the town looking for his uncle. Unable to find him, he had waited in ambush outside his house. When Verne appeared he had fired at him. A servant heard the noise, and rushed out to help Verne while the passers-by restrained Gaston.

Verne was carried into the house and his doctor was called. The bullet had shattered the bones in his foot and was hard to extract. The author's condition was serious.

That evening his lawyer Robert Godefroy, who had also sailed on the *St. Michel* with Verne and Gaston, wrote to Hetzel junior in Paris:

9 March. My dear friend, this evening at half-past five, Gaston who had escaped from the mental hospital, fired two shots at Jules Verne. Happily only one bullet hit. Verne is wounded in the foot, slightly I hope. I am hurrying to send this note for you to arrive tomorrow. I beg you to hurry. Yours Godefroy.

The next morning Hetzel's private secretary in Paris sent a telegram in the same terms to Hetzel senior, who was at his villa in Monte Carlo. His son was also there, as his father was slowly dying of creeping paralysis.

From Blois, Paul Verne came at once when he heard the news. At first there was no public mention of Gaston, but soon the news was common knowledge.

At first this strange incident created a stir, but then the papers fell silent. Their discretion was shared by the Verne family. In her biography published in 1928, Marguerite Allotte de la Fuÿe was deliberately misleading about what happened. Gaston was not named. He became a wretched youth, 'who from excessive work had been overcome by an attack of brain fever, dashed out in the street brandishing a revolver. Who can say what aberration it was that made him level it at the novelist, whose books he had read so raptly from childhood onwards?'

This is the question we can still ask today. Gaston was actually twenty-six years old, hardly the adolescent she suggests. He was an intelligent young man, an exceptional student who was preparing for what his family expected to be a brilliant diplomatic career. Perhaps he had become deranged under pressure of work. But mental illness has always a long history and does not suddenly appear. The doubts of Honorine's aunt about the stability of the Verne family back in 1861 here take on a new significance. Gaston himself must have been disturbed from his teens. Marcel

Moré has suggested that he was motivated by jealousy of his uncle and that his uncle's financial support had only been more deeply resented. The undercurrent of envy which can be read into his diary of their last cruise becomes more significant in the light of this murder attempt. Naturally enough Paul Verne's family even to this day will not speak about Gaston to anyone.

Whatever may have turned his mind, the unfortunate Gaston was locked away in a mental home in Blois by his family. He never recovered. During World War I he was moved to another institution in Luxembourg where he died.

In a later novel *For the Flag* Verne gives a vivid description of a mental asylum, albeit in America, set high on a bluff overlooking a river. This is the actual situation of the mental home in Blois. The bizarre scenes inside such a place which Verne describes in this book may well have been based on what he knew about such places because of his nephew's illness. There he writes about insanity:

> Ordinary madness, when it is not incurable, can only be cured by moral means. Medicine and therapeutics are impotent, and their inefficacy has long been recognised by specialists . . . It has been justly said that madness is an excess of subjectivity, that is to say, a state in which the mind devotes itself too much to its interior working, and not enough to impressions from the outside.

The mad inventor in the story 'lived only within himself, a prey to a fixed idea whose obsession had brought him to his present state'. The unhappy parallel between the mental patient and the creative artist must have struck Verne forcibly. His own neurotic symptoms – 'restlessness, varying moods, irritability, eccentricities of character, melancholy, apathy, repugnance to either amusement or serious occupation' – were those he gave to the unfortunate Thomas Roch. Perhaps the only thing that stopped Verne going mad was his very 'serious occupation', his incessant work.

The wound in Verne's foot was a serious one, and a long series of painful operations followed. The wound was held open in the hope that the bullet might be expelled. But it never was. The shattered bones set badly and his foot never fully healed. The shooting left him lame and for the rest of his life he walked with a limp. During his recuperation he was heavily sedated. And it was at this time he wrote one of his few poems of later years, a 'Sonnet to Morphine'.

While he was recovering two deaths occurred to distress him. Eight days after Gaston's attack on him Hetzel died – on 17 March 1886. He was nearly seventy-two years old. The funeral was held in Paris, and Verne was unable to go. But the first letter he wrote after the attack was to Hetzel junior, expressing the sorrow Honorine and he felt at the loss for Madame Hetzel and himself.

Louis-Jules Hetzel succeeded his father as the head of the publishing house in the rue Jacob. The connection with Verne continued in the old way, the son taking over the role of critic, adviser and friend, which his father had played since 1862. Two books were published in 1886: *Robur the Conqueror* and *The Lottery Ticket* and another two the following year. A brush with death was not enough to put a stop to Verne's indomitable industry.

But on 15 February 1887 his mother died at Nantes aged eighty-six. Verne was still laid up, so Honorine and Michel went without him to her funeral. Some months later, when he was somewhat better, Verne travelled down to Nantes to settle the probate of his mother's will. He sold the house at Chantenay which had had such a special place in his early life. By then the property was part of a suburb of an expanding Nantes and was surrounded by factories. Verne was saddened by the sight.

> The air that once used to be filled with the scent of flowers and fruit trees is now vitiated by a pall of black smoke. But what can one do? It seems that civilisation must adopt the guise of harsh necessity.

He left Nantes, never to return, taking with him as a gift from his sister the portrait of his father. She wanted him to have it 'so that the wise old man could gaze down on his eldest son in his retreat'. But such intimations of mortality did not overwhelm the writer's spirit. Verne was only fifty-nine. His body might be wounded, but his mind was as active as ever. He was determined to struggle on.

Chapter Sixteen

The Republican Councillor

THOUGH HIS HEALTH GAVE HIM INCREASING TROUBLE, VERNE was still an active man and full of energy. His literary output was well maintained: after 1886 he was to write some thirty-three of his books. But literature had never occupied all his time, and now he looked around for something new to do. Late in 1887 he decided to go into local politics. Worse still, so far as his family was concerned, he was to run for city councillor in Amiens on an 'ultra-red' party list.

Though his background was truly conservative, Verne's own sympathies had always been liberal, indeed anarchist. Thus, early in 1887, he had said that he would vote for Jules Ferry, the leading anti-clerical Republican. Then, later in the year, he horrified his family by deciding actually to join the Radical Republican list of the mayor of Amiens, Frédéric Petit. Honorine, who lived for her religion and her social round in Amiens, was quite dismayed. What would people think? Had Jules gone mad? Ever since his family have played down this new departure. Mme. Allotte de la Fuÿe makes little of it, as does his grandson in his more recent biography. What then was the real truth of the matter?

The idea of Verne's candidature was the result of old friendships, with his lawyer Robert Godefroy, and his wife's cousin Alphonse Paillat, who also stood that year on Petit's Republican list.

The party situation in Amiens in 1888 was complex. There was the Conservative Union, the Republicans, the Republican Alliance, the Radical Opposition, Independents, Patriotic Protest, Individualists, Workers' Electors, Sincere Republicans,

Independent Republicans, and last but not least, Absentionists. This could have been a formula for chaos, recalling the political situation which Verne describes in *Propeller Island*. But in fact two main parties confronted the local electors: the Conservative Union and the Republicans. But as Amiens was 'Red', the Republican party list headed the poll, and Petit himself had been mayor since 1880.

If he were to be certain of election Verne would have to stand as a Republican. He made his approach to the party through his friend Robert Godefroy, who wrote to Petit on 31 January 1888:

Jules Verne desires to enter the Municipal Council on the list patronised by citizen Frédéric Petit. The fact is that 10 years ago this would have seemed bizarre, because the aimiable writer, staying away from all political matters, would not have been taken for a wild Republican. Quite the contrary, his Orleanist sympathies were well known to me. But so what? He suffered like so many others under the tyrannies of childhood memory. Verne was born before 1829; his youth was passed therefore under the reign of Louis-Philippe, that golden age of the bourgeoisie whose benefits he heard boasted of by all his family. Despite this, he was a Republican in 1848: he has told me himself that in Nantes he distributed literature in favour of the Provisional Government candidates. But this enthusiasm was not just a youthful folly. I don't have to tell you the rest of this story, for you know it.

Today, intelligent man that he is, he recognises that the Republic is wanted by the great majority of the country, and that a revolution is impossible; coups d'état are not the way for holding on to power. He rallies round now quite openly, because personal ambition cannot be seen in this. If you think that his name is capable of attracting, I don't say votes, but followers, allowing you to draw up a convenient list, he is at your disposal.

Like all political virgins, Verne has asked me what are his chances of being elected, because if he were not to be, he would not dare to allow his name to appear on a poster. I have assured him, as I have everyone else, that your success will be overwhelming.

You yourself, my dear Petit, will see that it is wise and

politic to obtain as a collaborateur a man of incontestable talent and great fame who will do the council great service, that this will paralyse your deadly enemy *Le Journal d'Amiens*. The unexpected appearance of Verne's name will decide, I am sure, any hesitating voters, you will have nothing to do to complete the 36 whom you have called 'the gentlemen of no importance', and whom you already have in your hand. I have assured Verne, who has the greatest admiration for you, that you are too large-minded to pull-up over small details, such as, for example, his opinion on the matter of laicisation, that it can be put aside, as the law is charged to deliver the Communes of this care. Aquila non capit muscas. Forgive me, but I've been dying to use a Latin tag. Therefore, if you wish to interview Verne, write to him to come to the Mansion House; he is waiting for such an invitation and desires it.

His friend's pleading seems to have carried weight. After talking to Verne, Petit put him on his list of candidates for the election on 8 May 1888. Some of his party were a little uncertain about their new ally, and had to be reassured about what Petit called 'M. Verne's historic liberalism'. On the election day, Sunday, 6 May, Petit's paper *Le Progrés de la Somme* published the following note:

> Some accuse M. Jules Verne of being an Orleanist. This isn't true.
> Outside of his private friendships which no one has seen, M. Jules Verne, the pride of our city, has always conducted himself as a loyal Republican.
> His presence on the same list as M. Frédéric Petit is a guarantee of his opinions.

Verne had of course been friendly with the Orleans family in Le Tréport, but this was long before they had been exiled in 1886. He had never been involved in Royalist politics, and was not an Orleanist in the sense that his enemies meant. But neither was he a Republican in Petit's sense.

Petit was a radical socialist, whose opinions should have been anathema to one of Verne's background. Petit's 'Red' administration in Amiens had in fact worked hard for improvements of one kind and another: the theatre had been reconstructed, a new municipal post office erected, as well as local schools and other improvements. He had been connected with the Commune in 1871, but had not been arrested. His paper after 1871 supported Thiers. In November 1874 he had set up the Republican Union in Amiens. He was elected to the Municipal Council and became mayor in 1880. He died in 1895 still in that position.

Verne's connection with such a figure smacks perhaps of an opportunist attempt to secure his own election. Certainly on 8 May (after the first ballot in which Verne had received 6,598 votes from an electorate of 14,678 voters) *Le Progrès de la Somme* carried a letter from Verne which also appeared in the *Journal d'Amiens*:

Since *Le Progrès de la Somme* was published on Sunday morning, it was too late for me to be able to reply before the poll. I do not know what authorises your paper to think that I have ever changed my political opinions which I have had all my life.

I belong to the conservative faction and it was as a conservative that I was admitted to the list of M. the Mayor of Amiens in an effort to obtain a purely administrative mandate.

This admission, it seems to me, is all to the honour of M. Frédéric Petit and I know that I am acting as a good citizen in offering him my assistance in the struggle against municipal lack of compromise.

Now there is nothing equivocal between the electors and myself. Sincerely . . .

Perhaps not, but there was between him and his family and friends. On 11 May 1888, he wrote explaining himself to his childhood friend, Charles Maisonneuve:

My old silly ass, you want some explanations? Here they are: my real intention is to make myself useful, and to make a success of some urban reforms. Why must politics always be mixed up with Christianity over administrative questions? You know me well enough to know that, on the essential points, I have never submitted to any influence. In social matters, my taste is for order, in politics my ambition is to create, within the present movement, a party of reason, proportion, respect for life. You know well that I have never hidden what I think of the exile laws, I am resolved, in the same way, to defend, on every occasion, every one's freedom of conscience. So what you are kind enough to call my 'prestige' will never be at the service of any unrespectable cause. I might add that since infirmity obliges me to lead a more sedentary life, it is useful for me to keep in touch with public affairs and my fellow men. It's a professional matter. A number of my colleagues are extremists, but they will calm down. Others are men of sense – so much the better. Others are fools – better still. Their remarks will amuse me. I need it. Believe me, my dear Charles, your old friend.

On the second ballot on 13 May, Verne was elected with 8,591 votes from 14,000 voters. He was to be re-elected three times, in 1892, 1896 and 1900. In all he served sixteen years (1888–1904) as a Municipal Councillor. He conscientiously attended all meetings, except after 1903 when his declining health made this difficult. Outside of his literary work, the municipal affairs of Amiens completely absorbed him.

The new Council was installed on 18 May. Frédéric Petit made a speech outlining his programme. His previous administrations had done a great deal for Amiens, which Verne approved of. However the reporter from *Le Progrès de la Somme* noted that when Petit's speech ended with the rallying cry 'The Republic', everyone applauded him, except Jules Verne. (This was not a minor matter: when Cardinal Lavigerie, the Archbishop of Carthage and Algiers, toasted the Republic at a naval reception in November 1890, it caused a great scandal among conservative and Royalist Catholics.)

Two days later Verne applied to sit on the Fourth Committee of the Municipal Council, which dealt with education, the fine arts, the museums, the theatre, fêtes and street names. This cultural committee was the ideal place for Verne, and he threw himself enthusiastically into the new work. He was also to be involved in other committees, including one concerned with providing financial support for the family of Boucher de Perthes, the pioneering archaeologist who had been largely responsible for the then revolutionary ideas about early man which many were finding so disturbing.

Verne's contributions at Council meetings were numerous. His special interests were education, the theatre and urbanism. Actual politics seem to have interested him hardly at all. Though his colleagues were genuine radicals, he himself was always a moderate. Over the matter of the local medical school he won a notable victory over M. Fiquet who succeeded Petit as mayor in 1895, defeating the more radical elements who supported the mayor.

One of his main duties was to supervise the municipal theatre and provide an annual report on its finances and affairs. In January 1891 there was some discussion about allowing the regular seat holders in the theatre, women as well as men, to vote on matters of theatrical administration. Verne pointed out that the females who attended theatre were of all kinds. Did his colleagues want to mix together 'les dames comme il faut et les dames comme il en faut' (ladies who were proper and women who were 'necessary')? M. Vivien replied that if the Council were to concern itself with the virtues of all the fair residents of Amiens it would be very busy indeed. 'My dear colleague, you are telling me?' Verne cynically retorted.

More progressively he proposed replacing the gas lamps in the theatre with electric lights.

It became his habit to attend the theatre every evening it was playing to encourage the actors. He would arrive, often accompanied by Honorine, and eat sandwiches in his box during the interval. He never stayed for the last act, however, but crossed the road to dine at the Continental Hotel and was home to bed by ten o'clock.

His theatrical tastes ran to comic opera, and he admired Léo Delibes, Bizet and Massenet. He regretted the decline in the quality of the plays given at the theatre, but two years later he deplored the lack of interest among the people of Amiens in these efforts to entertain them. In 1903 he put the low return in receipts from the theatre down to the counter-attraction of Barnum's Circus.

Not that he didn't love the circus himself. In a series of reports he pleaded the cause of travelling shows which had no proper site in Amiens to perform in. He persuaded the Council to build a magnificent circus seating 4,000 people. This large building, in the ornate garlanded style of the period, had a colonnade around the outside, one column of which hid the chimney from the steam generators which provided the electric light for the building. This was Verne's own idea. The circus was built on the place de Longueville. Verne himself had the pleasure of opening it on 23 June 1889, at the same time as the Eiffel Tower was opened in Paris at the International Exhibition.

On the street names committee he was always anxious to preserve the old names, and the names associated with heroes and local worthies. Needless to say, he even wanted the city to retain *St. Michel* on one road, and not only because it was that of an archangel, one suspects.

But urbanism was his particular preoccupation on the Council. For instance, he wanted something done in 1888 about the fumes from the steam trains crossing the town. When the Council wanted to spend a bequest on erecting a clock in the very centre of the town, Verne pointed out that it would interfere with the tramways, and that no one really wanted the clock anyway. The trams themselves concerned him also. He wanted the overhead wires taken away in the squares, and the trams fitted with batteries.

There were proposals for either an extension of the theatre, or an open space in the free space behind the theatre. An open space it became, to Verne's delight.

Many of his ideas about urbanism and town planning found their way into an essay on Amiens in the year 2000, which he wrote in 1875. Far from being a vision of the future, that lecture had been in fact a critique of the present. His ideas were in many ways very up to date, because he was concerned with the aesthetic effects of changes in the city as well as with improving life without harming the environment.

In 1891 he reported on the facts about the Crampel Mission which had been lost in the area between Chad and the Congo. Another expedition was raised to look for it to which the Council subscribed. The idea of the Barsac Mission in his last book may have been suggested by this incident.

The political questions that he was involved in were few enough. In 1894 the President of France, Carnot, was assassinated by an anarchist at Lyons. The Council decided to send a delegation to the funeral, but Verne in his remarks did not seem particularly to care about the national mourning. His own sympathies, as shown in the character of Kaw-Djer in *The Survivors of the Jonathan*, were with the anarchists. Nevertheless, no matter how much their ideal of perfect freedom of 'direct action' might appeal to his deepest nature, in 1895 he was to reveal himself to be against the action of the trade unions which were just beginning to establish themselves in France.

Furthermore, in February 1898 a Council meeting to discuss the rallying of conservatives to the Republic broke up in disorder when an anarchist intervened. The police were heavy handed in restoring order, and questions were asked about the matter at the next meeting of the Council. Verne thought the results were 'excellent' and congratulated the police on the action which they took. Whatever anarchic feelings he may have privately harboured, order in the streets was another matter.

Verne's son-in-law, Colonel de Francy, has said that at this time Verne toyed with the idea of entering national politics. Raoul Duval wanted him to become a senator. So did his brother Paul, who could not bear to think of him retiring from an active life. Others such as Louis Salvador and Demetrios Zanini also urged him into this course. Zanini offered to finance his campaign for the Senate in 1892, 'an election which would be followed in no time at all by his election to the Presidency of the French Republic'. Heady dreams, but they were not for Verne. As he wrote to Paul: 'What a madman Zanini is. I should be madder if I believed him.'

He might have had such ambitions in 1888, but in 1892, 'Demetrios can say what he likes but it is over. Finished and done with! Four years ago I might have imagined that I could seize hold of some ambition. No, Paris will not see me again. It would only make me unhappy to go there.'

He might not achieve the French Academy either because he lived outside Paris. But he did not mind. Public office and acclaim were his. His mood, however, became increasingly sombre. He might not go to Paris, but unhappiness, it seems, sought him out even in Amiens. What was the source of this melancholy strain in his life?

Chapter Seventeen

The Carpathian Castle

VERNE'S MORE SOMBRE MOOD IN HIS LATER YEARS WAS increasingly reflected in his writings, even though these dealt with similar ranges of subjects, themes and places. For Verne's tremendous output continued into his old age. One or two books a year began to seem too many for just one man. Inevitably the rumour arose that he no longer did his own work, and that he was really a company of writers *Jules Verne et Cie*. This was not the case, all his books were his own, except for those written with André Laurie. The production between 1887 and 1895 was very mixed, and could indeed have seemed the work of a team. Yet in some of these novels, especially *The Carpathian Castle* (1892), Verne dealt with very personal themes, using material even from his own private life.

History and the struggle for freedom were still dominant subjects. In *North Against South* (1887) he dealt again with the American Civil War, siding with the enslaved Negroes of the South. *The Road to France* (1887) was an historical novel set at the time (1792) of the triumph of the French revolutionary army over the Prussian troops at the battle of Valmy, of which a vivid description is given. The theme of French nationalism was a new one for Verne, reflecting perhaps his increasing interest in real politics. A novel dealing with the revolt of the French in Canada, *Family Without a Name* (1889) dealt with the harsh treatment meted out by the British after the rising of 1837 failed. When the book was reprinted in Quebec in 1967 the entire edition of 5,000 copies was sold out within days. Some French Canadians at least had no doubt about the relevance of Verne's novel to their renewed struggle to establish and maintain their identity in a predominantly English-speaking Canada. The theme of British imperialism also provided the background to a novel set in Ireland, *Foundling Mick* (1893). Beginning realistically enough with scenes of the land war and eviction, the novel soon becomes a straightforward success story. Mick founds a business called Little Boy and Company, the company being another urchin, whose life he had saved. Verne's own impressions of Ireland from his brief calls ashore were bolstered by the books of Anne-Marie Bovet, an acute observer of the realities of life in an Ireland gripped by the Land War. Irish characters anyway are numerous in Verne's novels (17 characters in six novels chosen at random).

Geographical adventures still formed a large part of his output. *Two Years Holiday* (1888) was the only story Verne wrote which was specifically for children. One of the characters called Briant is said to be based on the young Aristide Briand, later Prime Minister of France, whom Verne met in Nantes a few years before writing it. A Robinsonade involving shipwreck and survival, the book also includes what the critic Kenneth Allott calls 'school-boy politics', these being largely a reflection of Verne's own political experiences in Amiens. As with adult politics, the rivalries and divisions soon lead to trouble, which is only resolved by the appearance of a common enemy. Verne's limitations as a novelist are pointed up by contrasting this book with William Golding's *Lord of the Flies*, where the same desert-island material is given a far more subtle and sombre treatment.

His novel of circus life *Caesar Cascabel* (1890), written at the height of his interest in the circus at Amiens, was also an adventurous travelogue through Alaska and the Russian Far East. Here again the glimpses of Russian rule in the distant provinces of the Empire provide an undercurrent of political comment. It is strange though to be reminded that Russia once had a large foothold on the American continent, and that the Iron Curtain might have been drawn across Vancouver Sound.

The Russian Far East was also the setting for *Claudius Bombarnac* (1892) which deals with a journalist sent out to cover the opening of the Trans-Asiatic Railway – an imaginary line which continued the Trans-Caspian across the Pamirs and through the Gobi Desert to Pekin. The novel was published the year that work began on the better-known Trans-Siberian, and was inspired by the real-life adventures of the French automobilist and journalist Napoleon Ney on the Trans-Caspian. Since the days of his first novels about transcontinental travel, the actual speed of travel had increased considerably. So much so that Verne now felt that circling the world was merely a matter of sitting in a seat.

These books were suggested to Verne by their various settings, but to the same period belong two more intimate novels, *Mistress Branican* (1891) and *The Carpathian Castle* (1892), in which Verne's personal life seems to be reflected.

The first of these books was the story of a devoted wife's search for her missing husband in the coral seas of the Pacific. It may have been inspired by the efforts of Lady Franklin to find her explorer husband lost in the wastes of the Arctic, and by the strange story of the schoolmistress's expectations of her husband's return which he recalled from his childhood. Mrs. Branican represents one aspect of womanhood, the fidelity of marriage. The title caused some concern to his publisher. Would his readers not take the meaning of 'Mistress' very literally? Verne agreed that English readers might, but with the authority of Dickens behind him, for he had the expression in one of his novels, his French readers would not.

This raises the question of the possibility of 'another woman' in Verne's own life. The public life of Jules Verne was exemplary, and no one would have suggested the likelihood of his keeping a mistress if his family biographers had not given us the lead already. Mme. Allotte de la Fuÿe, for one, in her book drops several discreet hints on this topic. As she is elsewhere so reticent about scandal, we may well assume that the evidence in this matter was, so she felt, too strong to be ignored.

'Mermaids are my only love,' he remarked. Perhaps it was not quite true. It has been asserted that, for a few brief seasons, a mortal woman was able to capture the heart that he kept so well hidden. But no one has left the least record of her voice or appearance . . . So perhaps he spoke the truth when he remarked that the sirens of the *Mysterious Island* were his only mistresses.

In truth, however, he did have a close friendship with a lady, but it seems she was no more than a friend, someone to provide the occasional intellectual stimulation which he lacked at home. And it may well be that Verne himself, in one of his own novels, has given us 'a record of her voice and appearance' and some clue to this siren. Elsewhere writing about the early 1890s, Mme. Allotte de la Fuÿe writes:

> But where a writer's innermost feelings are concerned, his readers must be content with what he himself has consented to reveal: and if we feel impelled to seek in Jules Verne's work the amplified memory of a secret and, perhaps, wholly intellectual passion, we are most likely to find it in his *Carpathian Castle*, written at this same period. The romantic climate of this novel sets it apart from the others, and gives grounds for such a supposition.

She also tells us that the death of this 'siren' cut short 'a precious correspondence'.

This is all very tantalising, especially as we have some idea of the sort of evidence she had before her. Jean Jules-Verne, in his more recent book, tells us that at the time she was writing her biography, he himself had actually sent Mme. Allotte de la Fuÿe the name of the lady concerned.

He tells us that during visits to Paris Verne was accustomed to stay with friends, sometimes with this lady. Her name, according to Jean Jules-Verne, was Madame Duchesne. She lived in Asnières, which was then a quiet, remote area, about an hour's drive from Paris, best known as a summer boating place. It was the Maidenhead of Paris, with little villas, inns and discreet hotels, one of the best of which was, at one time, the Château d'Asnières. He carefully notes that it was his brother who actually recalled the woman's name, as he himself had forgotten it. Certainly it seems that Honorine was well aware of her existence, for when she died Mme. Duchesne left a large legacy to Verne, which he refused.

Jean Jules-Verne has been unable to trace anything more about her. Luce Courville, who runs the Verne museum in Nantes, tells me that she was unable to trace any record of a Madame Duchesne at the Hôtel de Ville in Asnières. Nor was I myself able to locate her grave there. The name was not unknown locally, there was even a rue Duchesnay. But the woman herself still eludes us.

Had Verne found an old relation – for the name Duchesne is an old Nantes one – or was she a childhood friend? Both Mme.

Allotte de la Fuÿe and Jean Jules-Verne are convinced that this was a 'wholly intellectual' passion. She was the same age as Verne, and with her he could talk over his interests in a way which he could not do with Honorine. It seems that Honorine, when she heard about the affair, made light of it. 'The last thought of Mme. Duchesne was for Jules Verne,' writes his grandson, 'and her death caused him deep unhappiness.'

She died, it seems, about twenty years before Verne did, which would make it the year 1885. His novel *The Carpathian Castle* was drafted between 1886 and 1889. It was published after very careful revision in 1892. Verne attached great importance to the book, and urged his publisher to try and have it serialised in one of the leading papers. Nothing came of this, and the book appeared as a single volume in October 1892.

The story is set in Transylvania, not yet known through the novels of Bram Stoker. An ancient castle, which the local people of Werst believe to be haunted, is seen to have smoke coming from it. This is investigated by an old shepherd and a doctor, who have strange adventures while trying to enter the castle. Strange shapes fly through the sky, lights illuminate the night, and the doctor is held to the ground by a mysterious force while the shepherd is knocked off the walls by a shock.

A stranger arrives in the village, the Count Franz de Telek. While living in Naples the young count, a callow youth from Roumania, had become absorbed in music and opera. He had fallen in love with a singer at the Naples San Carlo opera house named La Stilla. But La Stilla had another admirer, a strange man named Gortz who followed her around Europe, never trying to speak to her, but attending all her appearances just to hear her sing. He was accompanied by another mysterious companion. La Stilla decides to give up her career to escape from this man, who has terrorised her with his attentions, and she gratefully accepts the offer of marriage from the Count de Telek.

But on the night of her last performance, at the climax of her great aria, she collapses and dies on the stage. She is buried by a mourning Naples. But the Count receives a note from the Baron blaming him for her death. After that the Baron de Gortz disappears.

Now in Werst the young count is fascinated by the superstitions of the villagers, even though he does 'not believe there are supernatural beings, either good or evil'. But when he hears that the castle once belonged to Baron Rodolphe de Gortz he is amazed. Then in the inn where he is staying, the Count dreams he hears the voice of La Stilla. He is determined to investigate the mysterious castle. He and his servant approach it, arriving at nightfall. On the battlements he catches a brief glimpse of La Stilla. Leaving his man outside, he gets into the castle, but soon finds himself confined in a dungeon, taunted by her voice. He escapes, and overhearing the Baron and his companion, an electrical inventor of genius, learns something of the secrets of the castle. The climax of the novel is reached when the Count confronts the Baron. He is listening to La Stilla sing, and her image appears on a small stage. But it is all an illusion arranged by mirrors. Her voice is coming from a phonograph. The castle is blown up, the Baron is killed, and the young count is taken from the ruins, his mind deranged for months by the experience. But he soon recovers, and the rest of the Baron's collection of phonographs of La Stilla singing, which he had secretly recorded with his inventor friend's help from his box in the theatre during the last months of her life, restores him to sanity.

A peculiar story for Verne, a gothic novel fitted out with the trappings of the latest science. When he began the novel, the phonograph which Edison had invented in 1877, had been improved by the introduction of wax covered cylinders. Edison had not as yet turned his attention to the film camera – it was not until 1895 that the cine camera became really practical due to the work of the Lumière brothers. Falling between these two dates, Verne is able to make use of an improved phonograph, but since no hint of the possibilities of the film camera seems to have reached him, he falls back on the Praxinoscope of Emile Reynaud, which could be seen at the Théâtre Optique in Paris. This device by means of mirrors and lamps managed to give a semblance of motion to still pictures. Reynaud had obtained a patent for it in 1887, though the actual invention dated from 1882. The book in no way presages film or television – indeed the idea of a phonograph for visual images was better done in Robert Cromie's *Plunge into Space*, for which Verne wrote an introduction in 1891, a year before he published his own novel.

Of course, Verne's interest in the book was not wholly technical, but emotional. In her biography Mme. Allotte de la

Fuÿe refers to the singer in the novel as 'Stella', which has led some to speculate as to whether this might be another key to the mystery behind it. Certainly the musical background is very important in the book, and must have meant a great deal to Verne. I myself wonder if the woman in his life was not in some way associated with theatre in Paris, perhaps even with the Théâtre Lyrique, of which Verne was the sometime secretary. Whoever and whatever she was Mme. 'Stella' Duchesne provides a mystery in Verne's life as yet unsolved.

His mood was increasingly bleak, as Mme. Allotte de la Fuÿe observes:

> One wonders what supreme reward had slipped through Jules Verne's fingers. He seemed, at that time, to be struggling against a secret despair, that not all the affectionate attentions of those around him could dispel. Outside the house, he made a show of gaiety. But at home he grew silent, locking up his secret sorrow within himself, as the great clam that Aronnax saw closed tightly on the pearl within. Whatever tragedy was enacted behind that silence, he allowed no whisper of it to survive him.

His family worried about him. To shake him out of his black mood his brother Paul suggested that he revisit Nantes. He could stay at Chantenay and the change would do him good. Also his nephews, Guillon-Verne and Fleury, the Nantes shipowners, were about to launch a ship named after him, and would be delighted if he would do the honours. 'We are awaiting your arrival for the christening of your ship,' his sister wrote. 'The family records at Chantenay won't be complete unless you propose the toast.'

The day came. But Jules Verne was not there. His brother had to launch the ship and toast her future in his place. Jules had stayed at home in Amiens, perhaps because the scenes of his childhood and first love were now too unbearable to revisit. However, soon after he wrote, apologising for not being there and wishing 'good luck to my ship'.

> I was deeply sorry to miss the ceremony, as I shall miss Maxime's wedding – I shall be replying to his fine letter. But

I am overwhelmed by too many grave sorrows to be able to take part in the family rejoicings in Nantes. All types of gaiety have become unbearable to me, my nature has changed deeply, and I shall never recover from the blows that fate has dealt me.

The stark emotional bleakness of Verne's last decade was relieved only by the persistence of his vivid imagination and his capacity for fantastic story-telling.

His brother was the only person in his life of whom Verne seems to have been completely confident. He relied on Paul for support and encouragement, as well as for practical help over the nautical details of his books.

In June 1894, for instance, he was appealing to Paul for help to finish his new book *Propeller Island*, the first volume of which was already complete. He wanted to ascertain whether Paul thought it was possible, speaking theoretically of course, to steer the island without using a rudder, but by a system of propellers on either side, driven by engines developing a million horsepower. He was sending him the final part of *The Wonderful Adventures of Captain Antifer*, the story of a treasure hunt with scenes in Scotland and elsewhere for a pirate hoard buried by a Pasha. The treasure was left on a volcanic island, Graham Island, which had risen from the sea on the route between Turin and Milan, off the south-west coast of Sicily. The book is an entertaining one, but as R. T. Gould, a British expert on Polar exploration, pointed out 'the ordinary cartographer cannot but rub his eyes when he comes to the passage where Antifer's gifted son-in-law, having as his only data the positions of three other islands forming a triangle with sides several thousand miles in length, succeeds in determining the location of the (sunken) treasure island by means of a direct geometrical construction on a twelve-inch globe'. A wonderful feat indeed.

Having finished the book, Verne admitted to Paul that he was utterly done in. 'I shall wilt. Tonight we had a storm and a torrential downpour, but the heat persists.' Work on *Propeller Island* went ahead with Paul's assistance and was complete a few months later.

By September he was able to send Paul the galleys for him to check. Young Hetzel, who came down to Amiens twice a month to talk about books and business, thought it was a highly original

book. Verne himself appears as the King of Malecarlie, a character
modelled on the exiled Emperor of Brazil, Don Pedro; in the
illustrations the king clearly has Verne's features.

I've read the *Memoirs of the Prince de Joinville*, and I can understand
you finding them fascinating. Heavens, yes. They are quite
simply delicious, and they are all our own youth. I have written
to the Comtesse de Paris, sending her my most sincere com-
pliments. Louis Salvador still writes to me. In the book which
follows *Propeller Island*, I shall bring in the Balearic Islands, and
that will give me the chance to speak about his magnificent
enterprise in that archipelago.

He thought that the second volume of *Propeller Island* would be
far more interesting than the first, because of its satirical nature.
'It will all be based on manners and events of the day, but I am
still a novelist first and foremost, and my books will always be
fictitious to the outward view.'

And it was as a novelist that he longed for election to the
Académie Français. But it never came. Verne had to be content
with the knowledge of entertainment that he had given to millions
of readers. His 'new kind of novel' had established itself. Science
fiction, in substance though not by that name, was by now an
established literary form.

A new aspect of his work after the attempt on his life, was the
help he received from his son Michel. He would now discuss his
ideas with Michel, and Jean Jules-Verne recalls them being
closeted together for hours on end. Later still, towards the end of
his life, Michel provided him with a secretary to take down his
dictation when his sight failed him.

Working with his father encouraged Michel to try his own hand
at writing. To improve his chances of publication these stories
were sent out to editors as being by 'M. Jules Verne', which
could mean either Monsieur Jules Verne, or Michel Jules Verne.

Michel's first story was 'The Year 2889', a day in the life of
an American journalist in the next millennium. First published
in *The Forum*, a New York magazine, the story was later reprinted
in *Yesterday and Tomorrow*, a collection of Verne's shorter fiction
which Michel edited in 1910.

This version of the story is probably the original one, as the earlier American one has been altered, and lacks the rather risqué dénouement when the editor's wife pops out of the wall in her bath, a Gallic touch which was restored in the French version.

In Paris Michel still frequented the *Chat Noir*, the artists' café where he would have been able to see a shadow theatre screen display the ideas of the writer Albert Robida about the future. The '*Telephote*' in his story is an adaption of that screen, and many of the ideas about the future also appear in Robida's works *Le Vingtième Siècle*, *La Guerre au XXe Siècle*, and *La Vie électrique*. Robida was also well known for his satire on Verne, the wildly funny *Voyages très extraordinaires de Saturin Farandoul* (1879). Robida was a genius of the Heath-Robinson variety – witty and fantastic, even when dealing with warfare, rather than technical and sinister.

The projecting of advertisements onto clouds, by which the American newspapers make their money in 2889, had been introduced at the Chicago Exhibition in 1894, and soon after in New York city by the *New York World*.

The other story by Michel Verne was 'An Express of the Future', which was published in England by the *Strand Magazine*, and more than three times in Russia. This story was about the promotion of a pneumatic tube train service across the Atlantic to New York – a giant version of the device which many older stores used to have for carrying dockets to the cash desks. This idea was not new. Such trains had been described in the *Scientific American* in 1867, and the Broadway Tunnel had been opened in 1870. André Laurie had used the idea in 1889 in his novel *De New York à Brest en sept heures*, but that had not been translated into English. After this Michel's business interests seem to have taken off again, and he gave up writing. He realised perhaps that science fiction was his father's special preserve, one recognised everywhere.

Chapter Eighteen

Science and Fiction

VERNE PUBLISHED *Propeller Island* IN 1895, THE SAME YEAR THAT
H. G. Wells brought out the first of his 'scientific romances',
The Time Machine. These two authors are the immediate sources of
all modern science fiction. With Wells the genre received the
second great impetus of genius. These last few years of the
nineteenth century, years of gaiety and decadence, of the
emergence of the electric generation, are a good moment in time
from which to look back at Verne's real achievements as a writer,
both in relation to others such as Wells, and to literature and
science as a whole.

There were, of course, many minor writers in the same period
whose work is now unread and unreadable – Verne's friend Robert
Cromie is one of them. Verne and Wells have survived because
of very genuine literary qualities, but as both were well aware
they were quite different in their approaches to their materials.
Wells, writing in the preface to his *Collected Scientific Romances,*
pays tribute to Verne:

These tales have been compared with the works of Jules Verne,
and there was a disposition on the part of literary journalists at
one time to call me the English Jules Verne. As a matter of
fact there is no literary resemblance between the anticipatory
inventions of the great Frenchman and these fantasies. His
work dealt almost always with actual possibilities of invention
and discovery and he made some remarkable forecasts. The
interest he invoked was a practical one; he wrote and believed
and told that this thing or that could be done, which was not
at that time done. He helped his readers imagine it done and

to realise what fun, excitement or mischief might ensue. Many
of his inventions have 'come true'. But these stories of mine
collected here do not pretend to deal with possible things; they
are exercises of the imagination in a quite different field.

This was a very accurate description of the differences between
the two. Verne himself, in two different interviews, one with
Robert Sherard in 1903, and another with Gordon Jones in 1904,
had some comments to make on his English rival. When Sherard
asked him his opinion of Wells, Verne was ready:

Je pensais bien que vous alliez me demander cela. His books
were sent to me, and I have read them. It is very curious, and, I
will add, very English. But I do not see the possibility of
comparison between his work and mine. It occurs to me that
his stories do not repose on very scientific bases. No, there is no
rapport between his work and mine. I make use of physics. He
invents. I go to the moon in a cannon ball, discharged from a
cannon. He goes to Mars [*sic*] in an airship, which he constructs
of a metal which does away with the law of gravitation. Ça
c'est très joli, but show me this metal. Let him produce it.

In talking to Jones some months later, Verne admitted that
Wells was one of the few living writers he admired, after a
moment's reflection about how he should express it.

There is an author whose work has appealed to me very
strongly from an imaginative stand-point, and whose books
I have followed with considerable interest. I allude to Mr. H. G.
Wells. Some of my friends have suggested to me that his work
is on somewhat similar lines to my own, but here I think they
err. I consider him, as a purely imaginative writer, to be
deserving of very high praise, but our methods are entirely
different. I have always made a point in my romances of basing
my so-called inventions upon a groundwork of actual fact, and
of using in their construction methods and materials which are
not entirely without the pale of contemporary engineering skill
and knowledge.
    Take, for instance, the case of the *Nautilus*. This, when
carefully considered, is a submarine mechanism about which

there is nothing extraordinary, nor beyond the bounds of actual scientific knowledge. It rises or sinks by perfectly feasible and well-known processes, the details of its guidance and propulsion are perfectly rational and comprehensible. Its motive force is no secret: the only point at which I have called in the aid of imagination is in the application of this force, and here I have purposely left a blank for the reader to form his own conclusions, a mere technical hiatus, as it were, quite capable of being filled in by a highly-trained and thoroughly practical mind.

The creations of Mr. Wells, on the other hand, belong unreservedly to an age and a degree of scientific knowledge far removed from the present, though I will not say entirely beyond the limits of the possible. Not only does he evolve his constructions entirely from the realm of the imagination, but he also evolves the materials of which he builds them. See, for example, his story *The First Men in the Moon* (1901). You will remember that here he introduces an entirely new anti-gravitational substance, to whose mode of preparation or actual chemical composition we are not given the slightest clue, nor does a reference to our present scientific knowledge enable us for a moment to predict a method by which such a result might be achieved. In *The War of the Worlds* (1898), again, a work for which I have the greatest admiration, one is left entirely in the dark as to what kind of creatures the Martians really are, or in what manner they produce the wonderful heat ray with which they work such terrible havoc on their assailants.

Mind, in saying this, I am casting no disparagement on Mr. Wells's methods; on the contrary, I have the highest respect for his imaginative genius. I am merely contrasting our two styles and pointing out the fundamental difference which exists between them, and I wish you clearly to understand that I express no opinion.

Both Wells and Verne himself emphasise the practical basis of his books. Yet this claim is deceptive. The American science fiction writer John Taine, himself a professional scientist, comments very aptly on the real relationship between Verne and the science of his time. He admits that for the most part scientific journalism in nineteenth-century Europe was superior to anything in America at the time. And that this would have been a fertile source of ideas.

To appreciate this, imagine what might have happened to science novels if Jules Verne had chanced on the really new and potentially revolutionary science of his time. In the 1860s Clerk Maxwell's mathematical prediction of wireless waves was current.* Verne was then in his thirties. In 1887 Hertz produced wireless waves in his laboratory. In the 1890s television was accurately forecast in reasonable detail by a prominent English electrical engineer.† All that deterred him, he said, from realising his forecast was the colossal expense. Verne at this time was still active. When these things were new, they offered as imaginative a mind as Verne's an opportunity to surpass the Arabian Nights. Yet Verne, to whom they were accessible had he looked in the right places, missed them. Doubtless science fictionists are overlooking equally good leads today.

So, ironically, though it was Wells who was the trained scientist (under Huxley at South Kensington), his work was basically more imaginative than the untrained Verne's. Verne admitted he was no scientist. He picked up ideas and made use of them. Often they were ideas already practical and not notions on the frontiers of knowledge – submarines, not radio waves. Often the ideas he used appealed to him as a writer, but were nonsense as science.

Some instances of his errors have been mentioned in the course of this book. Most arose from the confused and hasty nature of his notes, and the speed with which he worked on nearly every novel he published. If he had not been tied to two books a year, the detail of what he wrote would have been much improved. But

---

* Clerk Maxwell's *A Treatise on Electricity and Magnetism*, stating the basic laws for electro-magnetic radiation, the basis of radio, television and radar, appeared in 1873.

† He means A. Campbell-Swinton. Actually a form of television does appear in a Verne story, albeit one unpublished in book form during his life, and not translated into English until recently. This was in *The Day of an American Journalist 2889*. But this story may well have been really written by his son Michel.

in what he wrote Verne tried to present the possibilities of scientific development in a romantic light. His relationship with the science and technology of his time was a close one, even if confused at times.

But what of Verne's relationship with modern science fiction? Can he be called with justice 'the inventor of science fiction'. Or must that title still be retained by Hugo Gernsback, the American who coined the term in the 1920s?

I believe he can. Verne's stories contain elements of speculative interest quite lacking in much of the science fiction of the 1920s. Writing to please, rather than to a political thesis, his novels are certainly better than the later ones of H. G. Wells. (Though Verne is not a novelist in the same way as the author of *Mr. Polly* was.) As a writer and story-teller Verne is superior to most of his contemporaries, and indeed to most writers of speculative fiction down to recent years.

And yet as he grew older, Verne's books fell in popularity. Sales and revenues contracted. In France André Laurie and R. H. Rosny, among others, were now writing his kind of book more successfully in commercial terms. In England, Stevenson (who regarded Verne as mere entertainment for boys), Rider Haggard, Wells and Conan Doyle were taking over his field of adventure, mystery and scientific romance. In America the dime-novelist Luis Senarens with his Frank Reade series appealed to a wider market that cared little for the attention to exact detail which Verne put into his books. (There is no foundation for the claim by Sam Moskowitz that Verne borrowed from Senarens: they both worked from the same sources, taking their ideas for a giant helicopter from La Landelle.) Mark Twain in *Tom Sawyer Abroad* (1894) guyed Verne with an unexpected balloon journey which carried Tom and his friends from Hannibal over the Atlantic and the Sahara to land in Egypt. The confusion of time, the mad professor, the mysterious airship: these features of Verne's novels were burlesqued without pity. If Verne were to astonish the jaded *fin de siècle* temperament he would have to stretch himself.

And he did, for some of the novels of his last decade, though little known (some were not even translated in his lifetime), are among the most interesting he ever wrote, including as they do the return of Robur as *The Master of the World* in 1904.

If Verne was no scientist, many have said he was no writer

either. Certainly in France what he wrote was not regarded during his life as literature. It was merely entertainment. But like a lot of 'mere entertainment' his work has proved to have a surprising survival value. He is still widely read today, when much of George Sand or even Balzac has declined into obscurity.

In the last decade or so, since the appearance in 1966 of the first volumes of Verne in paperback in France, there has been a tremendous revival of interest in him by avant-garde critics and writers such as Roland Barthes and Michel Butor. The significance of Verne for 'the new novel' may seem surprising, but they have found in Verne not only an interest in the surface of things but also a new mythology of science. According to such writers, Verne has the highest claims upon our attention.

In socialist countries there has also been a great deal of interest taken in Verne, especially in the U.S.S.R. and Hungary. Their idea of Verne may be quite different from that current in the rest of Europe and America – for them he is still the great prophet of the space age, rather than the creator of initiatory romances.

In English-speaking countries Verne has been almost forgotten. Barely half a dozen of his titles remain in print, despite the effort in the 1960s by I. O. Evans to retranslate his entire works. However, Mr. Evans by cutting out large pieces of what seemed to him 'irrelevant' material of no interest to the modern reader, has given us a 'Boy's Own Verne', again a man quite different to either the Verne of the French critics, or of real life: Mr. Evans' Verne was 'little troubled by sex', a strange condition for a Frenchman.

Verne is often described as a 'Breton' with a 'Celtic' imagination. Neither is true. His father, who was the shaping influence on his youth, was not a Breton. Nor did his mother's family have much in common with the peasants of Morbihan. There is nothing fey or airy about Verne's mind. His novels are concrete and factual, quite the opposite of the products of the Celtic imagination in modern Breton or Irish literature. He has nothing in common with either Anatole Le Braz or J. M. Synge. Matthew Arnold, who defined with subtle sense the feeling of true Celtic literature, would probably have thought Verne something of a Philistine. And Verne himself, for what it is worth, saw himself as a French writer in the French tradition.

As a writer, Verne is naturally variable. But this is only to be expected. At his best he is extraordinary, at his worst he is abysmal. Yet none of his books is without some redeeming interest, either of imagination, or of geographical or scientific excitement. His entire oeuvre becomes of increasing interest as the nineteenth century recedes. His novels are a dream of the nineteenth century, a parallel world, the world as he imagined it was or might become.

Chapter Nineteen

The Master of the World

IN 1896 VERNE PUBLISHED *For the Flag*. THE PLOT WAS AN involved one, in which one of the leading characters is an inventor named Thomas Roch, who has become a monomaniac after his latest invention, an explosive called Fulgurator, is rejected by the French government as well as several other governments. He is kidnapped by a mysterious count from the mental home in which he has been confined.

It may be an indication of Verne's slackening imagination that the villain of the piece bears a family resemblance to Captain Nemo, even down to a submarine pen in a cavern under an island – this time in the Bermudas. (The finale of the film version of *Twenty Thousand Leagues Under the Sea* borrowed the ending of this novel as well as *Mysterious Island* to create an explosive conclusion.)

The mad inventor recovers his sanity in a moment of crisis when he patriotically refuses to fire on the flag of the French fleet investing the island. But earlier he had tried to sell his invention to Germany and Britain, a reflection in Verne's mind of his country's real rivals. An inventor of a super-explosive would usually bring to mind Alfred Nobel and dynamite. But after the publication of *For the Flag* in July 1896, Verne was sued for libel by a French inventor named Turpin, who had indeed had dealings with the French government in 1885 about an explosive he had created. Feeling aggrieved over his treatment, he had published a pamphlet about his Melinite, only to be imprisoned for revealing state secrets. In May 1894 he had announced he was taking another invention to Germany.

There is no doubt that Turpin had been in Verne's mind when

writing the book. In November 1895 he had told his publisher that he was forwarding the manuscript of his new novel, 'you know, the one about Turpin that I told you about'. But whatever its inspiration the actual plot bore no resemblance to the facts of Turpin's career.

The case was heard in Paris and Verne had to travel up to prepare his case and attend the hearings. This was to be his last visit to the capital and it might have been made in happier circumstances. His lawyer was the young Raymond Poincaré (later a President of the Republic). First Hetzel, and then Verne, was called to his chambers in the rue des Mathurins. 'Jules was given a marvellous reception by his lawyer,' Paul Verne reported to the family in Nantes. 'Maître Poincaré has been a great reader of his novels, and remains an enlightened admirer of his work.'

When the case was heard in November 1896, Verne and Poincaré won. And on appealing against the verdict in December, Turpin again lost. The *Journal d'Amiens* printed, with what must have been great relish, the judge's summing up and vindication of the celebrated local author. (At a later date Verne was to be surprised and pained at the position Poincaré adopted over the Dreyfus affair. A natural anti-Dreyfusard, Verne had been completely satisfied about that particular verdict of French justice.)

Perhaps because of all the publicity, *For the Flag* was to sell 12,000 copies, twice as many as the other novel Verne published in November of that year, *Clovis Dardentor*. This amusing trifle – mere knockabout as Verne admitted – was dedicated to his grandsons, Michel, Jean and Paul, and paid an oblique tribute to the childless Louis Salvador (whom he had met on his Italian trip) in the central character, whose books provided Verne with the background material on the Balearics, which was the setting of the book.

He was far more taken with the idea of his next book. Writing to Paul in October 1895, he said he was working as hard as ever. He never went out. 'Age, illness and worry are conspiring to turn me into someone whose bottom never leaves his chair.' Nevertheless he was 'terribly excited about my continuation of the Poe novel' and was almost into the second volume already.

The Poe novel was *The Narrative of Arthur Gordon Pym*, a strange narrative of bizarre adventures in the Antarctic, which had strong autobiographical elements. Verne, writing about Poe in 1863, had claimed that the novel was incomplete and hoped that some day a writer would finish it off. In 1895 he took up his own challenge. Starting from a new beginning with the narrative of an American naturalist, and skilfully incorporating details and hints from Poe's original tale, Verne provided a typically extraordinary explanation of the 'sphinx of the ice-fields', the great white figure which suddenly looms up before Pym at the end of Poe's story.

Verne made the sphinx literally 'a lodestone mountain', a magnetic mass which attracted all the iron in the area to itself. This was an old legend. Worked into Poe's novel and Verne's conclusion were elements taken from the ideas of Captain Symmes, to whom he owed notions in earlier novels.

On 1 September, before taking himself sailing 'to get myself shaken around a little', Verne sent Hetzel the first part of the novel. This appeared in June 1897; the second part came out in November. As he explained to Hetzel:

> It will be a kind of counterpart to *Captain Hatteras*, although there is nothing in the two books – plot or character – to make them alike. It will come at the right time, since people are talking about voyages and discoveries at the South Pole. My point of departure is one of Edgar Poe's strangest novels, *The Narrative of Arthur Gordon Pym*, but it will not be necessary to have read Poe's novel to understand mine. I have used everything that Poe left in suspense and have developed the mystery surrounding certain characters. I have one good *trouvaille*: one of my heroes who, like everyone else, thought that Poe's novel was entirely fictitious, comes face to face with a matching reality. Needless to say, I go much further than Poe did. Let me know what you think; I hope that my readers will be very interested.

He thought his story was truer to life and more interesting than Poe's, but his excitement was not shared by the public. *Hatteras* since 1866 had sold 36,000 copies: the new novel sold only 6,000.

This notion of completing other authors' books took hold of him again a year or so later when he wrote a sequel to Wyss's *The Swiss Family Robinson*, called *Second Fatherland* (1900). Wyss had been his childhood favourite. Children often wish that their favourite books went on and on, with the same things happening all the time. As an old man Verne was able to gratify this wish by providing for himself what he must have longed for as a boy.

This novel sold only 4,000 copies, very little better than might be expected for a book by a completely unknown author. By now Verne's foreign publishers were beginning to pick and choose among his books. His long time publishers in Britain, Sampson Low and Marston, could not bring themselves to publish *The Superb Orinoco* (1898). A dozen of his last books were never published during his life or after in English – not until the abridged editions prepared by I. O. Evans in the 1960s.

These neglected books, the sales of which were very low in France, have however many points of great interest. *The Superb Orinoco*, which I. O. Evans calls an inferior book, is one of the more curious. Verne had begun to write it as far back as 1894. Exploration during the nineteenth century produced few heroes from France: one of these was Jean Chaffanjon. In 1888 Chaffanjon, sponsored by the French government, had undertaken an extensive exploration of the Orinoco, finally discovering in 1891 the true sources of the river (or so he claimed, but he was either deluded or a liar, and the source was in fact not reached until 1951 by another French expedition).

His reports had been published in the journal of the Geographic Society, as was his lecture to the members on his return home. He also published a book about his travels. Intrigued by this great achievement by a French explorer, Verne wrote a novel about a girl disguised as a boy searching for her lost father. The vivid travelogue cannot disguise however the old Vernian theme of the lost father that appeared first in *The Children of Captain Grant*. Real facts produced in Verne's imagination another chapter in his personal explorations.

It was while finishing his Orinoco book that Jules heard that his brother Paul had suffered a series of heart attacks. Then, suddenly on 22 August 1897, Paul died at Blois. Jules, too ill to attend the funeral, was deeply shocked. Some months later he told his nephew Maurice, 'I never thought I would survive my brother.'

Despite this great loss and his own increasing ill health – bronchitis and rheumatism, as well as fits of dizziness – Verne toiled on. Writing to Hetzel (9 November 1897) he said he was like a well-oiled machine, he was still 'stoking the fires' of his imagination. The final revisions of the Orinoco book were only part of his work load.

He had plans for a new book to be called *The Will of an Eccentric*. Written during 1898, it was published in two volumes in August and November 1899. By now printing techniques had improved enough for Verne to be able to have his books illustrated by documentary photographs as well as by the more usual art work. Woodcuts had by now been replaced by electrotypes, which were not as attractive as the old woodcuts had been. But the photographs in the text of the novel give a very queer experience, almost one of alienation. Readers may have felt that the fiction was being reinforced, but nowadays one may feel that reality is being made fictional. Verne was moving towards the devices of the 'new novelists'. It is still astonishing to turn the pages of the original illustrated edition and find his hectic narrative interrupted by sober views of Chicago and other strikingly modern American cities. At that date middle western American buildings were the architecture of the future, as Verne realised. Chicago was the home of the skyscraper: the Marquette Building had been completed in 1894. The interplay between fantasy and reality is very strange.

Moreover the book mentions X-rays in Chapter Three. The novel, written during 1897 and 1898, is set in April 1897. Röntgen had discovered X-rays on 5 November 1895. Results of his experiments were published on 28 December 1895. The famous picture of the hand with a ring was made on 21 January 1896. Thus Verne might seem right up to date, if it were not for the fact that he attributes the discovery to a Professor Eling in Prussia. Once again he had been led astray by an inaccurate journalistic account.

The novel itself, however, had nothing to do with skyscrapers or X-rays, but was a description of the United States as it then was, over which was played a huge game of fox-and-goose. The idea was amusing, but what a chance was lost by throwing away the incidentals. In this novel the automobile appears for the first time in a Verne book.

The Brothers Kip, published in July and November 1902, was a tale of fraternal love inspired by his affection for his brother Paul. A tale of mystery and murder in the South Seas in which the two brothers are falsely condemned to a penal colony in Tasmania for a murder they did not commit. The echoes of the Dreyfus affair are obvious, though Verne based his story on a book by one of the Rorique brothers, another *cause célèbre* of the period. But instead of using France's own colony in Cayenne, which was notorious in legend as Devil's Island, he uses a British colony so as not to upset his domestic readers. Perhaps for this reason the book was never translated, even to this day. From Tasmania the brothers escape with the aid of exiled Irish Fenians – once again Verne sides with the freedom fighters, though he can have known little about the dynamitards of the IRA. The real murderer is finally detected and the brothers exonerated by an old idea that a dead man's retina retains an image of the last thing he saw, in this case the faces of the real killers.

This notion had been made use of by Villiers de l'Isle Adam in *Claire Lenoir*, published in 1887, though written ten years earlier. Verne had a copy of this book in his library dated the year of publication. In *Claire Lenoir* the retinal image is an illusion. But Verne followed the information in the second supplement to the *Dictionaire Larousse* and in La Grange and Valude's *Encyclopedie d'Ophthalmologie* that a scientist called Giraud-Teulon had fixed retinal images by using an alum bath. But in the novel the 'correct' procedures get confused. For Verne makes no use of an alum bath and the images are not obtained immediately after death.

These 'retinal images' were in any case on a par with Schiaparelli's 'Martian Canals', and existed in the eyes of the beholder rather than the corpse. This idea was also used by the author of *The Clansman* and by Kipling in his story 'At the End of the Passage'. Le Moyne Snyder claims that the idea continues to be held by some murderers, despite the efforts of scientists to enlighten them. This was not science, or even science fiction: it was merely nonsense.

In his old age Verne was the object of much journalistic attention. Marcel Hutin, a journalist from Paris, asked Verne during an interview about his new book for 1901:

My new book will be called either *The Great Forest*, or *The Aerial Village*. In it I am going to study the habits of the monkeys of Equatorial Africa, as Garnier [*sic*] did with his researches in Libreville, but the conclusions I shall put forward will be those of a believer, and entirely opposed to the theories of Darwin.

and also:

> I am trying to reconstruct a race intermediate between the most advanced of the apes and the lowest men . . . I deal with the question broadly and fancifully, and anyhow, I am far from reaching the same conclusion as Darwin, whose ideas I do not share at all.

The American scientist's name was Garner by the way, an error on the journalist's part which persisted in Verne's book. Few people have read the novel since it was published. It sold 6,000 copies, making it a little more popular than many of his other later books, but the scientific background to the story make it one of the most interesting of Verne's later novels.

The inspiration for the book came from two contemporary sources, Dr. R. L. Garner and Eugène Dubois. The first was an American who had been doing pioneering research into the languages of monkeys and apes. In *The Speech of Monkeys* (1892) Garner described his early work in zoos with captive monkeys and apes. He believed that he had discovered the rudiments of a basic language among these animals, and in the hope of extending his discoveries he took himself off to Africa. Dr. Garner, despite his strange ideas, has the historical distinction of being the first scientist to study any of the great apes in the wild.

He left New York in July 1892 for the port of Gabon where he arrived on 18 October 1892. He travelled down the Ogowe River in search of a suitable site for his work. This he eventually found on the south shore of Lake Fenan Vaz, about twenty miles from the sea-coast. (That it was also near a mission of the White Fathers is something he failed to mention in his book.)

He set up an iron cage, for at this time it was commonly believed that gorillas were dangerous animals. For 112 days he observed the local chimpanzees and gorillas, and made excursions into the forests further south. His second book *Gorillas and Chimpanzees* (1895) described several chimpanzees he kept in Africa and also what he saw and heard about the gorillas. He was at pains to set right the many erroneous ideas held about the great apes, perpetuated by those scientists who had not troubled to observe them in their wild state. His native informants distinguished various types of apes, and in addition gave me a minute account of the appearance and habits of the fourth kind which I believe to be another species of gorilla. They claim that he is more intelligent and human-like than any of the others; and they say that his superior wisdom makes him more alert, and therefore more difficult to find. He is said always to live in parts of the forest remote from human habitations.

This is where Eugène Dubois came in. In 1894 on the basis of discoveries of skull fragments featuring heavy brows and a receding forehead, Dubois had announced the existence of *Pithecanthropus*. This ape-man was seen as the so-called 'missing-link' which Ernst Haeckel had postulated – a painting of a family of ape-men had been given to him by his friends as a sixtieth birthday present. A reconstruction of the Java ape-man was shown in the Dutch pavilion at the Paris Exhibition in 1900 (in which Michel Verne was involved). The ape-man was the great sensation of the day.

Ape-men and men-like apes in Africa – could there be a missing link between men and apes lost in the African forests? These were the elements around which Verne created his novel. Actually the idea of a 'missing-link' was based on a misunderstanding of what Darwin had written. Men, he thought, were not descended from the present-day apes, but both men and apes shared a common ancestor. There is no link missing between men and gorillas. Verne like many others was unclear about this, hence the rejection of Darwin in his interview with Hutin.

In the novel two explorers in the Congo come upon an empty iron cage in the jungle and the diaries of a Dr. Johansen, who had been continuing Garner's work. (Verne seems not to have read Garner's book, but to have read about him in French journals where the views of the missionary White Fathers about the American were accepted.) One of their bearers captures a young ape which utters an articulated word.

Soon the explorers are captured and taken to the village in the tree-tops where the ape-men live. There they discover that Dr. Johansen has become Mselo-Tala Tala their king and they witness bizarre scenes of worship by the ape-men which parody the Papal ceremony of the sedalia, in which the Pope is carried around St. Peter's. The novel is said, even by Verne, to be anti-Darwinian. And yet the ape-men have a real existence, they do display some rudimentary religious feeling and a man is capable of degenerating to their level.

Altogether a peculiar and disturbing novel, especially in Verne's treatment of their proto-religion. He is either attempting a crude approximation of what an ape-man faith might be, or he is making a parody of his own religion. His own motives may well have been confused. In treatment the novel approaches a little too closely to the Tarzan books. One wishes that Verne instead of treating the subject 'broadly and fancifully' had attempted a more serious recreation of what might be involved in the discovery of a living ape-man. (Some idea of the culture shock that might be involved can be gained from Dr. Bernard Heuvelman's account of his own discovery of a frozen 'ape-man' in Minnesota in 1968.)

The same failure of fictional treatment affected the other novel he published in 1901, about the great sea serpent, *Les Histoires de Jean-Marie Cabidoulin* – later reissued as *Le Serpent de Mer*, and translated as *The Sea Serpent*. This book too had a fascinating scientific background.

Like the giant squid of which he had written in 1869, and which he is said to have seen himself in the Channel, the sea-serpent was one of those wonders of the oceans which had been the subject of ridicule and dispute for centuries. Despite many well-authenticated sightings by reputable witnesses, most scientists did not take it any more seriously than the legendary kraken.

Then in 1892 Dutch biologist Dr. A. C. Oudemans published a great quarto volume of 892 pages devoted entirely to *The Great Sea Serpent*. This placed the subject on a scientific footing for the first time by collecting and collating all the reports the author could discover which seemed to relate to the creature. His theory was that the sea-serpent so-called was actually a great long-necked mammal related to the seals. Oudemans' idea became the popular theory on the Continent, though in England and America many still clung to the older idea that the sea-serpent was a surviving plesiosaur from the great age of the reptiles 70 million years ago.

After 1892 the sea-serpent was taken seriously at last. Reports began to appear in reputable journals by well-known scientists and there was much discussion of the mystery in papers and magazines during the 1890s. All of this inspired Verne once again to return to this enduring great mystery of the sea.

His chief character in the novel is a Breton sailor who sets out in old age on a voyage around the world hoping to catch sight of the sea-serpent which has eluded him all his life. The old sailor Jean-Marie Cabidoulin derived his name from the man who had kept the inn *Les Trois Malices* who had reported Verne going aboard the *Coralie* on his escapade as a cabin-boy in 1839. Verne's mind must have been running over the years of his childhood, because the names of the crew are a roll-call of all his old school-mates and friends in Nantes and Chantenay. An exciting end to the novel fails to save the tedium of the earlier parts of the book.

His new novel for 1903 *Bourses de Voyage (Travelling Scholarships)* was quite different. This is the story of a party of schoolboys on a travelling scholarship cruise among the Antilles. Again it seems the old man remained true to the dreams of the schoolboy he was once who had longed to sail across the Atlantic to those legendary islands. But the book failed to find foreign publication at the time, and in France had sold only 4,000 copies before his death.

The next year, 1904 brought two more books. The first was *A Drama in Livonia*, another novel of judicial error. The plan for the book had been made in 1894, and was written the following year for publication in 1896. But the cautious Hetzel postponed it for fear it might be thought too controversial at the height of the Dreyfus affair. Though Verne and his son Michel, an ardent Dreyfusard, had differing opinions about the affair, it seems that Verne at last suspected that there might be something wrong. But the idea of legal error in his novels goes back a long way, to Detective Fix and the Indian judges he had described in 1873. But this novel set in a disturbed province of Czarist Russia, despite some exciting scenes and lively characters, also went untranslated. And in France a mere 4,000 readers were interested in Verne's account of a struggle for justice against arbitrary laws.

However these now almost forgotten novels were followed by one of his best known *The Master of the World* (1904), in which the sinister Robur returns to terrorise the world. This book had a curious development, as originally it was to have been rather blandly entitled *The Adventures of an American Detective*. This period was of course the era of Sherlock Holmes and his rivals, and Verne may well have wanted to try and write a really popular novel once again by catching at the latest vogue. But as he worked on the book, it changed into something else, a science fiction novel of his old sort. As he explained to his Italian correspondent Mario Turiello, it was to be the continuation and dénouement of Robur. It would also be 'the last word in automobilism'.

For the second time, a motor car appears in Verne's work, which had begun so long ago with the very latest thing in balloons. If nothing else this demonstrates the vast technical and social changes that had taken place since 1863. Then Verne had been a prophet of the benefits of modern science. Forty years on, he felt very differently. Now science had become a threat to the world.

In 1886 Robur had been represented as the science of the future. Now he returned as an embodiment of what that science might really mean. Written in the form of a detective story with John Strock of the Federal Police as the hero, the book is immensely superior to *Robur the Conquerer*. The dramatic climaxes are well developed, especially the scenes over Niagara Falls and in the thunderstorm which destroys *The Terror*, as Robur calls his futuristic flying machine which also doubles as the fastest racing car in the world and a miniature submarine. Verne makes good use of his knowledge of America in the scenes by Niagara and Lake Erie, which as he notes in the novel, he had visited in April 1867.

Whether Robur's new machine *The Terror* was really 'the last word in automobilism' is another matter. In the novel the idea of a multiple vehicle is very effective. Nothing like this then existed: the book appeared eighteen months before the first trial flights of the Wright brothers. Was it then an inspired and original vision of the future? I am afraid not.

Verne took the wrong route in making *The Terror* an aeroplane with flapping wings which imitated the flight of birds. True there had been many experiments with ornithopters during the previous twenty years. The most famous of these (from a French point of view) had been the experiments of the Frenchman Clement Ader. These had interested the French government but the trials came to nothing, despite the fact that Ader had 'flown' his plane 'Avion III' for a few seconds in 1893. Flown, that is, in the sense of raising it off the ground. He was the first man to do this. But this was not sustained or controlled flight such as the Wright brothers pioneered in America. Nevertheless Ader has an honoured place in the French *Musée de l'Air* outside Paris and inspired Verne's ideas for *The Terror*.

But even the idea of a multiple vehicle was not really new. In a previously-mentioned novel by Jacolliot called *The Fire Eaters*, there appears just such a machine called *The Swan*. This long novel (860 pages) had been published in 1886, but was little known by 1904. Doubtless Verne had read it when it was originally published, or when it was serialised in 1895, and later taking the idea had developed it in his own unique manner. *The Fire Eaters* is diffuse and rambling. As a novel *The Master of the World* is incomparably better.

The Master of the World, published in November 1904, was followed by *The Invasion of the Sea* early in 1905. This, too, had its origin in earlier years, in an article about creating an inland sea in Algeria which had appeared in *Musée des Familles* in July 1876. Verne was still loyal to his old sources of information. The idea was to connect up the Gulf of Gabes with the low-lying regions of desert behind it. In the novel the survey is made despite harassment by the Tuaregs. Work begins on the canal. The sea bursts in, however, and the area is flooded in an apocalyptic ending.

But these published works give only a small impression of the vast amount of work which Verne accomplished during the last decade of his life. By this time he had great difficulty in writing by hand, so Michel sent down from his company in Paris stenographers capable of taking his dictation, and had his later books typed up for him to revise before publication. Many of the novels of these years were discussed at length with Michel, and his involvement with the editing and publication of his father's posthumous novels deserves some discussion here, even if it means advancing some years in time.

Michel Verne, as a principal heir, was anxious to protect his father's estate. The month after his father died, Michel drew up an inventory of his father's manuscripts which was published as a letter in *Le Figaro* (2 May 1905) and *Le Temps* (3 May 1905). Later with a view to a civil suit with *Le Journal* some years later he drew up another list in a memorandum for his lawyer. Verne left unpublished the following materials:

1st – nine plays in verse
  – seven plays in prose
  – three novellas

 – an untitled novel
 – two historical accounts

All of these were written before *Five Weeks in a Balloon*, that is before 1863.

 2nd – two novels, also written before 1863, but which have features in common with his later work
 – Journey in England and Scotland
 – Paris in the Twentieth Century
 3rd – eleven volumes in the *Extraordinary Journeys*, six in one volume, two in two volumes.

This made ten volumes, not eleven. But Michel also made another error. When the books were published they made three series of two volumes. The first two were easily identified as *The Golden Volcano* and *The Thompson Travel Agency*. The trouble which led to the legal dispute arose over the authenticity of *The Survivors of the Jonathan*. Moreover the very last Verne book published *The Astonishing Adventures of the Barsac Mission* also had a curious history. But to take these in order of appearance.

In 1905 Michel saw through the press *Le Phare du bout du Monde*, which was translated in 1923 as *The Lighthouse at the End of the World*. This handwritten, inked-over manuscript was complete and ready for the press. Set in Tierra del Fuego, it describes the struggle between three lighthouse keepers on Isla de los Estados in 1859 against a gang of desperate pirates. Some of Verne's information on Patagonia, or Magellania as he called it, was partly supplied by a lady correspondent in South Africa. We know this because a letter to her was sent by mistake to Mario Turiello in Italy, who sent it back to Verne. Unfortunately he does not seem to have noted her name, so we have no way of knowing what role she played in Verne's life or how he came to know her.

Verne was often pains-taking in his efforts to get up his facts about a place, no less so in the next book *The Golden Volcano* (1905). The Yukon goldrush had been one of the great romantic episodes at the turn of the century, and naturally enough Verne was intrigued by the regions of Alaska and Canada running up to the Arctic Ocean. Some of the information he needed he got from the explorer Etienne Richet, whom he had met in person at a meeting of the Société Industrielle d'Amiens in 1899. A few years earlier, on 2 February 1896, Richet had been surprised to receive a letter from Verne when he was about to leave on an expedition to British Columbia.

After wishing the explorer well, Verne expatiated on his hopes for a French-speaking empire in the St. Lawrence Valley which would counter the predominant influence of the Teutons in North America. This political idea had been given expression in his novel *Family Without a Name* in 1889, and is still very much alive today in the separatist movement in Quebec to which De Gaulle and Malraux gave their political and cultural support.

At his lecture in Amiens in 1899 Richet had been talking about the Yukon, where the gold rush was already under way. Present were General de Brye, and three officers who were among the most famous explorers in France at that time, Marchand, Baratier and Gourand.

Richet became quite friendly with Verne, and gave the writer a Buddha from Angkor-Wat for his study. That room he remembered was decorated with portraits of Nansen, the polar explorer, Brazza, who opened up the French Congo, Marchand, du Comte de Brettes and the Duke d'Uzés. Verne it seems, had made his study a little shrine to modern exploration.

The novel which grew out of his interest in the Yukon was more extravagant than these sober origins suggested. Two cousins from Montreal are searching for a claim inherited from their uncle. They join up with two girls (also cousins) on their way to the Yukon. However their claims are washed out by a flood. Inspired by a dying man's story of a golden volcano far to the north, they set out to find it. Having foiled the villain Hunter, they find the volcano. But things go wrong. The volcano blows up. The gold showers into the sea. Hunter is killed by a falling nugget. Another apocalyptic conclusion: 'the gold goes up in smoke, like so much else in this vile world'.

Though the locale was very topical, the novel does not seem to have attracted much attention. Nor did the next book, *The Thompson Travel Agency*. Such firms had come a long way since Thomas Cook was organising his cruise on the Nile and his journey round the world in 1872. In 1907 anybody of moderate means could take an excursion to a country which would have been beyond reach a generation before. The novel dealt with an unscrupulous firm which tempts an Anglo-American party onto a cruise aboard a creaky ship which eventually sinks while voyaging among the Atlantic islands. Love triumphs between Robert Morgand (who is really a nobleman, the Marquis de Gramond) and the American Alice Lindsay.

The next book was a return to a genuine piece of science fiction. *The Hunt for the Golden Meteor* (1908) did find an English publisher, not Verne's old friends Sampson Low and Marston however, but the smaller and more distinguished firm of Grant Richards. (But the novel must have done badly in England, for Richards did not take up any other Verne titles.) The inventor Zephrin Xirdal invents a machine which generates a 'neutral helicoidal ray' (a phenomenon unknown to science) which creates an energy void. With this he plans to pull out of space a solid gold meteor. His uncle makes a killing on the stock exchange in gold mine shares when this leaks out. But the inventor is dismayed by the greed around him and the disputes that arise over the meteor. He deflects the meteor and it falls into the sea.

By a strange coincidence the novel came out the year that a real meteor crashed into the forests of Siberia, blasting miles of trees and creating aerial effects which were seen around the world. The reality was more astonishing than even Verne had imagined.

The novel features, perhaps as a tribute to Honorine or perhaps not, a perfect wife in Mrs. Hudelson. 'Unfortunately wives like this are rarely found outside novels,' Verne comments.

One of the illustrations (by Roux) in the novel seems to have been based on Verne's own house, and *The Secret of Wilhelm Storitz* (1910) actually includes an exact description of the house in rue Charles Dubois. The novel was about an invisible man (Wells' novel of that title had appeared in 1897). Storitz uses his power of invisibility to frustrate the marriage of a girl who had spurned him, an interesting contrast to what happens to Wells' character. The jilted lover was a figure very close to Verne's heart.

The Pilot of the Danube (1908) was also set in Eastern Europe but in the Turkish Empire. The winner of a fishing competition offers to break a record by living off what he catches while sailing down the Danube. He is really the leader of an underground movement against the Turks, and is soon involved in machinations between the rebels and the police. This detective story was written at one go in the course of a few weeks. Michel Verne had travelled along the Danube through Austria, Hungary and Rumania and Bulgaria. His account of his travels was the immediate inspiration of the novel, but Verne drew on a book by J. E. Driault on the eastern question which he had Hetzel send him down from Paris.

With *Hier et Demain* (*Yesterday and Tomorrow*), published in 1910, Michel had reached the stage of making books up out of his father's literary remains. This was a collection of stories and sketches written over many years. It included the most revealing story of his old age, 'The Eternal Adam', which he was working on when he collapsed in 1905. More about that in the next chapter. Here a brief glance at the other stories. These were 'Mr. Ray Sharp and Miss Me Flat', a musical fantasy of little interest. Also a very early story 'The Fate of Jean Morenas' which Michel must have liked very much as he later filmed it. The book also included his own story 'The Day of an American Journalist'; and 'The Humbug', written it is thought in 1863.

'The Humbug' is a curious story, about an American con-man whose stock-in-trade is the fossil skeleton of a giant. Phileas T. Barnum (1800–91) used to give a lecture with that title relating his experiences in gulling people: 'There's a sucker born every minute,' he used to say. It has been suggested that Verne's story was written after 1884 and that it was based on the bizarre claim of Florentino Ameghino to have discovered a fossil giant in Argentina. It was nothing of the sort, naturally. But Verne may have had in mind such celebrated American novelties as the 'fossil sea-serpent' exhibited in New York and London in 1845 by Dr. Albert Kock. This had been confected out of genuine fossil bones, which were later bought by the British Museum. Also there was the even more celebrated Cardiff giant, a 'fossil man' which created a sensation for a short season until it was proved to be a hoax.

And finally *The Survivors of the Jonathan* (1909) and *The Barsac Mission* (1919). The story of the Barsac mission had a complicated history. Among his papers Verne left the manuscript of a one-volume novel called *Voyage d'Etude*. The second chapter of *The Barsac Mission* as it now stands has this title, but the first chapter dealing with a bank raid in London suggests another kind of novel. As *The Barsac Mission* appeared as a two-volume novel, we might infer that Michel Verne had written at least half of the present text. He seems to have used as a basis for this a file of notes which was also among his father's papers entitled *Une Ville Saharienne*, which was seen by Emile Berr a journalist from *Le Figaro* a few days after Verne's death. *Voyage d'Etude* was a complete manuscript though. Michel in his memorandum noted the existence of 'a stenographic version' which was incomplete and needed important corrections.

Such an editing procedure might be understandable, but it seems there may have been another hand involved in this novel. *The Barsac Mission* was serialised in 1914, but not published in book form until after the war in 1919. But by 1912 it had already been plagiarised.

The book in question was *The Mysterious Plane (Le Mystère Plane)* by George Montignac. Though set in the Florida wilderness, the novel includes many features of the Verne novel, including the secret city, the sinister villain, the search party and the mysterious flying machine. Most remarkable of all are 'les guêpes', the wasps which feature as flying weapons in both books. George Montignac's other work consists almost entirely of boulevard plays and farces, not novels. Had he been hired by Michel to help with the revision, or rather rewriting of the novel? Had he been dissatisfied with either his pay or the delay in the novel appearing? His own novel is dated August 1912.

This is uncertain territory. There were claims by people to have worked with Verne in his last years, but Montignac did not claim this. The parallel between the two novels was pointed out in 1972 by Jacques van Herp, but since then there has been no more about it. Jean Jules-Verne, who might well know the truth, says nothing about the matter in his reticent biography of his grandfather.

Michel Verne was a man of great talent. As we have seen he had already written stories, which were published under his father's name, such as 'An Express of the Future' and 'The Day of an American Journalist'. Later in the twenties he was to produce and direct four films based on his father's novels. His own imagination, as shown in his short stories, was on a par with his father's and it would have been more open of him to have taken the credit for what was really his own work.

The matter of who wrote what might not be important were it

nor for the extravagant claims made for the book. The novel was not translated until 1960, when I. O. Evans produced a version for the new collected edition. He suggests that it illustrates 'Jules Verne's imaginative genius as well as his ability to keep abreast of the latest scientific and technical advances and to weave them into his narrative.' If anyone was being up to date it was Michel Verne and George Montignac, and of course his illustrator George Roux.

The vision of the secret city and the illustrations of it are quite magnificent. In designing the city Roux seems to have been directly inspired by the latest advances in architecture, for his fortress and factories owe something to the designs of the model factory at the Werkbund exhibition at Cologne in 1914 by Walter Gropius, with the same flat roofs, small windows and open stairs. Verne was well served by his designers to the very end (Roux had first worked on a Verne book in 1886).

The references to Marconi and the invention of radio (helped, of course, by the discoveries of the Frenchman Branly) suggest that the book was written about 1899; by 1914 the state of the art had advanced far beyond the primitive instrument described in the novel to such great effect in liberating the captives.

It would be wonderful to see this book (with Roux's pictures) as the summation of the ideas of Jules Verne. Perhaps we may. For though the final version may have been largely the work of his son and a collaborator, they were directly inspired by the great visionary. The strange figure of Harry Killer was drawn from the French millionaire Jacques Lebaudy and his schemes to found a colony in the Niger Bend. Also there was the fate of the expedition through the same area led by Paul Voulet in 1899, who was shot after being relieved of his command and murdering his replacement. The overtones of French imperialism in the book are quite true to life. But for something closer to a final testament of Jules Verne we must look elsewhere, to *The Survivors of the Jonathan* and to 'The Eternal Adam'.

Recent work as yet unpublished on the manuscript of *The Survivors of the Jonathan* seems to show that this too underwent revision at Michel's hands before publication. The novel is set, as was *The Lighthouse at the End of the World*, in Tierra del Fuego, and was originally called *Magellania*. At the turn of the century this was about the last unexplored region of the world, and because it was disputed by Chile and Argentina had no regular settlements. It had seen few explorers, outside of the British Navy who mapped the Straits of Magellan, and a French scientific mission in 1882, which Verne relied on for his background material.

Here on Hoste Island Verne's novel settles on a philosophical anarchist and atheist called the Kaw-Djer, the Benefactor, by the natives. An emigrant ship is wrecked in the straits and of necessity the Kaw-Djer becomes their leader. The people have divided into communists under Dorick, conservatives under an Irishman named Patterson, and socialists under Beauval who becomes governor of the island and is a failure.

The Kaw-Djer undertakes a coup d'état and makes himself leader of the colony. After this the anarchist finds himself having to organise a society, which he detests doing. When all the problems seem to have been solved, other complications arise. Gold is discovered. Outsiders intervene, riots ensue and the Kaw-Djer has his police fire on the mob. Horrified by this turn of events, he finally settles with the Chilean government to exchange gold rights for home-rule. He then steps down in favour of a young successor and sets off for the even more remote island of Cape Horn, to live in the lighthouse which he has built there, to prevent further wrecks.

This lighthouse actually exists at that remote quarter of the world (and Verne had already told a story about it in the earlier novel about the region). The novel itself is drawn in many other ways from real facts. The impressive figure of the Kaw-Djer seems to have been based by Verne on his friend the anarchist and geographer Elisée Reclus. Reclus had written about South America, on anarchism as a philosophy of life, and also about anarchist colonies. Among the islands in the same region of Cape Horn is L'Isle Hermite (named after a French explorer). The idea of a bearded reclusive anarchist hermit living there was the sort of punning association that appealed to Verne.

The hint that the Kaw-Djer may once have belonged by right among the mighty of the world was intended to bring to mind the mysterious fate of John Orth, as Louis Salvador's brother the Archduke Jean called himself when he went to sea after the Mayerling affair. A prince who had thrown away his position in life to become a ship's master, John Orth disappeared while sailing around Cape Horn and was never seen alive again.

This incident may have provided the germ of the novel, but the serious aspects of the novel derive both from the political ideas of Reclus as well as from Verne's own experiences as a politician in Amiens. The conclusion of the book is sombre, as the Kaw-Djer escapes to the ultimate island: 'far from everyone, useful to everyone, he would live, free and alone – for ever'.

Nowhere else, indeed, would he have had the strength to support the burden of life. The most poignant tragedies are the dramas of the mind. For those who have endured them, those whom they have left exhausted, despairing, hurled from the foundations upon which they have built, there is no other refuge but the cloister or death.

In the end, Verne implies, we all die alone. The Master of the World, the Kaw-Djer's opposite in character, had failed in his megalomaniacal schemes to conquer the world. Now the Kaw-Djer also fails in his scheme, and escapes from a society he cannot change to die alone.

The Kaw-Djer had chosen the cloister. This rock, it was a cell with its impenetrable walls of light and space.

His destiny was after all as good as any other. We die, but our actions do not die, for they live on in their endless consequences. Travellers of a day, we leave eternal traces of our path upon the sand. Nothing happens except what is determined for us by those who have gone before us, and the future is made up of the unknown results of the past. Whatever the future might bring, even though the people he had created should vanish after an ephemeral existence, even though the earth itself should be destroyed and scattered through the infinity of space, the Kaw-Djer's work would not perish.

Nor will Verne's. *The Survivors of the Jonathan* was the last novel that Verne ever completed himself. And in this novel Verne reached his ultimate island. The Kaw-Djer abandons the claims of the continent of men. He retreats to the integrity of his own island, 'entire of itself' rather than a 'part of the main'. The last *voyage extraordinaire* was completed, and Verne's strange journey of the mind was nearly over.

Chapter Twenty

The Eternal Adam

THE FINAL CHAPTERS OF VERNE'S LAST BOOKS WERE BEING written with something like his old concentration despite anxiety and pain, but time and energy were running out.

On 7 October 1901, Jules and Honorine moved out of the large mansion in the rue Charles Dubois and returned to the smaller house nearby, 44 Boulevard Longueville, where they had lived when they first came to Amiens. Their old housekeeper had died shortly before, and the mansion was now much too large for them.

Though not a sentimentalist, Verne had grown attached to the great house. The doctor's house in *The Chase of the Golden Meteor* and Myra's house in *The Secret of Wilhelm Storitz* were based upon it. The old housekeeper who looked after John Strock, the detective in *The Master of the World*, was probably based on their faithful old retainer in tribute to her long years of service. Verne was not above making such direct use of real life for the smallest details of his novels.

In moving he allowed, perhaps deliberately, many souvenirs and mementoes of his life to be lost. Three years before he had destroyed many letters, manuscripts and account books. Possibly the old writer was covering his tracks while he still had the time: he had no wish for anyone to know just how true to life the dramas of his own mind had been.

By now his health was failing seriously. In photographs he is visibly waning. A cataract obscured his right eye, and the eyes themselves had begun to weaken. His wounded leg still gave him trouble. At seventy-six he was beginning to feel his age. The events of his life were receding in his memory, as he wrote in a letter to his brother-in-law in Nantes:

You ask me to send an autograph for the Cheguillaumes. Here it is. Will you pass it on to them. Chantenay? The Cheguillaumes? How far away they seem! Did I really once know them? Yes – but when? I think it must have been under Louis XII or Henri IV. And you ask me when we shall meet again? In the other world, my friend – that is, if I have proved worthy of it. Yet I am still working. Perhaps I shall reach my hundredth volume.

At this time he was working on *The Master of the World* for publication in 1904, but other books were in active preparation which would not be seen in print until he was long dead: the hundredth volume he hoped to reach finally appeared in 1910.

Rumours of his ill health began to circulate and paragraphs about his decline appeared in newspapers across the world. To reassure himself Marcel Hutin came to see him on 22 May 1901. Aside from his new book for that year, the strange *Aerial Village*, they discussed a new trip around the world being possible now that the Trans-Siberian railway was completed. Verne thought that such a journey would now take about thirty days. By then several attempts had been made to break Mr. Fogg's record, as we have already seen. Most recently, in 1901 had been the race of two Paris journalists, Henri Turot of *Le Journal* and Gaston Stiegler of *Le Matin*.

Stiegler had written to Verne beforehand, and as he passed through Amiens on his way home, Verne was on the platform with Honorine to wish him well. It was a touching scene, the frail old writer with his wife hovering anxiously around him, reliving the triumph of an earlier year. Verne reproached Stiegler for not bringing back, as Phileas Fogg had done, a Mrs. Aouda. But, Stiegler protested, he had never met her! He must have been travelling too fast for romance. His journey had taken 63 days, 10 hours and 20 minutes.

Another visitor at this time was an old acquaintance, the British writer Robert H. Sherard, who had brought Nellie Bly to see him in 1889. He came to visit him again because of the rumours of his ill health. He was relieved to find that things were not as bad as he had feared. Verne explained that one eye was completely gone, but that he could still see a little through the other.

It is cataract in my right eye, but the other eye is still fairly good. I do not want to risk an operation as long as I can still see enough to do the little work, the little writing, the little reading that I still do, for remember, sir, that I am a very old man now, past seventy-six. Since the reports of my blindness got about the sympathies of the world have been awakened. I have received numerous letters from all parts. Many people have sent me prescriptions for cataract, marvellous remedies. They tell me not to allow any operation to be performed; that these remedies of theirs will cure me without danger. It is very kind of them. I have been much touched, but, that I know, of course, that an operation is the only cure.

They went on to talk about his new books and about H. G. Wells, and of Verne's predictions, the importance he set by the names of his characters, the 'reportage Americain' and of his warm admiration for Dickens, Balzac and Sterne. A lively conversation, in fact. Sherard was moved by the meeting.

One had come to pity; it was with envy rather that one passed out into the grey and lonely world. For there beyond the velvet hangings stood the table, neatly laid with two covers vis-à-vis, by the side of the iris painted windows, which opened onto the sunny garden full of flowers. And by the sculptured hearth, on the mantelpiece of which a ruddy and resplendent samovar purred its note of intimate and familiar comfort, two armchairs stood side by side.

His sight grew dimmer, but still Verne did not have the operation to remove the cataract. As long as he could write and read even that little bit, he waited. He had also gone quite deaf in one ear, as he admitted to Mme. Du Crest in 1903, 'so that I am in no danger of hearing half the foolish and wicked things that people say. That is a big consolation'.

In Amiens today it is still recalled that on his afternoon walks Verne would sometimes pause behind one of the trees in the Boulevard Du Mail to relieve himself 'comme un chien'. This was a symptom of the insidious disease which was slowly killing him, as were the cataracts and his weakening sight. For Verne had diabetes, which causes excessive urination, as well as weakening of the eyes.

Verne was a sick man, but there was little that his doctor could do for him. Diabetes was then a fatal condition. Insulin, which treats the symptoms of the disease today, did not become available until the 1920s. One is struck by the strange fact that medical science, which had made such great strides during the nineteenth century in the prevention and treatment of diseases, was the one science which Verne never wrote about. Perhaps he was too much of a hypochondriac to dare to.

One Amiens citizen, André Desfeuilles, recalls Verne's kindness to him as a boy, for he invited him home one afternoon, and while Honorine, who knew his mother, fussed over him, Verne went off to get a copy of *Two Years Holiday* to present to him. It was a small gesture by the author to one member of his worldwide audience. As a gesture to him some of his British readers, through the Boys' Imperial League, presented him with a silver-mounted walking stick to help him move around.

Desfeuilles recalls seeing Verne sitting on the same bench in the Boulevard Du Mail every afternoon, watching the trains pass in the long green tunnel of the railway cutting in front of his house. One of these would have been the express to Brindisi that Phileas Fogg had caught with Passepartout in 1872. A sad, sick and lonely man, visibly declining, Verne's mental energy was still remarkable.

On the shelves of his library, newly set up in a room beside his bedroom again, *The Master of the World* was the last edition he was to see join the long line – at least three yards, as he pointed out to Robert Sherard – of the original editions of his books.

Yet in this last year or so of his life, Verne's mind remained lucid. His letters to Hetzel in Paris and to his young Italian friend Mario Turiello are evidence of this.

He had been writing to Turiello since 1894. These letters to his admirer in Milan show Verne in full possession of his faculties, even though sight and sound were failing him. On 1 May 1904, for instance, he wrote at some length, discussing with passion the trip of the French President through Italy (which he disapproved of as giving support to the Italian government against the Pope). Turiello had become editor of the *Journal de Naples*, and Verne hoped his literary talents would soon get due recognition. With him he discussed his sea-serpent book and other current projects.

His letters to Hetzel also reveal his state of mind at this time. On 2 September 1904 he reports that he is correcting the proofs of *The Master of the World*, and that in a few days he would send him the manuscript of the new serial for the *Magasin* for 1905, which was to be *The Invasion of the Sea*. This would be followed by *The Secret of Wilhelm Storitz*, which he hoped to see published while he was still alive.

A few weeks later, on 15 October 1904, he wrote again to Hetzel to say that he was sending the manuscript of *The Sea in the Sahara* (as the new novel was then called) and that he wanted to be informed of its safe arrival at once. For nearly thirty years he had been sending down to Paris his actual manuscript, and not a copy, and he always feared that it would be lost in the post.

On 7 December 1904, he wrote about the title of the new book. But he concluded, 'We have discussed all this.' Hetzel, in fact, came to Amiens twice a month to discuss business and the progress of the various works in hand. The next day, after hearing from Hetzel, he said he thought *A New Sea in the Sahara* was the best title. And on 12 December what was to be the last letter of all:

My dear Jules, I sent you yesterday two parcels of the proofs of *The Invasion of the Sea*. If you have the time to send them back, I will revise them, otherwise be good enough to see that the corrections are properly done. One point: according to my notes, and doubtless according to Bechu, Toureg is written without an *s* in the plural. The same for Targui, the Toureg, the Targui. A good handshake from your old friend, Jules Verne.

So to the end Verne was worrying over the minutest details of his books, concerned always with accuracy. (Actually a Targui is an individual of the Toureg tribe; the error on his part arose from his sources.) It is interesting to see that Hetzel settled the questions of the titles for the books, selecting one from a list proposed by Verne. Here Verne is being a little less than his meticulous old self over the proofs, for usually he called for several sets. Perhaps his stamina for such work was running down.

On 20 December he was writing again to Mario Turiello. He apologised for not writing before, but he had been suffering a great deal of pain and liked to deal with his letters himself. (He did not admit that the pain was due to a diabetic attack.) He had read Turiello's article in the *Journal de Naples* about his work and it had given him great pleasure. He had also read his new book on Leopardi and hoped that Turiello's talent would soon be rewarded. He wondered if his friend had read *The Master of the World* yet: 'it is the ne plus ultra of automobilism'.

As the new serial began appearing in the *Magasin*, Jules Verne celebrated his seventy-eighth birthday on 8 February 1905. A month later, on 17 March, he suffered another diabetic attack. Eight days of increasing pain followed.

On 20 March news reached Paris that Verne was dying. Members of his scattered family hurried down to Amiens to be with him. His younger sister Marie wrote to her family in Nantes after her arrival:

Here I am in Amiens, my dear husband, as you will have learned by now from my telegram, and in the next room to Jules. Our poor friend is certainly very ill, nothing but a miracle can save him. His right side is completely paralysed. However he can still move his head. He is very calm. He seemed happy to see me. He told me so. He had a bad attack of diabetes a fortnight ago, and between Sunday night and Monday, it suddenly got worse. Last year, without our knowing, he had a similar attack, but once it was over, he paid no more attention to it. It is touching to see all the care and affection Honorine lavishes on her husband, but of course, Jules has always done only what he wanted to do. The dear man is taking it all with the utmost serenity, and is quite ready to die. He has seen this moment coming for a long time now, and after the first crisis he said to his wife: 'Next time, you can bring me the priest before you call the doctor, that's all there is to it!' She did as he asked. Jules gladly confessed his sins, and even remarked to the priest, who comes to see him every day: 'You have done me good. I feel regenerated.'

With his relatives gathering around him, Verne hoped that the old family quarrels would be forgotten. Michel came from the south of France with his wife and children. Jules did not seem to be in so much pain now, and was carefully tended by Honorine in her great soft bed in the front ground floor room.

Day by day the paralysis spread. He no longer recognised those around him. He slowly faded as the paralysis reached his brain. Marie felt that he was no longer her brother with his marvellous intelligence, but only an empty body.

In Nantes a family dinner to celebrate an engagement had already been arranged and could not be cancelled. But his relatives worried about whether they were doing the right thing. Doubtless the dying man would not have minded their harmless fun. But all around the world people were moved by Verne's state. The Havas News Agency carried reports of his condition above even those from the siege at Port Arthur. The *Petit Journal* in Paris reported that he had revived enough to recognise his three grandsons.

When Hetzel arrived, however, he could get no sign of recognition from his friend. During the night of Thursday, 23 March, his left side became totally paralysed. Towards two o'clock in the morning his sufferings ceased and he fell into a coma.

Reporting on his condition the day before, the *Journal des Débats*, concluded that 'Contrary to what has been said, Jules Verne is not a Protestant. Born in Nantes in 1828, he belongs to an old Catholic family, and has received the last consolations of that religion.'

It may seem a strange rumour that Verne could have been taken for a Protestant, but understandable. He was not a Catholic novelist, his books are not the creations of a Catholic sensibility. His readers had rightly detected his underlying scepticism and his deterministic belief in science, and had easily assumed that his was a Protestant imagination with little remaining interest in religion.

Some confirmation of this would have been found in the story Verne completed shortly before his death. Called 'The Eternal Adam', the story was to be his testament, his own 'mémoire d'outre tombe'. It was to be included by his son in a collection of short stories published in 1910. Today it is one of Verne's almost forgotten masterpieces. In the story Verne develops the idea of an eternal cycle of events continuously repeating themselves. This deterministic idea had already been elaborated by Nietzsche, and reflects the pessimism so obvious in the fate of the Kaw-Djer. The idea is wholly repugnant to orthodox Catholic belief (for it is an explicit denial of the intervention of Salvation in History). This does not seem to have struck Michel Verne when he published it, or indeed, any other members of the family who insisted on the odour of sanctity in which the great man passed away.

'The Eternal Adam' is a bleak denial of the eternal god. At the time of his death Verne's intellect had broken completely at last with the stern god of his father's faith. But the heart has its reasons. No cradle Catholic ever fades completely from the influence of his childhood verities. The consolation of the last rites of the Church may well have satisfied the emotions of the writer whose imagination had flown beyond them into the infinite void, as at the end of the last of the strange journeys:

Such were the meditations of Zartog Sofr, as he bent over this venerable manuscript.

This narrative from beyond the tomb enabled him to imagine the terrible drama for ever played throughout the universe, and his heart overflowed with pity. Bleeding from the countless wounds from which those who had ever lived had suffered before him, bending beneath the weight of those vain efforts accumulated throughout the infinity of time, Zartog Sofr'-Ai-Sr gained, slowly and painfully, an intimate conviction of the eternal recurrence of events.

Jules Verne died at eight o'clock on the morning of Friday, 24 March 1905; he was eighty-seven.

Only months before, at Kill Devil Hills in Carolina, an aeroplane had taken to the air under fully powered control. Born in the heyday of the clipper ship, Verne had lived on into the dawning of the new age of technology which the spirit of his life's work had predicted. Only months later, in the *Annalen der Physik*, an officer of the Swiss patent office named Albert Einstein would suggest his partial theory of relativity. The simple causality of the Newtonian world in which Verne had lived was also over. The complex relativistic modern age dawned as Verne died. Born into the certainties of faith, Verne died in doubt. He had seen the liberal hopes of his youth slowly betrayed, both by politics and by a science only too ready to serve the ends of war rather than peaceful progress. The romantic adventurers of his early novels were in the end replaced by the far more complex figures of the Kaw-Djer with his atheism and anarchy, and the Zartog Sofr'-Ai-Sr with his discovery that progress was a complete illusion. Among the most popular writers of his age, Verne's own character had evolved along with his century's, from certainty to doubt.

The funeral was held on 28 March 1905. It was an elaborate affair, with parties of soldiers and schoolchildren, politicians and clergy. Among the great crowd that followed the bier to the cemetery was a strange Englishman. He had learnt one phrase off by heart, which he repeated to the family as he shook each of them by the hand. 'Courage, courage, dans la dure épreuve qui vous atteint.' Be brave in the sore trial you face. Was it, some of them later wondered, the ghost of Phileas Fogg?

Honorine died on 29 January 1910, aged eighty, and was buried beside Jules. Memorials were later erected to Verne in both Nantes and Amiens. But neither of them quite equals the remarkable memorial which Michel raised over his father's grave in 1907. Created by Albert Roze, it shows the bearded Verne, his hair tossed by the sea winds, breaking free of shroud and tomb, rising with a magnificent gesture from the dead. Above it are cut his name and the words:

ONWARD TO IMMORTALITY AND ETERNAL YOUTH

Appendix

Round the World Records

1870 – George Francis Train: '80 days'
1889 – Nellie Bly: 72 days, 6 hours, 11 mins, 14 secs
1890 – George Francis Train: 67 days
1891 – Elizabeth Bisland (Mrs. Whetmore): 73 days
1892 – George Francis Train: 60 days
1901 – Gaston Stiegler: 63 days, 10 hours, 20 mins*
1901 – Henri Turot: ?
1901 – Charles Fitzmorris: 60 days, 13 hours, 29 mins
1903 – I. W. Sayre: 54 days, 9 hours, 30 mins
1903 – Henry Frederick: 54 days, 7 hours, 20 mins
1907 – Col. H. Burnley-Campbell: 40 days, 19 hours, 30 mins
1911 – André Jaeger Schmidt: 39 days, 19 hours, 43 mins, 37 secs
1913 – John Henry Mears: 35 days, 21 hours, 35 mins
1924 – unknown flier: 40 days, 5 hours
1926 – Evans and Linton Wells: 28 days, 14 hours, 36 mins, 51 secs
1928 – John Henry Mears and C. B. D. Collyer: 33 days, 15 hours, 21 mins
1929 – Palle Huls: 44 days
1929 – *Graf Zepplin* (German airship): 21 days, 7 hours, 28 mins
1931 – Willy Post and Gatty: 8 days, 15 hours, 53 mins
1933 – Willy Post: 7 days, 12 hours, 49 mins
1936 – Jean Cocteau: 80 days
1936 – 3 American journalists: 18 days and 14 hours
1937 – Amelia Earhardt: ? (lost over the Pacific)
1938 – Howard Hughes: 3 days, 19 hours, 14 mins
1941 – James W. Chapman: ?
1947 – Bill Odom and Melton Reynolds: 28 hours, 26 mins
1948 – Thomas Lanphier: 4 days, 23 hours, 47 secs

* The opening of the Trans-Siberian Railway altered the route around the world, cutting days off the long sea journeys of Mr. Fogg.

1949 – B.50: 24 hours
1952 – Jean-Marie Audibert: 4 days, 19 hours, 38 secs
1954 – Françoise Haurie and Jean-François Bernede: 80 days
1956 – Gregoire Brainier and Micheline Roncari: 80 days
1957 – Jean-Claude de Lassé: 80 hours
1971 – S. J. Perelman: completed by plane
1971 – John Burningham: 80 days
1972 – S. S. *France*: 88 days
1972 – Pierre Mézerette: 69 hours, 1 min
1972 – Pierre Thonon: 75 hours, 55 mins
1972 – Jean Martel and Henri Charles Tauxe: 80 days
1977 – Claude Mosse: 80 days

Bibliography

The Works of Jules Verne

Les Voyages Extraordinaires
1863   *Cinq Semaines en Ballon*
1864   *Voyage au Centre de la Terre*
1865   *De la Terre à la Lune*
1866   *Voyages et Aventures du Capitaine Hatteras* (2 vol.)
1868   *Les Enfants du capitaine Grant* (3 vol.)
1870   *Autour de la Lune*
1870   *Vingt mille lieues sous les mers* (2 vol.)
1871   *Une Ville flottante*
1872   *Adventures de Trois Russes et de Trois Anglais*
1873   *Le Tour du Monde en Quatre-Vingts Jours*
1873   *Le Pays des Fourrures* (2 vols.)
1874   *Le Docteur Ox*
1874–75   *L'Ile mystérieuse* (3 vols.)
1875   *Le 'Chancellor'*
1876   *Michel Strogoff* (2 vols.)
1877   *Les Indes Noires*
1877   *Hector Servadac* (2 vols.)
1878   *Un Capitaine de Quinze Ans*
1879   *Les Tribulations d'un Chinois en Chine*
1879   *Les Cinq Cents Millions de la Bégum*
1880   *La Maison à Vapeur* (2 vols.)
1881   *La Jangada*
1882   *L'Ecole des Robinsons*
1882   *Le Rayon Vert*
1883   *Kéreban le Têtu* (2 vols.)
1884   *L'Archipel en Feu*
1884   *L'Etoile du Sud*
1885   *Mathias Sandorf* (2 vols.)
1885   *L'Epave du 'Cynthia'* (written with André Laurie)
1886   *Robur le Conquérant*
1886   *Un Billet de Loterie*

1887   *Nord contre Sud* (2 vol.)
1887   *Le Chemin de France*
1888   *Deux Ans de Vacances*
1889   *Famille-Sans-Nom* (2 vol.)
1889   *Sans Dessus Dessous*
1890   *César Cascabel* (2 vol.)
1891   *Mistress Branican* (2 vol.)
1892   *Le Château des Carpathes*
1892   *Claudius Bombarnac*
1893   *P'tit-Bonhomme* (2 vol.)
1894   *Mirifiques Aventures de Maître Antifer* (2 vol.)
1895   *L'Ile à Helice* (2 vol.)
1896   *Face au Drapeau*
1896   *Clovis Dardentor*
1897   *Le Sphinx des Glaces* (2 vol.)
1898   *Le Superbe Orénoque* (2 vol.)
1899   *Le Testament d'un Excentrique* (2 vol.)
1900   *Seconde Patrie* (2 vol.)
1901   *Le Village Aérien*
1901   *Les Histoires de Jean-Marie Cabidoulin*
1902   *Les Frères Kip* (2 vol.)
1903   *Bourses de Voyage* (2 vol.)
1904   *Un Drame en Livonie*
1904   *Maître du Monde*
1905   *L'Invasion de la Mer*
1905   *Le Phare du Bout du Monde*
1906   *Le Volcan d'Or* (2 vol.)
1907   *L'Agence Thompson and Co.* (2 vol.)
1908   *La Chasse au Météore*
1908   *Le Pilote du Danube*
1909   *Les Naufragés du 'Jonathan'* (3 vol.)
1910   *Le Secret de Wilhelm Storitz*
1910   *Hier et Demain* (stories)
1919   *L'Etonnante Aventure de la Mission Barsac* (2 vol.)

Stories
1851   *Les Premiers Navires de la marine mexicaine*
1851   *Un Voyage en ballon*
1852   *Martin Paz*
1854   *Maître Zacharius*
1855   *Un Hivernage dans les glaces*
1864   *Le Comte de Chantelaine*
1865   *Les Forceurs de Blocus*

1875   *Amiens en l'an 2000*
1886   *Fritt-Flac*
1889   *In the Year 2889* (largely by Michel Verne)
1910   *Hier et Demain* (containing *la Famille Raton*; M. *Ré-dièze et Mlle Mi-bémol*; *la Destinée de Jean Morénas*; *le Humbug*; *la Journée d'un journaliste américain en l'an 2889* (revised French version of *In the Year 2889*); *l'Eternal Adam*.

Other Works
1867–68   *Géographie illustrée de la France et de ses colonies*
1870–80   *Découverte de la Terre: Histoire générale des grands voyages et des grands voyageurs* (6 vol.)

A complete bibliography of the published and unpublished works of Jules Verne can be found in the 'Orientation bibliographique' by François d'Argent and Pierre-André Touttain appended to *Cahier Jules Verne* (ed. Pierre-André Touttain) published by *L'Herne* (Paris, 1974). Verne destroyed his own personal papers before his death. However several collections contain letters and other manuscript materials. These are principally:

Bibliothèque Nationale, Paris: Fonds Hetzel, premier serie, nos.73–80, correspondence of Jules Verne with Hetzel père and fils, correspondence concerning Verne, contracts, receipts and accounts, documents pertaining to Verne, and correspondence with his heir Michel Verne.

Bibliothèque Municipale, Nantes: Musée Jules Verne, papers of Marguerite Allotte de la Fuÿe and the collection of Maxime Guillon-Verne, including letters to Paul Verne. This is the main centre for Verne studies, under the enthusiastic direction of Mlle Luce Courville, and it also includes a substantial collection of books, models, magazines and other materials pertaining to his life and times, and the science of the period.

Private collections: Jean Jules-Verne, early manuscripts; Mme Dumoret, letters; Mme Vaulon, other family letters.

Bibliothèque Municipale, Amiens: a small collection of books and articles concerning Verne. Also in Amiens is the Centre de Documentation de Jules Verne, run by Daniel Compère at 23 rue Caumartin.

Allott, Kenneth: *Jules Verne*. London: The Cresset Press, 1940; New York: Macmillan, 1941.
Allotte de la Fuÿe, Marguerite: *Jules Verne, sa vie, son œuvre*. Paris: Kra, 1928; Hachette, 1953 and 1966.
——: *Jules Verne*. London: Staples Press, 1954; New York: Coward McCann, 1956.

Almeras, Henri d': *Avant la gloire, leur débuts: Jules Verne.* Paris: Société français d'Imprimerie et de Librairie, 1903.

Andreev, Cyrille: 'Preface aux Oeuvres Completes en U.R.S.S.', *Europe* (Paris), avril-mai 1955.

——: *Три ж изни жюля верна.* Moscow: State Publishing House, 1960.

Audouard, Olympe: *Silhouettes parisiennes.* Paris: Marpon et Flammarion, 1883.

Bachelard, Gaston: *Le droit de rêver.* Paris: Presses Universitaires de France, 1970.

Barlet, H.: *L'Auteur des Voyages extraordinaires.* Paris, 1909.

Barthes, Roland: *Mythologies.* Paris: Editions du Seuil, 1957.

Bastard, Georges: *Verne, auteur des Voyages extraordinaires.* Paris: Dentu, 1883.

Baudin, Henri: *La science-fiction: un Univers en expansion.* Paris: Bordas, 1971.

Becker, Beril: *Jules Verne.* New York: G. P. Putnam's Sons, 1966.

Bellemin-Noël, Jean: 'Analectures de Jules Verne', *Critique* (Paris), août-septembre 1970.

Belloc, Marie A.: 'Jules Verne at Home', *The Strand Magazine* (London), vol. 9, February 1895, pp. 206–213.

Bellour, Raymond and Brochier, Jean J. (eds.): *Jules Verne.* Paris, 1966.

Betteloni, Vittorio: *Impressioni critiche e ricordi autobiografici.* Napoli, 1914.

Bitelli, G.: *Giulio Verne.* Bescia, 1955.

Born, Franz: *Jules Verne, der Mann, der die Zukunf erfand.* Eupen: Markus-Verlag, 1960.

——: *Jules Verne, the man who invented the future.* Englewood Cliffs, N.J.: Prentice-Hall, 1964.

Brandis, E.: *жюл верна, ево лжш и торч тчес тво.* (*Ioul Vern, evo jizni i torchtchestvo*). Moscow: State Publishing House, 1962.

Brissenne, A.: 'Jules Verne' in *Portraits intimes.* Paris: Armand Colin, 1899.

Butor, Michel: 'Le Point Suprême et l'Age d'Or' in *Repertoire.* Paris: Editions de Minuit, 1960.

Castelot, André: 'Ce merveilleux Jules Verne!', *Miroir de l'Histoire* (Paris), no. 199, juillet 1966.

Castle, Geoffrey: 'Introduction' in *20,000 Leagues Under the Sea.* London: Collins, n.d.

Chini, L.: *Giulio Verne.* Florence: Le Monnier, 1954.

Claretie, Jules: *Jules Verne,* Paris: Quantin, 1883.

Cohen, Victor: 'Jules Verne', *The Contemporary Review* (London), October 1956, pp. 220–223.

Compère, Daniel: *Approche de L'Ile de Jules Verne.* Paris: Minard. 1976.

De Amicis, Edmondo: 'Una visita a Jules Verne' in *Memorie*. Milan: Treves Fratelli, 1900.

Diesbach, Ghislain de: *Le Tour de Jules Verne en quatre-vingts livres*. Paris: Julliard, 1969.

Escaich, René: *Voyage a travers le monde vernien*. Bruxelles: La Boëtie, 1951; Paris: Plantin, 1955.

Evans, I. O.: *Jules Verne Master of Science Fiction*. London: Sidgwick & Jackson, 1956.

——: *Jules Verne and His Work*. London: Arco Books, 1965.

Frank, Bernard: *Jules Verne et ses Voyages*. Paris: Flammarion, 1941.

Franquinet, E.: *Jules Verne, Zinj persoon en zinj Werk*. Eindhoven: de Pilgrim, 1942.

——: *Jules Verne en zinj Wonderreizen*. Den Hag: 1964.

Freedman, Russell: *Jules Verne, Portrait of a Prophet*. New York: Holiday House, 1965.

Gould, Rupert Thomas: 'Jules Verne' in *The Stargazer Talks*. London: Geoffrey Bles, 1943.

Goupil, Armand: *Le Personage du savant dans l'œuvre de Jules Verne*. Mémoire de thesis: Facultie des lettres et sciences Humaine de Caen, 1965.

——: *Jules Verne*. Paris: Libraire Larousse, 1976.

Helling, Cornélis: 'Les personages réels dans l'oeuvre de Jules Verne', *Bull. Soc. Jules Verne* (Paris), no. 2, fevrier 1936, pp. 68–75.

Heuvelmans, Bernard: 'Le père contesté' in *Jules Verne*. Paris: Editions de L'Herne, 1974.

Honnegar, J.: *Jules Verne, Eine littarische Studie*. Unsere leit, 1875.

Horvath, Árpád: *Verne a technika álmódja*. Budapest: Tancsics Könyvkiado, 1969.

Huet, Marie-Hélène: *L'Histoire des Voyages extraordinaires*. Paris: Minard. 1973.

Jacobson, A. and Antoni, A.: *Des anticipations de Jules Verne aux realisations d'aujourd'hui*, Paris: Gigord, 1936.

Janatka, J. M.: *Neznamy Jules Verne*. Praha, 1959.

Jeoffroy, Pierre: 'Jules Verne, les voyant', *Paris-Match*, 11 octobre 1958.

Jules-Verne, Jean: *Jules Verne*. Paris: Hachette, 1973.

Kiszely, M. B.: *L'Image de la nation hongroise dans Jules Verne*. Debrecen, 1935.

Laissus, Joseph: *Jules Verne, l'extraordinaire voyageur, 1828–1905*. Paris: Gauthier-Villars, 1967.

Le Cholleaux, R.: *Jules Verne (les Contemporains)*. Paris, s.d.

Lemire, Charles: *Jules Verne 1828–1905*. Amiens: Berger-Levrault, 1908.

Ley, Willy: 'Jules Verne, the Man and his Works' in *Dr Ox's Experiment*. New York: The Macmillan Company, 1963.

Machery, P.: 'Jules Verne, ou le récit en defaut' in *Pour une théorie de la production littéraire*. Paris: Maspero, 1966.

Marcucci, Edmondo: *Giulio Verne e la sua opera*. Milano: Associeta Anonime Dante Alighieri, 1930.

——: *Les Illustrations des Voyages Extraordinaires de Jules Verne*. Paris: Société Jules Verne, 1956.

Martin, Charles-Noël: *Jules Verne, sa Vie et son Oeuvre*. Laussanne: Editions Rencontre, 1971.

Metral, Maurice: 'Jules Verne et son petit monde', unidentified Paris paper, winter 1958–59 (Archives Peter Costello).

——: *Sur les pas de Jules Verne*. Neuchâtel: Nouvelle Bibliotheque, 1963.

Mordianu, Dinn: *Jules Verne*. Bucharest: Tineremlin, 1962.

Moré, Marcel: *Le Très Curieux Jules Verne*. Paris: Gallimard, 1960.

——: *Nouvelles Explorations de Jules Verne*. Paris: Gallimard, 1963.

——: *Les Noces Chymyques du Capitaine Nemo et de Salomé*. Paris: Gallimard, 1967.

Ocagne, Maurice d': *Hommes et Choses de Science*. Paris: Libraire Vuibert, 1930.

Pavolini, A. F.: *Giulio Verne*. Roma: A. F. Formiggini, 1932.

Peare, Catherine O.: *Jules Verne, His Life*. New York: Holt, 1956.

Péter, Zoltan: *A Kepzelet Varazsloja Jules Verne Élete*. Budapest: Móra Ferenc Konyvkiadó, 1972.

Popp, Dr. Max: *Julius Verne und sein Werk*. Wien: Hartleben, 1909.

Ragon, Michel: 'Jules Verne visionaire de l'architecture', *L'Oeil* (Paris), no. 227, juin 1974, pp. 44–49.

Ransson, R.: *Jules Verne que j'ai connu*. Amiens: Academie d'Amiens, 1937.

Rauville, Hervé de: *Jules Verne*. Paris: Dupont, 1905.

Raymond, François and Compère, Daniel: *Le Development des Études sur Jules Verne* [in France]. Paris: Minard, 1976.

Ricca, F.: *Ricordando Giulio Verne*. Rieti: Faraoni, 1952.

Ristat, Jean: *Le Lit de Nicolas Boileau et de Jules Verne*. Paris, 1965.

Roussel, Raymond: *Comment j'ai écrit certaines de mes livres*. Paris: Jean-Jacques Pauvert, 1963.

Serres, Michel: *Jouvences sur Jules Verne*. Paris: Editions de Minuit, 1974.

Sherard, Robert H.: 'Jules Verne re-visited', *T.P.'s Weekly* (London), 9 October 1903, p. 589.

Slonim, M.: 'Revival of Jules Verne', *New York Times Book Review*, 22 May 1966.

Topin, Marius: *Jules Verne (Romanciers contemporains)*. Paris: Charpentier, 1876.

Touttain, Pierre-Andre (editor): *Jules Verne (Cahiers de L'Herne)*. Paris: Editions de L'Herne, 1974.

Vierne, Simone: *L'Ile Mysterieuse de Jules Verne.* Paris: Hachette, 1973.
———: *Jules Verne et le Roman initiatique.* Paris: Editions de Sirac, 1973.
Waltz, George H.: *Jules Verne, the biography of an imagination.* New York: Henry Holt, 1943.
Zlabek, Vaclav: *Fantasie-skutecnost.* Praha: Dvur kralove, 1921.

Index